The Redhouse Guide

to

THE AEGEAN COAST of TURKEY

by

JOHN FREELY

Photographs by
Anthony E. Baker

Published by the Redhouse Press,
Rızapaşa Yokuşu No. 50, Mercan, Istanbul

Front cover: Trajaneum, Pergamum
Back cover: Artemis, Selçuk Museum, Selçuk

ISBN 975-413-071-X

Printed in Turkey by Yeni Alaş Matbaacılık Şirketi,
Dr. Emin Paşa Sokağı No. 16/2, Cağaloğlu, Istanbul

TO

JAMES AND CARLA LOVETT

CONTENTS

LIST OF ILLUSTRATIONS

ILLUSTRATIONS

Map I Western Turkey

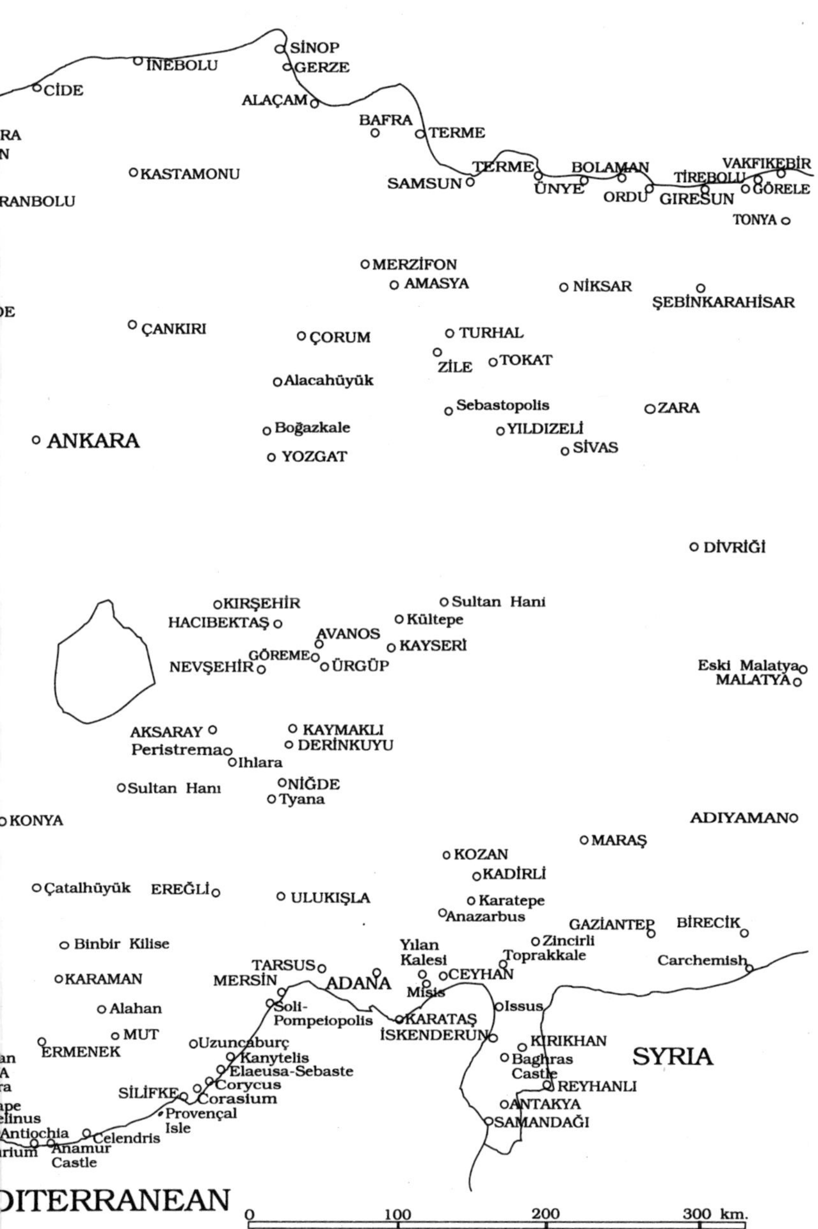
SİNOP
GERZE
İNEBOLU
CİDE
ALAÇAM
BAFRA
TERME
KASTAMONU
TERME
SAMSUN
ÜNYE
BOLAMAN
ORDU
TİREBOLU
GIRESUN
VAKFIKEBİR
GÖRELE
TONYA
MERZİFON
AMASYA
NİKSAR
ŞEBİNKARAHİSAR
ÇANKIRI
ÇORUM
TURHAL
ZİLE
TOKAT
Alacahüyük
Sebastopolis
ZARA
ANKARA
Boğazkale
YOZGAT
YILDIZELİ
SİVAS
DİVRİĞİ
KIRŞEHİR
HACIBEKTAŞ
AVANOS
GÖREME
NEVŞEHİR
ÜRGÜP
Sultan Hani
Kültepe
KAYSERİ
Eski Malatya
MALATYA
AKSARAY
Peristrema
Ihlara
KAYMAKLI
DERİNKUYU
Sultan Hanı
NİĞDE
Tyana
KONYA
ADIYAMAN
MARAŞ
KOZAN
KADİRLİ
Çatalhüyük
EREĞLİ
ULUKIŞLA
Karatepe
Anazarbus
GAZİANTEP
BİRECİK
Binbir Kilise
Zincirli
Yılan
Kalesi
Toprakkale
Carchemish
TARSUS
KARAMAN
MERSİN
ADANA
CEYHAN
Misis
Alahan
Soli-
Pompeiopolis
Issus
KARATAŞ
MUT
İSKENDERUN
KIRIKHAN
ERMENEK
Uzuncaburç
Kanytelis
Baghras
Castle
SYRIA
Elaeusa-Sebaste
Corycus
REYHANLI
SİLİFKE
Corasium
ANTAKYA
Provençal
Isle
SAMANDAĞI
Antiochia
Celendris
Anamur
Castle
0
100
200
300 km.

LIST OF SITE PLANS

AUTHOR'S NOTE

This is one of a series of guides to the various regions of Turkey. The present guide covers the northern Aegean coast of Asian Turkey from the Dardanelles to the valley of the Menderes, the river known in antiquity as the Maeander. The itineraries take one to all of the historic sites along this coast, with excursions inland along the valleys of the principal rivers, most notably that of the Maeander.

This note is followed both by an introduction to Turkish spelling and pronunciation and by a glossary of the Turkish words and technical terms used in this book. The appendices, which consist of an illustrated note on classical architecture, a chronology, and a selected bibliography, also provide the reader with useful information.

TURKISH SPELLING AND PRONUNCIATION

Throughout this guide, except in quotes from earlier travelers, modern Turkish spelling has been used for Turkish proper names and for things that are specifically Turkish. Modern Turkish is rigorously logical and phonetic, and the few letters that are pronounced differently than in English are indicated below.

Vowels are pronounced as in French or German; i, e., **a** as in father, **e** as in met, **i** as in machine, **o** as in oh, **u** as in mute. In addition, there are three other vowels that do not occur in English; these are **ı** (undotted), pronounced as the "u" in but, **ö** as in German or as the "oy" in annoy, **ü** as in German or as "ui" in suit.

Consonants are pronounced as in English, except the following:

c as "j" in jam; e.g. **cami** (mosque) = jahmy
ç as "ch" in chat; e.g. **çorba** (soup) = chorba
g as in get, never as in gem
ğ is almost silent and tends to lengthen the preceding vowel
ş as in sugar; e.g. **çeşme** (fountain) = cheshme

GLOSSARY

The following list includes both the Turkish words and the technical, architectural, and archaeological terms used in the text. The Turkish words in parentheses are the forms which the immediately preceding words assume when modified by a noun, e.g. Yeni Cami (the New Mosque), but Sultan Ahmet Camii (the Mosque of Sultan Ahmet).

acropolis upper city, usually fortified
ada (adası) island
Aeolic capital palm-leaf capital developed by the Aeolian Greeks
agora market square of an ancient Greek city
amphitheater a theater with an auditorium of circular or oval form surrounding an open arena; used in the Roman world for gladiatorial combats, etc.
anta (pl. **antae**) the slightly projecting pilaster of a cella wall
architrave a lintel carried from the top of one column to another, the lowest element of an entablature
ashlar square cut building stones
atrium the entrance court of a Roman building, roofed over around its periphery but open at the center
baldachin a canopy-like structure
basilica originally a Roman exchange and court of law; in Christian times a church with a central nave and side aisles of lower height
bedesten a Turkish market building usually used for the storage and sale of the most precious goods
bekçi watchman
belediye (belediyesi) town hall, municipality
beylik a Türkmen principality
boule city council
bouleuterion council house in an ancient Greek city
bulvar (bulvarı) boulevard
büyük big
cadde (caddesi) avenue

GLOSSARY

cami (camii) a mosque

capital the topmost member of a column

caravanserai inn for travelers

cavea the auditorium of a Greek theater, originally carved out of the side of a hill

cella the enclosed central chamber of a temple, also called the naos

chancel that part of a church reserved for the clergy

citadel inner fortress, usually on an acropolis composite capital: Corinthian capital combined with Ionic ovolo and volutes

Corinthian an order of architecture differing from the Ionic principally in its capital, which is decorated with volutes and acanthus leaves

cornice the upper member of the entablature

crepidoma the stepped platform of a temple

cunei the sectors into which the seats of a theater are divided by its aisles

çarşı (çarşısı) market

çay (çayı) tea; also a small stream

çeşme (çeşmesi) Turkish fountain

dağ (dağı) mountain

darüşşifa hospital

deniz sea

dere (deresi) stream or valley

diazoma (pl. **diazomata)** circumferential passageway separating tiers of seats in a theater

dipteral a temple surrounded by a double peristyle

Doric the order of architecture originally developed by the Dorian Greeks

drum one of the cylindrical sections of a column shaft

entablature the superstructure carried by a colonnade, comprising architrave, frieze and cornice

eski old

exedra (pl. **exedrae)** a semicircular niche

exonarthex outer vestibule of a Byzantine church

eyvan vaulted room with one side open to a court, iwan

frontal a façade

frieze the middle element of an entablature; also any horizontal zone adorned with reliefs

Gazi warrior for the Islamic faith

GLOSSARY

Gigantomachia war of or with the giants

göl (gölü) lake

groin vault an arched roof formed by the intersection of two semi-cylindrical surfaces

gymnasium school and athletic center in an ancient Greek city

hamam (hamamı) Turkish bath

han (hanı) inner city caravanserai

hecatomb ancient Greek or Roman sacrifice consisting of one hundred oxen or cattle

heroon shrine of a deified hero

hexastyle a temple with six columns at its end or ends

in antis between the antae

Ionic the architectural order developed by the Ionian Greeks

iskele (iskelesi) pier or landing-stage

kale (kalesi) castle or fortress

kapı (kapısı) door or gate

kaza sub-division of a Turkish province

kıble direction of Mecca

konak (konağı) large house

köprü (köprüsü) bridge

köy (köyü) village

küçük little

külliye (külliyesi) religious complex, usually including a mosque and all of the pious foundatıons attached to it

kütüphane (kütüphanesi) library

medrese (medresesi) Islamic school of theology, medresseh, madrasah

mescit (mescidi) small mosque, masjid

metopes recessed panels between the triglyphs in a Doric frieze

meydan (meydanı) village square or town center, maidan, meidan

mihrab niche in a mosque indicating the direction of Mecca

mimber the pulpit in a mosque

naiskos a small shrine-building

narthex vestibule of a church

necropolis burial ground of an ancient Greek city

nehir (nehri) river

GLOSSARY

Nike winged female figure personifying victory

nymphaeum monumental fountain

odeion concert hall in the form of a small theater, usually roofed; sometimes used for meetings of the city council

ogival pointed arch

opisthodomos rear porch of a temple

orchestra the space used by the chorus and at first by the actors in the Greek theater; circular in plan in classical theaters, but generally reduced to a horseshoe in Hellenistic theaters

order in ancient Greek architecture this usually consisted of a column with base, shaft and capital, the whole supporting an entablature

ovolo a rounded convex moulding

palaestra exercise ground of a Graeco-Roman gymnasium

parados (pl. **paradoi)** arched side entrance to the orchestra of a theater

pediment the triangular termination of a ridge roof

pendentive spherical surface that makes the transition from the cornice of a dome to its supporting arches

peripteral a temple whose cella is surrounded by a colonnade

peripteros a peripteral temple

peristyle a covered colonnade surrounding a building; or an inner court with a colonnade

podium a low wall or continuous pedestal on which columns or other monuments are carried

portico a colonnaded space, with a roof supported on at least one side by columns

pronaos front porch of a temple

propylon monumental gateway

proscenium colonnade between the orchestra and the stage building

prostyle a temple with columns in front

prytaneion the senate house in an ancient Greek city

pseudo-dipteral a dipteral temple with the inner row of columns omitted

quadriga four-horse chariot

şadırvan ablution fountain in a mosque courtyard

satrap Persian governor

skene the stage building that formed the back scene of a theater

sokak (sokağı) street

GLOSSARY

spandrel the space between the exterior curve of an arch and the enclosing right angle

squinch a surface carried across the corner of a room, often making the transition between two arches and the cornice of the dome

stadium running track where all athletic contests were held

stalactite in Ottoman architecture, a surface carved in the form of the icicle-like hanging deposits in a cave

stoa a long covered hall or porch with columns in front stylobate: the upper step of a temple, which formed a platform for the columns

su (suyu) water or stream

temenos the sacred enclosure or precincts of a temple

templum-in-antis a temple whose only external columns are between its antae

tımarhane insane asylum

transept the crossarm of a cruciform church

türbe (türbesi) mausoleum, turbeh, turbe

tympanum a wall that fills in an arch or pediment

Valide Sultan the mother of a reigning Ottoman sultan

volute the spiral scroll of the Ionic capital

xoanon sacred wooden image of a deity

yeni new

Yürük Turkish nomads

CHAPTER ONE

THE TROAD: ÇANAKKALE TO AYVALIK

The first part of our first itinerary will lead us south from Çanakkale to Assos on highway E87/550, which takes us through the western part of the Troad, the ancient land of Troy. This great peninsula forms the northwesternmost extension of Asia Minor, bounded on the north by the Dardanelles, on the west by the Aegean, and on the south by the Gulf of Edremit, known in antiquity as the Adramyttene Gulf. The second part of our itinerary will take us around the Gulf of Edremit from Assos to Ayvalık on the next peninsula to the south, the southern part of the region known in antiquity as Mysia. The countryside through which we pass is for the most part still unspoiled by modern development, and one can see why it so impressed the Romans when their legions first passed this way after the organization of the province of Asia in 129 B.C. As Cicero wrote of this bountiful region in one of his *Orations:* "In the richness of its soil, in the variety of its produce, in the extent of its pastures, and in the number of its products it surpasses all other lands."

After passing the turnoff for Troy, our route takes us up into the heavily wooded hills east of the Trojan Plain, flanked by stands of pine and valonia oak. At Taştepe we make a short detour on a road to the right. The road crosses the Scamander and then passes through Pınarbaşı, a village on the northern slope of Ballı Dağ, the hill that some Homeric scholars believed to be the site of Homeric Troy before Schliemann's excavations at Hisarlık. Beyond Pınarbaşı the road comes to a T at the village of Üvecik, with the left fork leading south to Geyikli and the right heading north to Kumkale. A short drive along the right fork brings us to Hasan Kulesi, a small castle built ca. 1780 by Cezayirli (the Algerian) Hasan Paşa, grand vizier under Selim III (r. 1789-1807). This is one of the very few extant examples in Anatolia of a pyrgos, the fortified dwelling of a local warlord like Hasan Paşa.

After our detour we return to highway E87/550, which we follow south as far as Ezine, the main town of the central Troad. Ezine stands astride the Akçın Çayı, the principal tributary of the Scamander, whose sources are on the northern and western slopes of Mt. Ida. Here we are in the heart of Homeric Dardania, the region listed in the Catalogue of Trojans as being ruled by Aeneas, a descendant of Dardanus who in Virgil's *Aeneid* became the founder of Rome.

At Ezine we leave the highway and turn right on a road signposted for Geyikli and Odunluk İskelesi. After a few kilometers we turn off on to a rough track signposted for ancient Neandria, one of the oldest cities in the Troad.

The site of Neandria is on the bare summit of Cığrı Dağı, a granite mountain forming a conspicuous ridge five kilometers long. The ancient city occupies the high crest of the ridge at an altitude of 520 meters. The impressive defense walls of Neandria, which date from the late fifth or early fourth century B.C., are three meters thick and enclose an area measuring some 1,400 meters from east to west and with a maximum north-south width of 450 meters. The well-preserved main gate is in the middle of the south side of the defense circuit. The site was tentatively identified as Neandria by Frank Calvert, the man who led Heinrich Schliemann to discover Homeric Troy, and this was confirmed by the German archaeologist Robert Koldewey when he excavated the site in 1889. Pottery finds on the site indicate that Neandria was founded in the late eighth century B.C., probably by Aeolian settlers from Tenedos. Neandria lasted until the final decade of the fourth century B.C., when its inhabitants were transferred to the new city of Alexandria Troas, which had been founded on the nearby coast by Antigonus I Monopthalmus, the One-Eyed, who succeeded Alexander the Great as King of Macedonia. The site has been abandoned since then, used by herders of the surrounding villagers to graze their cattle. (It is interesting to note that the coins of Neandria have on their reverse the figure of a grazing horse.)

The acropolis of the city was on a hilltop near the eastern corner of the defense walls. This eminence was surrounded by a polygonal wall of the sixth century B.C., a stretch of which has been preserved on the south slope of the hill. The only extant monument of Neandria is marked by a solitary wind-blown tree some 200 meters to the northwest of the main gate. Koldewey unearthed here the remains of an Aeolic temple of Apollo dating from the end of the seventh or the beginning of the sixth century B.C. This is one of two Aeolic temples of this type that have survived in Asia Minor, the other being at Larisa north of İzmir. The stylobate, or temple platform, measures 12.87 by 25.71 meters. Its cella, or sanctuary building, is 8.04 by 19.82 meters in its interior dimensions. The roof of the temple was supported internally along its central axis by a row of seven wooden columns, the stone bases of which are still in place. The columns were surmounted by handsome Aeolic capitals, now on exhibit in the Istanbul Archaeological Museum.

We now return to the road leading westward from Ezine to Geyikli and Odunluk İskelesi. As we do so we pass through the extensive ruins of Alexandria Troas, which are estimated to cover a thousand acres. But the site has been used for centuries as a quarry, so there is little definite to be seen other than the scattered ruins of unidentified buildings and a number of sarcophagi along the roadside. The only structure of any size still standing is the enormous ruined edifice known locally as Bal Saray, the Honey Palace. This is a Roman gymnasium and baths erected in A.D. 135 by Herodes Atticus, who lived in Alexandria Troas while he was chief administrator of the province of Asia under his close friend, the Emperor Hadrian (r. 117-38). A quarter of a century later, under the Athenian acropolis, he would build the magnificent odeion, or concert hall, that still bears his name.

According to Strabo, the original settlement on this site was an ancient Greek colony named Sigeia. A new and far larger city was founded on the site ca. 310 B.C. by Antigonus I, who named it Antigonia in his own honor. Antigonus was defeated and killed at the battle of Ipsus in 301 B.C. by Lysimachus, who succeeded him as king of Macedonia. Soon afterwards Lysimachus changed the name of Antigonia to Alexandria, one of fifteen cities named for Alexander by the generals who succeeded to his empire. But travelers, even in antiquity, were led by the proximity of Troy to call the city Alexandria Troas.

During the Hellenistic era Alexandria Troas became the wealthiest and most populous city in the Troad, for its strategic position near the entrance to the Hellespont made it a convenient place for the transshipment of goods passing between the Aegean and Asia Minor. During the reign of Augustus (27 B.C.-A.D. 14) a Roman colony was established here, reaching the height of its prosperity in the time of Hadrian, as evidenced by the huge gymnasium and baths erected by Herodes Atticus.

By the middle of the first century A.D. a small group of Christians had begun to gather in Alexandria Troas, one of at least a score of such communities that formed in Asia Minor at that time. These early Christian communities are mentioned in the Epistles of St. Paul and *Acts of the Apostles,* from which it is known that

Aeolic Capital from Neandria, Istanbul Archaeological Museum

Bath of Herodes Atticus at Alexandria Troas

Bath of Herodes Atticus, Print from Chandler

Paul visited Alexandria Troas twice during his missionary journeys, probably in the years A.D. 48 and 53. *Acts* 20:7-12 records a dramatic episode that occurred during Paul's second visit to Alexandria Troas:

> On the first day of the week we met to break bread. Paul was due to leave the next day, and he preached a sermon that went on till the middle of the night. A number of lamps were lit in the upstairs room where we were assembled, and as Paul went on and on, a young man named Euthchus who was sitting on the window sill grew drowsy and was overcome by sleep and fell to the ground three floors below. He was picked up dead. Paul went down and stooped to clasp the boy to him. "There is no need to worry," he said, "there is still life in him." Then he went upstairs and carried on talking until he left at daybreak. They took the boy away alive, and were greatly encouraged.

Alexandria Troas was still an important town at the beginning of the Byzantine era. Coins have been found from the reign of Constantine the Great (324-37), who had considered shifting the capital of his empire here, before changing his mind in favor of Byzantium.

Later in the Byzantine era Alexandria Troas is recorded as having the status of a bishopric, but otherwise it disappears from the pages of history, along with most of the other cities in the Troad. During the first half of the fourteenth century the Troad fell under the control of the Karası Türkmen tribe, who established a *beylik,* or emirate, one of a number that emerged in Anatolia with the decline of the Selçuks. Then in 1336 the Karası *beylik* was conquered by the Osmanlı Turks under Orhan Gazi (r. 1324-59), after which the Troad became part of the rapidly expanding Ottoman Empire. Thenceforth Alexandria Troas was known to the Turks as Eski Stambul, the "Old City," the name by which it is still known locally today.

European travelers to the Ottoman Empire write that Alexandria Troas was abandoned and in ruins. The most complete description of the site is that of Richard Chandler, who writes of it in his *Travels in Asia Minor, 1764-65:*

> Alexandria Troas was seated on a hill, sloping toward the sea, and divided from Mt. Ida by a deep valley....The port of Troas, by which we landed, has a hill rising behind it in a semicircle, and covered with rubbish. Many small granite pillars are standing, half buried, and much corroded by the spray....The city wall is standing, except toward the vineyard, and the battlements ruined. It was thick and solid, had square towers at regular distances, and was several miles in circumference. Besides houses, it enclosed many magnificent structures; but now appears as the boundary of a forest or neglected park....Above the shore is a hollow, overgrown with trees, near which Pococke [in 1740] saw remains of a stadium, or place for races, sunk in the ground; and higher up is the vaulted substructure or basement of a large temple. We were told that this had lately been a lurking place for bandetti; who often lay concealed here....Near it is a souterrain [cistern]; and at some distance vestiges of a theater and an odeum, or music theater....

Chandler goes on to describe the gymnasium and baths of Herodes Atticus, which then as now was the principal extant monument of Alexandria Troas, along with the remains of the aqueduct that brought water to it:

> The principal ruin, which is that seen from afar by mariners, commands a view of the islands Tenedos and Lemnos; and, on one side, of the plain of the Hellespont, and of the mountains in Europe. Before it is a gentle ascent, woody, with inequalities, to the sea, distant by computation about three miles. It is a very ample building, and, as we supposed, once the gymnasium, where the youths were instructed in learning and in the exercises. It consists of three open massive arches, towering amid walls, and a vast heap of huge materials....The history of this noble and once useful structure affords an illustrious instance of imperial and private munifence. An Athenian, Tiberius Claudius Atticus Herodes, presided over the free cities of Asia. Seeing Troas

> destitute of commodious baths, and of water, except as it was procured from muddy wells or reservoirs made to receive rain, he wrote to the emperor Hadrian not to suffer an ancient and maritime city to be destroyed by drought, but to bestow on it three hundred myriads of dracms for water, especially as he had given far greater sums even to villages. Hadrian readily complied, and appointed him overseer of the building. The expense exceeded seven hundred myriads [over 226,000 pounds sterling in 1764], and it was represented to the emperor as a grievance, that the tribute from five hundred cities should be lavished on one in an aqueduct. Herodes, in reply, begged him not to be displeased, that having gone beyond his estimate, he had presented the overplus to his son, and he to the city....

The road brings us down to the sea at Odunluk İskelesi, the Wood Pier, a tiny hamlet where there is a ferry service out to Tenedos, Turkish Bozcaada. Odunluk İskelesi is on or near the site of ancient Achaeium, a place name found only in Strabo, who mentions it in his description of the coast south of Cape Sigeum:

> After the Sigeian Promontory [Cape Sigeum] and the Achilleium one comes to the Achaeium, the part of the mainland that belongs to the Tenedians; and to Tenedos itself, which is not more than forty stadia distant from the mainland. It is about eighty stadia in circumference, and has an Aeolian city and a temple of Sminthian Apollo, as the poet [Homer, in Book I of *The Iliad*] testifies: "And dost rule mightily over Tenedos, O Sminthian!"

The region subject to Tenedos along the coast south of the present Odunluk İskelesi was more generally known as the Tenedian Peraea. The Tenedian Peraea comprised the territory of a number of cities founded along this coast in the archaic period (ca.700-479 B.C.) by Aeolian Greeks from Lesbos, who also controlled Tenedos itself. The patron deity of Tenedos and the Tenedian Peraea was Sminthian Apollo, Apollo the "Mouse God." The origin of this strange name is explained by Strabo in his description of Chryse, which he calls Chrysa, one of the cities of the Tenedian Peraea, whose foundation was traditionally attributed to the Teucrians, a people from Crete whom the Greeks believed to have been the first Hellenic settlers in the Troad:

> In this Chrysa is also the temple of Sminthian Apllo; and the symbol which preserves the etymology of the name, I mean the mouse, lies beneath the foot of his image. These are the works of Scopas of Paros; and also the history, or myth, about the mice is associated with the place: When the Teucrians arrived from Crete...they had an oracle which bade them to "stay on the spot where the earth-born should attack them;" and he says, the attack took place around Hamaxitus, for by night a great multitude of field mice swarmed out of the ground and ate up all the leather in their arms and equipment; and the Teucrians remained there; and it was they who gave its name to Mt. Ida, naming it after the mountain in Crete. Heracleides of Pontus says that the mice which swarmed around the temple were regarded as sacred, and for this reason the image was designed with its foot upon the mouse.

We now head southwards from Odunluk İskelesi along a secondary road, which takes us down the coast along what was once the Tenedian Peraea. A short way along we pass Dalyan, a seaside village on the site of the ancient harbor of Alexandria Troas, which is now silted up. Along the sandy shore we see a number of ancient column drums once intended for shipment to Istanbul as building material for one of the imperial Ottoman mosques, but abandoned here when they cracked while being loaded.

The road takes us southward as far as Gülpınar, a village just above Baba Burnu, the southernmost promontory of the Troad. A signpost points the way to the temple of Apollo Smintheus, whose site on the outskirts of the village was excavated in the 1980s by Turkish archaeologists. The temple is a pseudo-dipteral edifice of the Ionic order dated to the second half of the third century B.C. It had a peripteral colonnade of eight by fourteen columns standing on a stylobate measuring 24 by 43 meters. This was the principle temple of ancient Chryse, whose site has been identified at the nearby seagirt promontory of Göztepe.

The original Smintheum figures prominently in *The Iliad,* for it was here that the Achaians captured the beautiful Chryseis, daughter of Chryses, Apollo's priest at this sanctuary. After Chryseis was presented to Agamemnon, Chryses went to the Achaian camp and asked for the return of his daughter. When Agamemnon refused Chryses prayed to Apollo to avenge his dishonor, whereupon the god unleashed a terrible plague upon the Achaians. The Achaians appealed to Agamemnon to return Chryseis to her father, but he said that he would only agree if his mistress was replaced by "fair cheeked" Bryseis, the beautiful slave girl whom Achilles had captured. The enraged Achilles stormed out of the Achaian camp, beginning the fateful quarrel that is the opening theme of *The Iliad.* Meanwhile, Agamemnon sent Chryseis back to her father in a flotilla commanded by Odysseus, who has brought along a hecatomb of bulls and goats to be sacrificed at the Smintheum as an act of atonement to Apollo. The landing of the Achaians at Chryse is described in one of the most lyrical passages of *The Iliad,* as "Chryseis herself stepped from the seagoing vessel," after which "Odysseus of the many designs led her to the altar" where her father Chryses was waiting to embrace her. Chryses then appealed to Apollo to lift the plague from Agamemnon's army, after which he and the Achaians slaughtered the sacrificial animals and began a joyous feast of thanksgiving.

> All day long they propitiated the god with singing,
> chanting a special hymn to Apollo, these young Achaians,
> singing to the one who works from afar, who listened in
> gladness.
> Afterwards when the sun went down and the darkness came
> onwards
> they lay down and slept beside the ship's stern cables.
> But when the dawn came again with her rosy fingers,
> they put forward to sea toward the wide camp of the Achaians.

Fragments of the Temple of Apollo Smintheus, Chryse

Just beyond Gülpınar a turnoff on the right leads out to the southwesternmost point of the Troad at Baba Burnu. The village of Baba Burnu clusters around the periphery of a large and well-preserved Ottoman fortress, dated by an inscription to 1726. The village and the cape take their name from a sainted dervish whose tomb is out on the headland. Mariners sailing around the cape in former times would throw ashore sacks of food as offerings to the saint, thus supplying the succession of hermit dervishes who cared for his tomb. The headland was known to Genoese and Venetian navigators as Santa Maria, but the Greeks always referred to it by its ancient name, Cape Lekton. According to Strabo, Agamemnon erected an altar to the Twelve Gods on Cape Lekton, but no trace of this has ever been found. The cape is mentioned in Book IV of *The Iliad,* where Hera stops here briefly with Hypnos, god of sleep, while on her way to meet Zeus on the summit of Mt. Ida (Turkish Kazdağı). They paused for only a moment on "Lekton, where they first left the water and went/on over dry land, and with their feet the top of the forest was shaken."

We now drive eastward from Baba Kale on a secondary road that ends at Bademli, where we rejoin the main road from Gülpınar to Behramkale, a village on the shore of the Gulf of Edremit opposite the Greek island of Lesbos. A road leads uphill from the port of Behramkale to the upper village, which clusters around a great spire of rock surmounted by the acropolis of ancient Assos, the principal archaeological site in the southern Troad.

The ruins of Assos were first studied in 1881-83 by an Amercan expedition sponsored by the Antiquarian Society of Boston, with J. T. Clarke and F. H. Bacon directing the excavations. Most of the works of art and sculptural fragments found by the American expedition have been on exhibit for more than a century at the Boston Museum of Fine Arts, as well as a few in the Louvre and the Istanbul Archaeological Museum. As a result, Assos was well-known in the West, though seldom visited. The development of Behramkale as a seaside resort in the 1980s has attracted more visitors to the site. The site of ancient Assos has been reexcavated in recent years, with a Turkish team working on the acropolis and French archaeologists digging in the lower city, which is on the seaward slope below the sheer north face of the great rock on which the city was first founded.

The American excavators unearthed objects on the acropolis indicating that the site was first occupied in the Early Bronze Age. Clarke identified this Bronze Age settlement with the city of Pedasos mentioned by both Homer and Strabo. Homer mentions this city in Book VI of *The Iliad,* where he writes that "...the lord of men, Agamemnon, brought death to Elatos,/whose home had been on the shores of Satnoeis' lovely waters,/sheer Pedasos...." Homer refers to the city again in Book XXI of *The Iliad,* where he writes of "Altes, lord of the Leleges whose delight is in battle,/and holds headlong Pedasos on the river Satnioeis." This has led scholars to identify the Satnioeis with the Tuzla Çayı, the stream that flows past the north side of Assos. Strabo confuses the issue by saying that in his time (64 B.C.—ca. A.D. 25) Pedasos was deserted, whereas Assos was then a flourishing city. This has led the archae-

Ottoman Fortress at Cape Lekton, Print from Ximinix

ologist John M. Cook, an authority on the Troad, to reject the identification of Pedasos with Assos, although there is no other known site that fits the Homeric description.

In any event, archaeological evidence indicates that the city of Assos whose ruins we see today was founded in the seventh century B.C. According to Strabo, who quotes earlier Greek historians, Assos was founded by Aeolians from Methymna, a city on the northern tip of Lesbos just across the strait, on the site of the present town of Molivos. During the first half of the sixth century B.C., Assos came under the control of the Lydian kings, who ruled from their capital in Sardis. After the fall of Sardis to Cyrus the Great in 546 B.C., Assos and the other Greek cities of northwestern Asia Minor became part of the Persian province of Hellespontine Phrygia. After the defeat of Persia by the Greeks at the battle of Plataea in 479 B.C., Assos became a member of the Delian confederacy under Athens, and for the next century its history was much the same as the other Greek cities in western Anatolia.

The most illustrious period in the history of the city came in the second quarter of the fourth century B.C., when a wealthy banker named Euboulos ruled from Assos over a principality that extended around the shores of the Adramyttene Gulf as far as Atarnaeus. Euboulos was succeeded by the eunuch Hermeias, a benevolent despot known as the Tyrant of Atarnaeus, who had studied in Athens under both Plato and Aristotle. When Hermeias came to power in his principality he decided to establish a Platonic state in Assos. He thereupon invited a number of scholars in Athens to join him, most notably Aristotle, who headed a school of philosophy in Assos during the years 347-344 B.C. Aristotle married Hermeias' niece and ward, Pythias, who bore him a daughter while they lived in Assos. This idyl came to an end in 344 B.C., when Hermeias was captured by the Persians, after which he was tortured and then executed. Before he died, Hermeias sent a secret message back to Aristotle, saying that despite the torture he had endured "he had done nothing to dishonor philosophy." This moved Aristotle to write his only known poem, a paean of praise in honor of Hermeias.

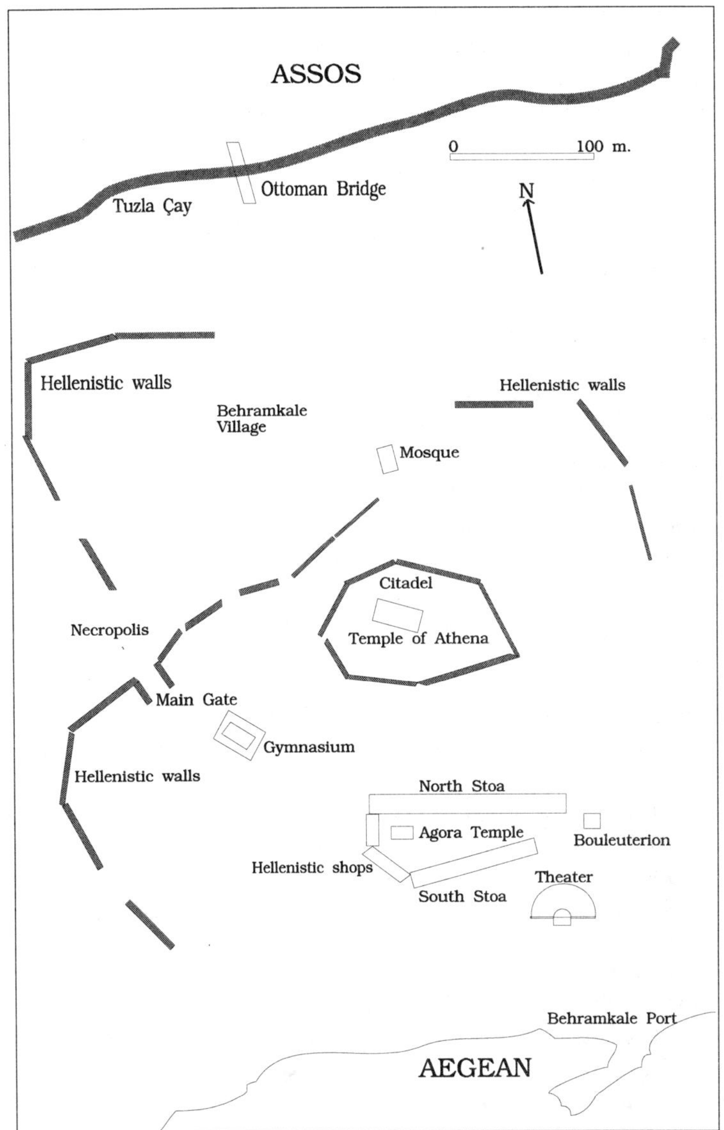
ASSOS
0 100 m.
N
Ottoman Bridge
Tuzla Çay
Hellenistic walls
Behramkale
Village
Hellenistic walls
Mosque
Citadel
Temple of Athena
Necropolis
Main Gate
Gymnasium
Hellenistic walls
North Stoa
Agora Temple
Bouleuterion
Hellenistic shops
Theater
South Stoa
Behramkale Port
AEGEAN

Aristotle then fled with his family and his student Theophrastus to Lesbos, where they remained for a year. During that year Aristotle and Theophrastus began their pioneering researches in zoology, botany and biology, laying the foundations for these branches of the life sciences.

Another notable from ancient Assos is the philosopher Cleanthes. Cleanthes was born in Assos in 331 B.C. and went to Athens to study with Zeno, founder of the Stoic school of philosophy. When he first came to Athens Cleanthes aroused suspicion in the Areopagus, the Supreme Court, because he had no visible means of support. When they learned that he worked at night as a drawer of water so that during the day he could study with Zeno, the court awarded a small pension to Cleanthes. Zeno would not allow him to accept it. After the death of Zeno in 264 B.C. Cleanthes became head of the Stoic school. His most enduring contribution to knowledge was his belief that the sun was the center of the cosmos, a concept that was revived eighteen centuries later by Copernicus in his heliocentric theory of astronomy.

The steep main street of the village leads up to the acropolis of Assos, from where we can survey the ancient city and its surroundings. There, from an altitude of 238 meters, we command a panoramic view that on one side ranges across the southern Troad to Mt. Ida and on the other looks across the Gulf of Edremit to the Mysian coast, with Lesbos rising out of the Aegean across the strait to the south.

The defense walls of Assos are among the most impressive remains of the ancient city. The outer walls date mostly from the mid-fourth century B.C., probably from the time of Hermeias. These walls were originally about three miles in circumference, but now only about half of the circuit remains standing, the best-preserved sections being to the west and northwest of the acropolis. The inner walls, which formed a citadel around the summit of the acropolis, date from the sixth century A.D., probably from the reign of Justinian (527-65).

At the peak of the acropolis is the temple of Athena, the most important monument in the upper city. Clarke and Bacon excavated the stylobate of the temple, which measures 14.03 by 30.31 meters, and carried away to Boston the surviving fragments of its frieze and superstructure, leaving only the bare platform and some scattered column drums and capitals, along with a few sculptural fragments. The American and Turkish studies have revealed that it was a Doric temple made of andesite, a reddish local stone. It had a peripheral colonnade with six columns at the ends and thirteen along the sides, with a pair of columns *in antis* in its pronaos, or front porch. Three of the columns in the peripteral colonnade have now been reerected, along with their Doric capitals. Completed ca. 530 B.C., this is the only Doric temple known to have been erected in Asia Minor during the archaic period. But it is a very odd Doric temple indeed, with a number of features showing a strong Ionic influence, as might be expected here on the Aegean coast not far north of Ionia. The most unusual of these features was its sculptural decoration. In addition to the reliefs on its metopes, its architrave too was sculptured, treated as if it were an Ionic frieze.

On the northern side of the acropolis, above the uppermost tier of the village, we see an early Ottoman mosque built of the same andesite stone as the temple of Athena. The founder of the mosque, is identified by an inscription as the Hüdavendigâr [an imperial Ottoman title meaning "Creator of the Universe"] Sultan Murat I (r. 1359-89). He conquered this region in the third quarter of the fourteenth century. Although of the simplest single-unit type, it is an impressive structure, with a dome seven meters in diameter. Over the door there is an inscribed cross and a Chi-Rho symbol in relief. The emblem of Christ and the dedicatory inscription in Greek indicate that the mosque was constructed from the stones of a Byzantine church, believed to be of the sixth century.

We now walk down through the village, noticing that all of the older houses are made from the same andesite as the temple of Athena and the mosque of the Hüdavendigâr. We then pass through an opening in the fence that surrounds the excavations below the acropolis, after which we walk around the northwestern arc of the defense walls to approach the lower city of Assos.

This brings us along an ancient road that passes through the necropolis of Assos, where a large number of huge sarcophagi are to be seen, some of them with their massive lids still in place. These sarcophagi were made from a porous local stone, much sought after for that purpose because it hastened the decomposition of the flesh of the deceased that in earlier times had been burned off in a funeral pyre. According to Pliny the Elder, the word sarcophagus, which in Greek literally means "body-eater," comes from this local Assos stone. He also claimed it was used in curing the gout, although he did not say how it was used.

After passing the necropolis the ancient road brings us into the lower city of Assos through the western gate in the defense walls, which here date from the fourth century B.C. A short distance in from the gate we come to the gymnasium, a structure in andesite stone dating from the second century B.C. This huge edifice still preserves its paved central courtyard, measuring 32 by 40 meters, originally bordered on all four sides by Doric colonnades. The

Doric Colonnade of Temple of Athena, Assos

Walls of Assos

northeast sector of the courtyard contains the remains of a church erected in the early Byzantine era, and in the southwest corner there is a cistern.

Continuing in the same direction, we come to the western gate of the agora, or market square, the center of the lower city, which together with all of its surrounding structures was built in the third or second century B.C. Here too the buildings are all of andesite stone, designed in the Doric order with Ionic elements. Just inside the gate to the right is the agora temple, its cella opening eastward into a pronaos fronted by four columns. The agora is bounded on its northern side by a stoa measuring some 110 meters in length, with a cistern in front of it. On the south side of the square, at a small angle tapering to the east, there is another stoa, this one about 70 meters long, with the remains of a Roman bath behind it. At the western end of this stoa there is a small heroon, or shrine of a deified hero. At the northeast corner of the agora we see the bouleuterion, or council chamber. It is a square structure 20 meters on a side, its roof supported internally by four columns.

We now make our way down to the theater, which is below the agora to the south. The theater was built in the third century B.C. and altered in Roman times, though it still retains its original Greek form, with its horseshoe-shaped orchestra.

We now return to the village of Behramkale, where most visitors to Assos spend the night in one of the hotels along the waterfront. Some stones from the mole of the harbor of ancient Assos can still be seen in the little fishing port of Behramkale. According to *Acts of the Apostles,* during his second missionary journey Paul joined Luke and the other members of his party here after travelling overland from Alexandria Troas. As soon as he arrived they set sail for Mitylene. As we read in *Acts* 20: 3-14:

> We were now to go ahead by sea, so we set sail for Assos, where we were going to take Paul on board; this was what he had arranged, for he wanted to go by road. When he rejoined us at Assos we took him aboard and went on to Mitylene. The next day we sailed from there and arrived opposite Chios. The second day we touched at Samos, and after stopping at Trogyllium, made Miletus the next day. Paul had decided to pass wide of Ephesus, so as to avoid spending time in Asia, since he was anxious to be in Jerusalem, if possible, for the day of Pentecost.

We leave Behramkale on the road to Ayvacık, which just below the town crosses the Tuzla Çay, the Satnioeis of *The Iliad.* Beside the highway the old road crosses the river on a hog-backed bridge with pointed arches, built by the Ottomans in the mid-fourteenth century.

At Ayvacık we return to highway E87/550, where we turn right to head towards İzmir. Beyond Ayvacık the highway approaches the Gulf of Edremit, and the stands of pine and valonia oak give way to shimmering groves of olive trees. Then the highway passes over the coastal ridge and winds down through a wild gorge, where we are suddenly confronted with a magnificent panorama of the Gulf of Edremit and the rolling hills on its southern shore, with the blue-green mountains of Lesbos rising out of the turquoise Aegean to the west.

The scenery along the north coast of the gulf is surpassingly beautiful, as the highway runs along the shore past olive groves, white sand beaches and pine-clad promontories. Above us to the left loom the majestic peaks of Mt. Ida, which rises 1,724 meters above sea level. The white villages perched on its flanks look like those one sees on the Aegean isles.

At Küçükkuyu a turnoff on the left is signposted for the so-called Altar of Zeus. This takes us up to the village of Adatepe, near which there is a huge rock that both Schliemann and the German archaeologist Judeich called the Altar of Idaean Zeus. There is virtually no archaeological evidence to support this identification. However, Schliemann was convinced that this was the place on the peak of Mt. Ida known as Gargaros, from which Zeus watched the ebb and flow of the fighting on the Trojan Plain far to the north. This is where Hera alighted after her flight from Cape Lekton with Hypnos, the god of sleep, having come to beguile Zeus so that her ally Poseidon could aid the beleaguered Trojans in their battle with the Achaians. Homer describes the scene in Book XIV of *The Iliad:*

> But Hera light footed made her way to the peak of Gargaros
> on towering Ida. And Zeus who gathers clouds saw her,
> and when he saw her desire was a mist about his close heart
> as much as on that time they first went to bed together
> and lay in love, and their dear parents knew nothing of it...
> underneath them the divine earth broke into young, fresh
> grass, and into dewy clover, crocus and hyacinth
> so thick and soft it held the hard ground deep away from them.
> There they lay down together and drew about them a golden
> wonderful cloud, and from it the glimmering dew descended.

Returning to the main highway, we continue driving eastward along the northern shore of the gulf. Near the head of the gulf we pass the village of Devren, which is on the shore almost directly under the main peak of Mt. Ida. Devren has been identified as the site of Antandros, one of the ancient cities of the southern Troad, of which nothing now remains except scattered architectural fragments built into the terrace walls of an olive grove.

Both Herodotus and the poet Alcaeus write that Antandros was inhabited before the Aeolian Greeks first settled on the northern Aegean coast of Anatolia, at the beginning of the first millennium B.C. Stephanos Byzantios, the Byzantine chronicler, writes that Antandros was for a time inhabited by the Cimmerians, the warlike people from the Crimea who in the mid-seventh century B.C. overran western Anatolia. By the fifth century B.C. the city was inhabited by Aeolian Greeks from Lesbos, for the name Antandros appears at that time in tribute lists as a colony of Mytilene. Herodotus writes that Xerxes passed through Antandros on his way from Sardis to the Hellespont in 480 B.C. Strabo notes that the Idaean peak directly above Antandros was called Alexandreia, after Alexander, better known as Paris, son of King Priam and Hecuba. According to mythology, Paris spent his youth tending sheep on the slopes of Mt. Ida above Antandros, and it was here that he judged the contest of beauty between Hera, Athena and Aphrodite. Paris awarded the prize to Aphrodite, and the jealousy that this aroused was one of the factors that eventually led to the Trojan War. Mt. Ida was also the setting for the love affair between Aphrodite and Anchises, a descendant of Dardanus who was a second cousin of King Priam. The love child of this romance, as Homer writes in Book II of *The Iliad,* was Aeneas, "whom divine Aphrodite bore to Anchises/in the folds of Ida, a goddess lying in love with a mortal." According to Virgil, Aeneas embarked on his voyage of exile from Antandros after the fall of Troy, as the hero tells the tale in Book II of *The Aeneid:*

> Lordly Ilium had fallen and all of Neptune's Troy lay a smoking ruin on the ground. We the exiled survivors were forced by divine command to search the world for a home in some uninhabited land. So we

> started to build ships below Antandrus, the city by the foothills of Phrygian Ida, with no idea where destiny would take us or where we would be allowed to settle....In tears I left my homeland's coast, its havens and the place where Troy had stood. I fared out alone on the high seas, an exile with my comrades and my son, with the little Gods of our home and the Great Gods of our race.

The highway now brings us to the head of the gulf, where a turnoff on the right leads to the coastal village of Akçay. This has been tentatively identified as the site of ancient Astyra, which Strabo describes as "a village with a precinct sacred to the Astyrene Artemis."

The highway continues inland until it reaches Edremit the largest town in the southern Troad. The town's name varies only slightly from that of the Greek city of Adramyttium, which the geographer Charon of Lampsacus considered to mark the southeastern limit of the Troad. The present town of Edremit undoubtedly lies some distance inland from the site of ancient Adramyttium, or so it would seem according to Strabo's description of the region around the end of the gulf: "And quite near Astyra is Adramyttium, a city colonized by the Athenians, which has both a harbor and a naval station." Even in early Ottoman times Edremit was on the shore of the gulf, or at least had a port there. At the beginning of the fourteenth century, when the region was part of the Karası *beylik*, Yahşi Bey of Saruhan built a fleet of several hundred barques in Edremit, using wood cut on Mt. Ida.

One of the earliest references to Adramyttium is in Xenophon's *The Anabasis*, or *The March Up Country,* which chronicles the adventures of the Greek mercenaries known as the Ten Thousand on their long homeward journey from Persia in 401-399 B.C. This reference occurs in the last chapter of *The Anabasis,* when Xenophon describes the route taken by the remnants of the Ten Thousand on their way south from the Hellespont to southern Mysia; as he writes:

> Then they marched through the Troad, and after crossing Mount Ida,

came first to Antandros, and then went along the coast to the plain of Thebe. They travelled from there by way of Adramyttium and Certanon to the plain of Caicus, and so reached Pergamum and Mysia.

The site of ancient Thebe has never been identified, but it is believed to be a short distance to the northeast of the present town of Edremit. This was the birthplace of Andromache, the wife of Hector. In Book VI of *The Iliad* Andromache tells Hector of how Achilles killed her father and her seven brothers when he sacked "Thebe of the towering gates." The city is mentioned by Sappho in one of her poems, "Andromache's Wedding". She writes of how Hector came there to take home his bride, "her eyes gleaming/from Thebe the holy...."

The only historic monument in Edremit is Kurşunlu Cami, a Selçuk mosque which, along with a small *türbe*, was founded in 1231 by Yusuf Bey. There is also a small museum in the town library, with a number of antiquities from archaeological sites in the region, along with a large collection of arms from the Ottoman period. The town gardens of Edremit are among the prettiest in Turkey.

We continue along highway E87/550, which after Edremit heads southwestward along the southern shore of the gulf. We now see Mt. Ida dominating the view to the north across the widening gulf, as we pass from the Troad into southern Mysia.

After a drive of 45 kilometers from Edremit we come to Ayvalık, a pretty port town on the southwesternmost promontory of the gulf. The suburbs of the town spread out on to Alibey Adası, a hydra-headed island connected by a bridge to the mainland. Alibey Adası and the smaller islets scattered around it in the strait between the mainland and Lesbos, seven nautical miles distant, were known to the Greeks as Hecatonnesi. Strabo writes that these isles were sacred to Apollo, "for along the whole of this coast as far as Tenedos Apollo is highly honoured." Strabo then goes on to mention a city and an island, both called Pordoselene, which from his description could be identified with the present Ayvalık and Alibey Adası.

> Near these islands [the Hecatonnesi] is Pordoselene, which contains a city of the same name, and also, in front of this city, another island, larger and of the same name, which is also inhabited and has a temple sacred to Apollo.

The history of Ayvalık is obscure up until the last quarter of the eighteenth century, when a stroke of good luck suddenly brought it into prominence. At that time the population of Ayvalık was almost entirely Greek, as was the case in most of the communities along the Aegean coast of Anatolia. The historic incident that changed the fortunes of Ayvalık occurred on 6/7 July 1770, when the Russians virtually annihilated the Ottoman fleet in a battle off Çeşme, at the end of the peninsula west of İzmir. The only Turkish captain who escaped was Cezayirli Hasan Paşa, who managed to sail his badly damaged ship as far as Ayvalık, where he ran it aground. The Greeks of Ayvalık rescued Hasan Paşa and his crew and escorted them to Çanakkale, from where a ship brought them safely back to Istanbul. Four years later Hasan Paşa was made grand admiral of the Ottoman navy and then in 1789 he became grand vezier. Hasan Paşa never forgot the Greeks of Ayvalık for saving his life, and when he became grand vezier he obtained from Selim III an imperial decree granting the town privileges that were enjoyed by few other places in the Ottoman Empire. According to the decree, all Muslims in Ayvalık were to be relocated in the surrounding villages; no Turkish soldiers were allowed in the town or even to pass through it; the townspeople were spared all arbitrary taxes and paid only a specified amount each year; and they had the right to appoint their own governor, who would be a Turk, and whom they had the right to dismiss if they felt it necessary. This privileged status attracted Greeks from all over the Ottoman Empire to Ayvalık. It soon became the most prosperous and progressive town in the region, with an academy in which 600 students received a classical education in the liberal arts, science and mathematics, using books published by their own press. Ayvalık retained its privileges until 1919, when the Greek army invaded Asia Minor and captured the town in the first battle of the Graeco-Turkish war. This was the beginning of the end for Hellenic Ayvalı, as it was known to the Greeks. At the conclusion of the war all of the Greeks of Ayvalık were deported to Greece in the population exchange that was agreed upon in the Lausanne Treaty of 1923, to be replaced by Turkish refugees from Greece.

Up until 1923 there were a score of Greek Orthodox churches in Ayvalık. Most of them were converted to mosques after the population exchange, the largest being Ayios Ioannis, which is now Saatli Cami (the Mosque with a Clock); and Ayios Yiorgios, now Çınarlı Cami (the Mosque with the Plane Tree). The two most notable exceptions are the church of the Taxiarchoi (Archangels), which has been restored as a museum of icons; and Ayios Nicholas, the former cathedral, which is also being restored as a museum.

In recent years many Greeks have been crossing from Lesbos to Ayvalık for their holidays, and in the summer months they fill the cafés and restaurants along the seafront and on Ali Bey Adası. And among the songs that they sing is a lament from the diaspora of 1923, remembering with painful nostalgia the lost world of Hellenic Ayvalı:

My eyes have never seen a village like Ayvali
Ask me about it, for I have been there.
It has silver doors, golden keys,
And beautiful girls as fresh as cool water....

CHAPTER TWO

MYSIA:
PERGAMUM

After leaving Ayvalık we return to highway E87/550 and continue driving toward İzmir, as we enter the part of ancient Mysia that extends eastward from the Aegean south of the Troad. The highway takes us south-southeast along the coast, with the mountains of Lesbos in view to our right across the strait. About 38 kilometers from Ayvalık there is a turnoff to the right for Dikilli, a little port where there is a car ferry service to Lesbos.

The site of ancient Atarnaeus is a short distance to the northeast of the Dikili turnoff. Atarnaeus is mentioned twice by Herodotus, the first time in connection with an incident that took place there ca. 510 B.C., and the second as being one of the places through which Xerxes marched his army on the way from Sardis to the Hellespont in 480 B.C. During the mid-fourth century B.C. the city was controlled by Hermeias, the Tyrant of Atarnaeus, and after his death in 344 B.C. it reverted to Persian rule for a decade before being freed by Alexander the Great. Atarnaeus remained independent throughout the Hellenistic period, but then under Roman rule it was absorbed in the territory of Pergamum, and by the second century A.D. it had declined to the status of a village. All that remains of Atarnaeus are parts of the supporting wall of its citadel and fragments of the outer defense wall of the city.

Beyond the Dikili turnoff the highway leaves the coast and turns eastward. We then turn left from the highway on to the road for Bergama, which is eight kilometers to the east up the valley of the Bakır Çayı, the River Caicus of antiquity.

Bergama is a Turkish town that has grown up around the ruins of ancient Pergamum. The oldest of these ruins, dating from the Hellenistic period, are on the mountain that rises just to the north of Bergama, while the remains of Roman Pergamum are in the town itself. The setting of the Hellenistic city is spectacular, its acropolis situated on the peak of the mountain more than 350 meters above the surrounding plain. This gigantic spire of rock rises precipitously from the plain on three sides, flanked by two tributaries of the Caicus, with the Selinus flowing around the mountain to the west and the Cetius to the east. All of these features made this a natural fortress controlling the Caicus valley, the heart of what came to be the Pergamene kingdom.

The oldest pottery shards found on the acropolis of Pergamum date from the eighth century B.C. These remains indicate that the first settlers on the acropolis were not Greeks, but by the beginning of historic times the settlement here had become thoroughly Hellenized. The Greek form of its name—Pergamos—means the inner citadel of a city, so used by Homer in referring to Troy.

There are a number of myths concerning the origin of Pergamum and the Pergamene kingdom. According to one of these myths, the first ruler of Mysia was Teuthras, who gave his name to the kingdom of Teuthrania and the capital of the same name, which was located farther down the Caicus valley to the southwest. Another myth concerns the princess Auge, daughter of King Aleos of Tegea, who was disowned by her father after she was seduced by Heracles and gave birth to the god's son, Telephus. According to Pausanias, in his *Guide to Greece,* Aleos locked Auge and Telephus in a trunk and threw them into the sea, after which they floated all the way to the northern Aegean coast of Asia Minor. There they were washed up at the mouth of the Caicus river and found by Teuthras, who married Auge and adopted Telephus as his son. Then when Teuthras died Telephus succeeded him as King of Teuthrania. One of the fabled exploits of Telephus was his defeat of an Achaian army led by Agamemnon, who in this version of the myth had mistakenly wandered into Teuthrania before he besieged Troy, probably a folk memory of an early Hellenic invasion of northwestern Anatolia, at some unknown time just prior to the dawn of recorded history.

The first recorded mention of Pergamum is by Xenophon in the last chapter of his *Anabasis,* where he describes how the Ten Thou-

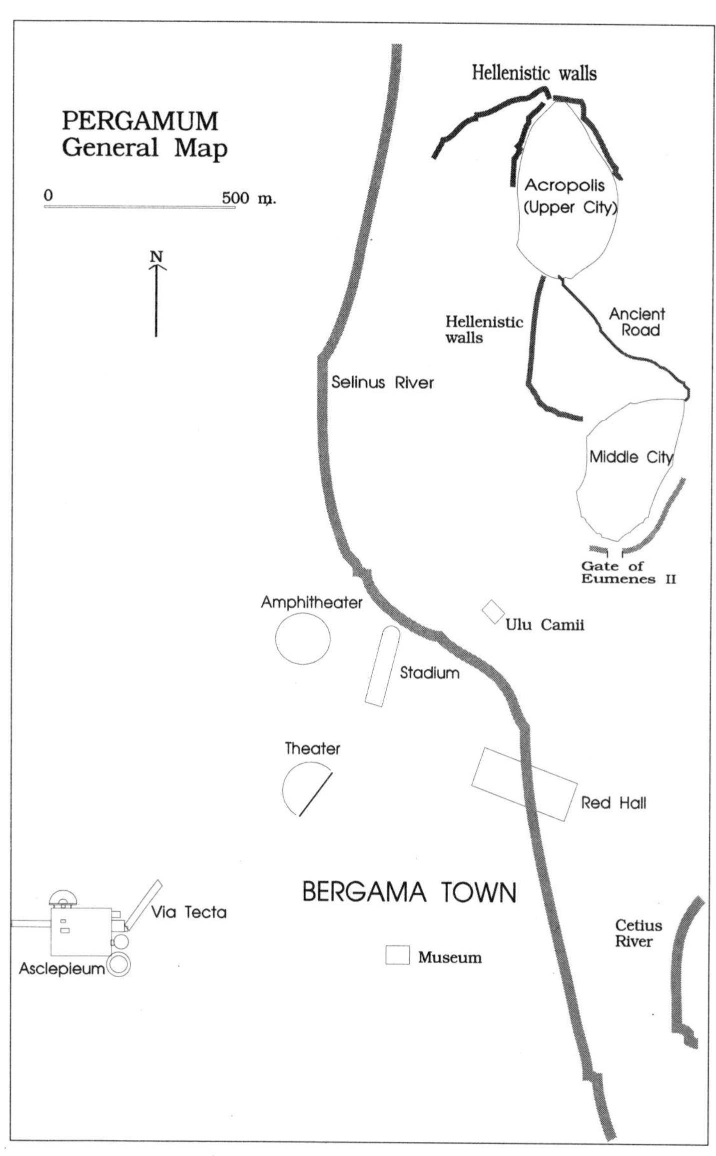
PERGAMUM
General Map
0
500 m.
N
Hellenistic walls
Acropolis
(Upper City)
Hellenistic
walls
Ancient
Road
Selinus River
Middle City
Gate of
Eumenes II
Amphitheater
Ulu Camii
Stadium
Theater
Red Hall
BERGAMA TOWN
Via Tecta
Asclepieum
Museum
Cetius
River

The Acropolis at Pergamum, Allom Print

sand made their way south "to the plain of Caicus, and so reached Pergamum and Mysia." This was in the spring of 399 B.C., when the remnants of the Ten Thousand joined forces with the Spartan general Thibron, who had come to aid the Greek cities of Asia Minor in a revolt against the Persian satrap, or governor, Tissaphernes. At Pergamum Xenophon was entertained by the widow Hellas, whose late husband Gongylus had been ruler of a small principality in the Caicus valley, and which after his death had been divided by his two sons. Hellas, realizing that her guests were in need of money, suggested that Xenophon and his men attack the fortified estate of a local Persian nobleman, which they succeeded in doing on their second attempt. Meanwhile Thibron had arrived in Pergamum, whereupon Xenophon gave over to him command of the Ten Thousand, and at the same time several Greek dynasts in the Caicus valley voluntarily surrendered to the Spartan general. Xenophon ends *The Anabasis* at this point, having given us a glimpse of life in the Caicus valley at the beginning of the fourth century B.C.

Pergamum appears briefly in history once again in the last quarter of the fourth century B.C. as a footnote to the story of Alexander the Great. After Alexander's victory at the battle of the Issus in 333 B.C., he took as his mistress the Persian princess Barsine. Seven years later she bore him a son named Heracles. Alexander sent Barsine and her son back to Pergamum, where they remained for nearly two decades, until Heracles was put to death on the orders of Antipater, the regent of Macedonia.

Aside from these two minor incidents, Pergamum does not appear in the full light of history until the end of the second decade of the third century B.C. It emerged then as an independent state after the wars of the Diadochi, the successors of Alexander. When Antigonus lost his life at the battle of Ipsus in 301 B.C., all of Asia Minor fell under the control of Lysimachus, King of Thrace. Soon afterwards Lysimachus appointed a Paphlagonian named Philetaerus to be his governor at Pergamum, leaving in his charge a large part of the royal treasury. After Lysimachus was defeated and killed in 281 B.C., Philetaerus managed to retain his position as governor at Pergamum, keeping the huge sum of money that had been deposited with him and using it for his own purposes. He then established an independent principality with its capital at Pergamum and adorned it with temples and other public buildings. He also made generous loans to neighboring cities to maintain good relations with them. At the same time he developed the Pergamene lands in the Caicus valley and created an army to defend his realm. Philetaerus died in 263 B.C. and was succeeded by his nephew Eumenes, whom he had adopted as his son.

The year after his succession Eumenes defeated the Seleucid king Antiochus I in a battle near Sardis. This preserved the independence of Pergamum from the Seleucid kingdom, the vast realm that had been founded in Syria by the Macedonian general Seleucus I Nicator, another of Alexander's successors. During the two decades following this victory Eumenes enlarged his principality to include the whole of the Caicus valley and most of the adjacent Aegean coast. Eumenes ruled until his death in 241 B.C. and was succeeded by his adopted son Attalus, a grandnephew of Philetaerus.

Attalus began his reign with a great victory over the Gauls, the barbaric Celtic tribespeople who had crossed over from Europe in 278 B.C. and for the next generation terrorized western Asia Minor. The Roman historian Livy writes thus of the Gauls and their defeat by Attalus in Book XXXVIII of his *History:*

> ...they [the Gauls] levied tribute throughout every part of Asia this side of the Taurus...and so great was the fear of their name...that even the kings of Syria [the Seleucids] did not refuse to pay them tribute. The first of all the inhabitants of Asia who ventured a refusal was Attalus...and beyond the expectation of all, fortune favoured his bold undertaking. He defeated them in a pitched battle.

This broke the power of the Gauls, ending forever the menace they had posed for the Greek cities of western Asia Minor. His great triumph earned Attalus the name of Soter, or Saviour, and led him to call himself King of Pergamum, the first of the Attalid dynasty to assume that title. He ruled for 44 years, the longest reign in the Attalid dynasty. Attalus spent much of this time in warfare with the Seleucid kings of Syria, struggling for supremacy in Asia Minor, but by the time he died in 197 B.C. the boundaries of Pergamum were much the same as when he began his reign.

Attalus had entered into good relations with Rome, and when this policy was continued by his son and successor, Eumenes II, it soon resulted in rich benefits for the Pergamene kingdom. A Roman army under Scipio Africanus invaded Asia Minor in 190 B.C., joining forces with Eumenes and his troops in an effort to break the power of the Seleucid kingdom, then ruled by Antiochus III. Scipio and Eumenes decisively defeated Antiochus at the battle of Magnesia early in 189 B.C., after which most of the former Seleucid possessions in Asia Minor were awarded by Rome to Pergamum. The territory of the Pergamene kingdom was thus greatly increased, stretching along the Aegean coast from the Hellespont to the Maeander River, including also the islands of Euboea, Aegina and

Andros. The territory in the interior comprised most of Asia Minor west of Ancyrathe—modern Ankara, extending from the Black Sea and the Sea of Marmara south to the Mediterranean. As the historian Polybius noted, Eumenes succeeded his father "in a kingdom reduced to a few petty towns, but this he raised to the level of the largest dynasties of his day." Eumenes used the vast wealth of this huge kingdom to adorn his capital with temples and other public buildings, including the famous library of Pergamum. During his reign Pergamum emerged as one of the leading cultural centers in the Greek world, surpassed only by Athens and Alexandria. It was a focal point for the advancement of Hellenism in Asia Minor. The city was also renowned for its school of sculpture, which produced some of the supreme masterpieces of Hellenistic art—works such as the "Dying Gaul," now in the Capitoline Museum in Rome.

Eumenes died in 159 B.C. and was succeeded by his brother Attalus II, who ruled until 138 B.C. Attalus continued the policies of his late brother, particularly the Pergamene alliance with Rome. He fought a long and difficult war against Nicomedes II of Bithynia, in which Pergamum eventually emerged victorious. Attalus was also a great builder and patron of the arts. He is remembered today principally for the magnificent edifice that he endowed in Athens—the Stoa of Attalus, which has now been fully restored. It is a fitting monument to the greatness of Pergamum in its golden age.

But the golden age did not long outlive Attalus II. He was succeeded in 138 B.C. by his weak and eccentric nephew, Attalus III, who neglected affairs of state to dabble in alchemy and botany and allowed his kingdom to be dominated by Rome. Toward the end of his life Roman power had grown so great that there seemed little future for an independent realm in western Asia Minor, and so in his last will and testament Attalus bequeathed his kingdom to Rome. When Attalus died in 133 B.C. his bequest was quickly accepted by the Roman Senate. But then a pretender named Aristonicus appeared on the scene, claiming to be a bastard son of Eumenes II, and many Pergamenes enlisted in his cause. A three-year war followed before the Romans finally defeated Aristonicus, who was captured and sent as a prisoner to Rome. Soon afterwards he was strangled. Rome then incorporated the Pergamene kingdom into the newly organized province of Asia, which came into being in 129 B.C.

Pergamum prospered under Roman rule, becoming an important center of trade. This led to a great increase in its population, which at its peak in the mid-second century A.D. numbered some 150,000, as the city spread out on to the plain to the south of the acropolis hill. A number of monumental edifices were erected in the lower city at this time, most notably the great healing shrine known as the Asclepieum, where the great physician Galen received his training and wrote the first of his medical treatises. But then in the third century the fortunes of Pergamum began to decline, as other cities in western Asia Minor began to surpass it in trade and commerce. Nevertheless, Pergamum continued to be one of the cultural centers of the Graeco-Roman world. Julian the Apostate studied philosophy here in 351, a decade before he began his reign as emperor (361-63), indicating that ancient Greek culture was still alive in Pergamum at that late date. But Christianity had already struck its roots in Pergamum by then, for it was the site of a bishopric, one of the Seven Churches of Revelation. As the Evangelist, writing in the last years of the first Christian century, says in *Revelation* 2:12-13:

> And to the angel of the church in Pergamos write: "These things saieth he which hath the sharp sword with two edges. I know thy works and where thou dwellest, even where Satan's throne is: and thou holdest my name, and hast not denied my faith, even in those days when Antipas was my faithful martyr, who was slain among you, where Satan dwelleth."

Like all of the other ancient cities of western Asia Minor, Pergamum was destroyed during the Persian and Arab invasions of the seventh and eighth centuries. It survived on a much smaller scale through the medieval period, captured in turn by the Crusaders, Byzantines, Selçuks and then the Ottomans, who under Orhan Gazi took the city in 1336. Known to the Turks as Bergama, the lower city on the plain revived under Ottoman rule and became the lively town one sees today. The ruins of the ancient city were first excavated in 1878 by the German Archaeological Society under the direction of Carl Humann and Alexander Conze, a project that continues to the present day.

Our route takes us through the center of Bergama and then across the Bergama Çayı, the River Selinus of antiquity. On the other side of the bridge we come to the extraordinary edifice known as Kızıl Avlu, the Red Court. The building takes its name from the red brick with which it is constructed; this was originally revetted with colored marble, of which only bands of molding and blocks of consoles remain. This enormous structure, which together with its courtyard covered an area originally measuring 260 by 100 meters, was excavated by the Germans in the years 1927-38. Much of its court is still hidden under the surrounding houses of the town. It is built directly over the river, which flows diagonally under the courtyard through a large double tunnel. The Red Court has been identified as a temple dedicated to the Egyptian deities Serapis, Isis and Harpocrates, and is dated to the first half of the second century A.D. During the early Byzantine period it was converted into a Byzantine church dedicated to St. John the Apostle. The main structure consists of a monumental basilica measuring 60 by 26 meters and surviving up to a height of 19 meters. This is flanked by two circular towers fronted by courtyards surrounded on three sides by stoas, with an outer courtyard to the west 200 meters long and 100 meters wide. The great entryway of the main structure is seven meters wide and 14 meters high. It opens into the marble-paved basilica, in whose center there is a shallow marble basin once used for ritual ablutions. Behind the basin there is a podium, 1.5 meters high, that supported the base of an enormous ten-meter-high cult statue of Serapis.

The high priest of Serapis approached this base via a subterranean passageway, after which he made his way up inside the statue to speak as if his was the voice of the god himself, uttering oracles. Serapis, god of the underworld, was worshipped here along with his associated goddess Isis and the god Harpocrates. On the west side of the courtyard there are a number of ancient architectural fragments, including several with inscriptions in Hebrew, as well as some Jewish gravestones from the Ottoman period.

After leaving the Red Court we follow signposts that direct us to the acropolis of ancient Pergamum, driving along a steep road that winds up to a car park within a short walk of the mountain's summit.

The ruins on the summit comprise the very oldest part of Pergamum, the citadel of the ancient city. During the Attalid period the citadel enclosed the royal palace, the theater, the arsenal, and several of the city's most important religious shrines. These institutions gave the citadel a sacred and ceremonial aura, in contrast to the more public character of the quarter farther down the mountain, which might be termed the middle city, to distinguish it from the lower city of Roman times on the plain below. The citadel walls date from the late fifth or early fourth century B.C. Philetaerus presumably restored the fortifications of the citadel when he took control of Pergamum, erecting within it a palace that would be enlarged by his successors in the Attalid dynasty. Eumenes I extended the defense walls of the city southward in two more or less parallel lines to the plain below, enclosing the new quarter that had developed during the first century of Attalid rule.

The pathway from the car park leads to what was once the gateway of the upper city, near the southeastern corner of the city. Just outside the gateway we see on our left the remains of a heroon. This was a peristyle building, that is, with a surrounding colonnade. It was probably dedicated to Attalus I and Eumenes II, who after their death were raised to the status of deified heroes.

We now pass through the remains of the propylon, the monumental gateway to the citadel, erected by Eumenes II. Inside the propylon an ancient street leads out to the north end of the narrowing citadel. On the right side of the street we pass a series of

The Red Court, Allom Print

The Red Court

foundations that have been identified as belonging to the palaces of the Attalid kings. There are five palaces in all, and each one of these has been attributed to one of the Pergamene rulers, partly on the basis of objects found in them and partly by conjecture. The first of these that we pass has been attributed to Eumenes II, followed in turn by those of Attalus II, Eumenes I, Attalus I, and finally that of Philetaerus.

Behind the palaces on the right side of the street we see first the remains of a complex of Hellenistic houses, and then a barracks and a defense tower. All these structures were undoubtedly used by the garrison of the citadel, whose arsenal formed a walled enclosure at the long and narrow northern end of the acropolis.

The principal sanctuaries of the upper city are all on the precipitous western side of the acropolis, arrayed in an arc above the theater. At the northern end of this arc we see the newly restored Trajaneum, a Corinthian temple built for the deified emperor Trajan (r. 98-117). It was completed ca. 125 by his successor Hadrian, who after his death in 138 was also worshipped in this sanctuary. The Trajaneum is of the type known as hexastyle peripteral, with six columns at the ends and nine along the sides, and with a pair of columns *in antis* in its pronaos. The temple stands in the center of a vast temenos, or sacred enclosure—an area measuring some 60 by 80 meters, bordered on its sides and rear by towering colonnades. The columns to the rear stand on a retaining wall five meters high, so that the colonnade would be visible from the theater terrace below. The reerected columns are crowned with several varieties of palm leaf capitals, which are late variants of the so-called Pergamene capital. Colossal cult statues of Trajan and Hadrian stood at the rear of the temenos flanking the temple. The heads of the statues of both emperors were discovered early in the excavations and are preserved in the Pergamum Museum in Berlin.

Directly above the central axis of the theater we see the ruins of the temple of Athena Polias Nikephorus, the Bringer of Victory to the City. All that remains of the temple is its crepidoma, or stepped platform. There is reason to believe that Zeus was worshipped here

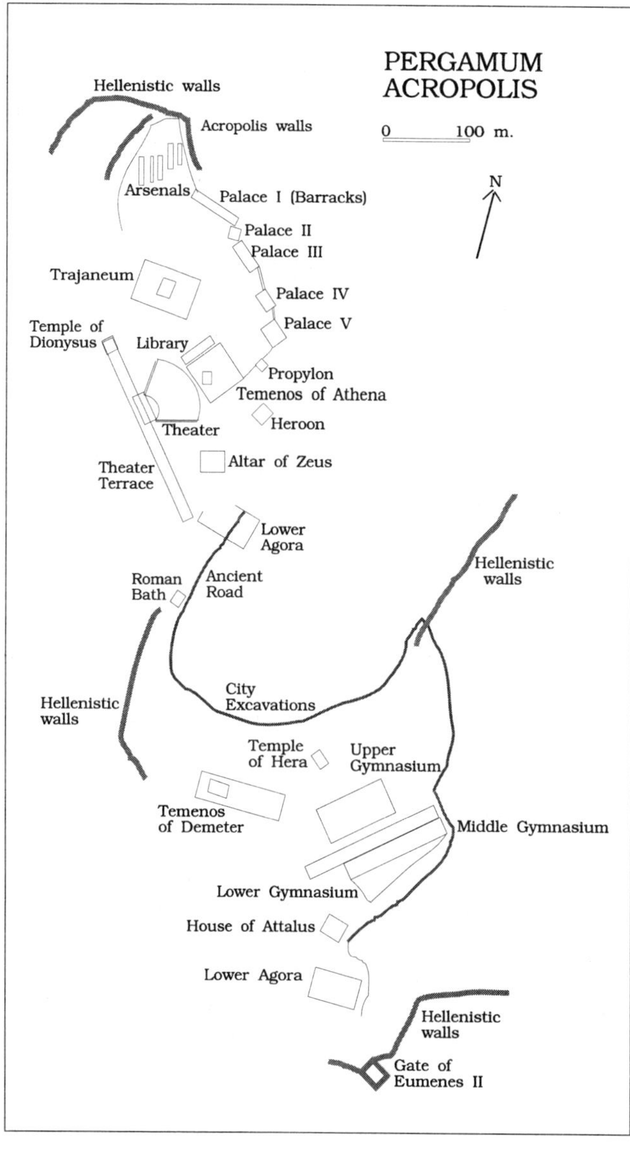
PERGAMUM
ACROPOLIS
0 100 m.
N
Hellenistic walls
Acropolis walls
Arsenals
Palace I (Barracks)
Palace II
Palace III
Trajaneum
Palace IV
Palace V
Temple of
Dionysus
Library
Propylon
Temenos of Athena
Heroon
Theater
Altar of Zeus
Theater
Terrace
Lower
Agora
Hellenistic
walls
Roman
Bath
Ancient
Road
City
Excavations
Hellenistic
walls
Temple
of Hera
Upper
Gymnasium
Temenos
of Demeter
Middle Gymnasium
Lower Gymnasium
House of Attalus
Lower Agora
Hellenistic
walls
Gate of
Eumenes II

along with Athena. This is the oldest extant temple in Pergamum, dating from the early third century B.C. It is one of the rare Doric temples in Asia Minor, a peripteros with six columns at its ends and ten along its sides. It has two columns *in antis* in both its pronaos and its opisthodomos, or rear porch. Its cella is divided by a wall into two equal chambers. The temple stood at the open front end of a temple nearly as large as that of the Trajaneum, bordered on the other three sides by two-storied stoas, in each of which the lower story was in the Doric order and the upper one in the Ionic. These stoas were later additions; the one on the north was erected by Eumenes II, while those on the south and east sides were probably built later in the second century B.C. The magnificent two-storied propylon was at the south end of the east stoa. Within the pediment of this entryway was a frieze that included sculptures of the owl of Athena and the eagle of Zeus, reassembled in the Berlin Museum from fragments discovered on the site. The double-aisled northern stoa had on its lower story a central colonnade with Pergamene capitals. The marble parapets of the upper stories were decorated with reliefs representing the captured weapons and chariots of conquered enemies, most notably the Gauls. Within the temenos there stood a number of bronze statues on marble bases, most of them commemorating the great victory that Attalus I won over the Gauls at the beginning of his reign. A number of these bronzes were later copied in marble, the most famous being the "Dying Gaul."

Adjoining the temenos of Athena on the south are the remains of the celebrated Library of Pergamum, built by Eumenes II at the same time as he erected the north stoa of the temple. The library, which was dedicated to Athena, the goddess of wisdom, was approached through the upper stories of the stoa. According to ancient sources, the Pergamene library possessed some 200,000 scrolls. This means that most of these works must have been stored elsewhere, for it is estimated that the rooms here had space for less than a tenth of that number. These scrolls were made of parchment, an invention attributed to both the Pergamenes and the Ionian

The Trajaneum

Greeks, replacing the papyrus used by the Egyptians. The fame of the Pergamene library rivalled that of Alexandria, a tribute to the love of learning of the Attalid kings, who were known throughout the Greek world as patrons of scholarship. Apollonius of Perge, one of the greatest mathematicians of the Hellenistic period, studied for a time at Pergamum as a guest of Attalus I, to whom he dedicated some of his works. The fate of the Pergamene library after the Attalid period is uncertain. Mark Antony promised to give it to Cleopatra to make up for the destruction of the library at Alexandria, but it is not known whether he ever did so. It would appear that most if not all of the collection remained at Pergamum, for the city continued to be a great center of learning up until late antiquity. This would not have been possible without the full resources of the library.

The reading room of the library is the largest of the four extant chambers. One can still see there the wall sockets that supported the shelves where the scroll collection was kept. Also visible is a pedestal that once supported a large statue of Athena. The pedestal was originally three meters in height and the statue itself was three and one-half meters tall, giving one some idea of the grand dimensions of the room. The statue, which is now preserved in the Berlin Museum, is a marble copy in reduced size of the colossal chryselephantine (gold and ivory) cult figure of Athena Parthenos, the Virgin Goddess, which stood in the Parthenon of Athens, a work of the great sculptor Pheidias.

Just to the south of Athena's sanctuary are the remains of a Hellenistic stoa. South of that is the great Altar of Zeus, of which only the stepped platform remains. The altar was unearthed by Carl Humann in 1881 and was later reconstructed in the Berlin Museum from fragments found on the site. It remains one of the supreme masterpieces of Hellenistic architecture and art.

The Altar of Zeus was built by Eumenes II soon after his victory over Antiochus III at the battle of Magnesia in 189 B.C., and commemorates his own victory and the earlier triumph of Attalus I over the Gauls. Like the temple to its north, the altar was dedicated to both Zeus and Athena. It stood in the center of a vast temenos measuring 69 by 77 meters. Aligned precisely with the temple of Athena, which loomed above it on its terrace some 50 meters to the north, both edifices could be seen in one harmonious view. The monument was set on a five-stepped crepidoma of nearly square form. Above this in turn were a three-stepped podium, a frieze, and a colonnaded stoa in the form of an enclosing wall. This wall and its Ionic colonnade extended around the north, east and south sides of the monument, leaving two projecting wings to flank the magnificent stairway on the western side. A score of 20-meter-wide marble steps led up to the open rectangular area on which the altar, a marble offering table set on a three-stepped podium, was erected. The colonnade extended completely around the periphery of the enclosing wall and across the top of the steps. A similar portico was planned for the central court around the altar, but was never completed.

The sculptural decoration on the Altar of Zeus was meant to symbolize the heroic role of the Attalids and their mythical ancestors as the saviours of Hellenic civilization in its struggle against barbarism. The enclosing wall that surrounded the altar on three sides was carved with reliefs depicting incidents from the life of Telephus, son of Heracles: his birth, his landing with his mother Auge in Mysia, his adoption by King Teuthras, his succession to the throne, his defeat of Agamemnon's army, his founding of Pergamum, and finally his death. This decoration symbolized the semi-divine origins of the Attalid dynasty and its ancient connection with the heroes of the Homeric epics. The frieze under the Ionic portico was adorned with a Gigantomachia, the mythical battle between the Olympian gods and the ancient giants. This vast scene, some 120 meters long and 2.3 meters high, contained about fifty Olympian deities and an equal number of giants—the most complete representation of the Greek pantheon in existence. One art historian has estimated that the reliefs represent the efforts of some forty sculptors, who together produced the most extraordinary work of art that has survived from the Hellenistic age in Asia Minor.

It has been suggested that the Altar of Zeus may have been

The Altar of Zeus

what the author of *Revelation* was referring to his letter to the church in Pergamum, where he writes of the city as the place "where Satan's throne is." When the Evangelist passed through Pergamum in the last years of the first century A.D., the Altar of Zeus was still standing in all of its pagan glory; the Olympian deities wese still being worshipped in their magnificent temples and altars on the Pergamene acropolis.

Just below the Altar of Zeus to the south, at the southernmost end of the acropolis, we come to the market square known as the upper agora. This irregular-shaped area, little more than half of a square, is formed by a Doric stoa dating from the third century A.D. At its northwestern end we see the remains of the agora temple, a little structure with mixed Doric and Ionic elements erected in the second century B.C. It was probably dedicated to either Zeus or Hermes. The agora is cut through its center by an ancient street that led down from the acropolis to the middle city, which we will explore after we visit the theater.

The northwestern end of the upper agora opens out on to the theater terrace, a long and narrow shelf that stretches for nearly 250 meters to the north below the tiered seats of the auditorium. The terrace was bordered on its western side by a Doric stoa, which was one story high on its inner side and three on the outside, where it was supported by a retaining wall with internal chambers. This wall, together with the stoa above it, was in places five stories high because of the very steep slope of the hillside. The view from the terrace is stupendous, looking out over the valley of the Caicus stretching off towards the Aegean coast--the land that comprised the realm of Pergamum when it first became an independent state.

At the northern end of the terrace a flight of 25 steps leads up to the ruins of a small Ionic terrace dedicated to Dionysus, worshipped here as the god of the theater. The original andesite temple was erected in the first half of the second century B.C. The present structure dates from the second decade of the third century A.D., when it was rebuilt in marble and dedicated to the deified emperor Caracalla (r. 211-17), who was worshipped here as the "new

Dionysus." It is a prostyle temple, the colonnade of its pronaos arrayed with four columns in front and two on the sides, counting corner columns twice. The temple faces south from its podium at the top of the steps, 4.5 meters above the level of the theater terrace.

The theater is one of the most impressive in Asia Minor surviving from the Hellenistic period. It was originally constructed in the third century B.C., then rebuilt by Eumenes II and altered once again in Roman times. The cavea, or auditorium, forms part of the natural contour of the steeply sloping west front of the acropolis rock. From the top of it, the principal sanctuaries of the upper city of Pergamum would have been dramatically visible to the audience as they entered from the theater terrace. The auditorium is exceptionally steep, with 80 rows of seats ascending the slope through an elevation of 36 meters. Because of the topography the cavea comprises a much smaller angle than in a typical Greek theater. The seats are arranged in three tiers separated by broad horizontal passages called diazomata, with narrow stairways dividing these into six or seven cunei, or wedges. There were seats for some 10,000 spectators, with the king's marble box still in place just above the center of the front row. The orchestra extends out on to the theater terrace, where in Hellenistic times a wooden skene, or stage building, was erected on the day of a performance. It would be dismantled immediately afterwards, so as not to obscure the superb view.

We now follow the ancient road from the upper agora to the middle city. The middle city represents an expansion of Pergamum by Eumenes II, who extended the line of fortifications from the citadel to form a new quarter about halfway down the mountain. On the way down we pass an archaeological zone that was first explored in 1973, a site known as the City Excavations. Its purpose was to study the form and growth of Pergamum beyond the official buildings and thus to learn more about the daily life of the Pergamenes. The first of the structures in this group that we come to is a bath on the right of the road about 100 meters from the

Theater and Temple of Dionysus

upper agora. Originally erected in the Hellenistic period, it was rebuilt in the Roman era.

Another 100 meters along we come to the main area of the City Excavations. The most important structures unearthed here are a Roman bath and gymnasium complex, an odeion and a heroon, the latter known as the Marble Hall. These three buildings appear to have been erected ca. 70 B.C. by, or in honor of, a wealthy Pergamene philanthropist named Diodoros Pasparos. His portrait bust is now in the Bergama Museum in the lower town, replaced in the heroon by a plaster bust. The eighteen reliefs in the heroon are also plaster copies of the originals in the museum•Among these are representations of weapons and armor, a fighting cock, a warrior (now headless), and an erect phallus—symbol of good luck and prosperity. Other structures unearthed in the City Excavations include a tavern, a shop that sold wine and olive oil, a sanctuary of a Dionysian cult, a peristyle house with a bath, and a well house, along with a large number of ramshackle Byzantine houses dating from the twelfth century to the fourteenth.

The road winds on beyond the City Excavations and eventually brings us to the middle city. The surviving monuments here include the lower agora, three gymnasia, four temples, two public fountains, and a number of other structures, including altars, stoas and propylaea, or monumental entryways.

The temple of Demeter stands below the road at the northwestern corner of the middle city. This is the oldest of the temples in the middle city, founded by Philetaerus and his brother Eumenes in memory of their mother Boa. Later additions were made by Queen Apollonia, wife of Attalus I. It is of the type called a *templum-in-antis,* that is, with columns only between its antae—the extensions of the side walls of the cella. This interesting little structure combined all of the Greek architectural orders; its columns were Doric and their capitals were Aeolic, with Ionic and Corinthian elements added in the Roman period. The temenos of the temple was surrounded on three sides by stoas erected by Queen Apollonia. The one on the southern or downhill side was supported by massive retaining walls. Apollonia also added the propylon at the west end of the temenos, its columns surmounted by Aeolic capitals that have recently been put back in place.

The second of the four temples of the middle city is a short distance to the east of Demeter's temenos. This was dedicated to Hera Basileia, the Queen of the Gods. It is a small four-columned Doric prostyle edifice, probably erected by Attalus I. East of the temple there is a stoa and to its west an exedra, or semicircular niche. Within the exedra there is a marble altar dedicated to the Anatolian god Men. This was excavated elsewhere on the site and reerected here, though it has no connection with the temple of Hera. Although of modest size, the temple of Hera stood in a prominent position at the top of the middle city and could be seen from a considerable distance.

Between the temenos of Hera and that of Demeter we see the remains of a tiny temple dedicated to Asclepius, the healing god, whose main sanctuary in Pergamum is in the lower city. The temple here was first erected in the third century B.C. as a Doric edifice, but in the latter half of the second century B.C. it was rebuilt in the Ionic order. In its present form it is a six-columned prostyle temple, with four columns in front of its pronaos and two on the sides.

The largest secular building complex in the middle city is the gymnasium, which is situated on three terraces tiered one above the other. The upper gymnasium was built by Attalus II and the lower two by Eumenes II, with all three of them rebuilt during the Roman period. The upper gymnasium was reserved for grown men, the middle for ephebes—youths undergoing military training in addition to their other studies, and the lower one for young boys. The upper one, known as the Ceremonial Gymnasium, occupied a terrace measuring approximately 200 by 45 meters, with a central courtyard 74 meters long and 36 meters wide. The courtyard was surrounded by a two-storied stoa, originally in the Doric order but rebuilt in the Corinthian order during the Roman era. The structures to the east and west of this courtyard formed part of a baths complex, which in the Roman era was an integral part of all gym-

Upper Gymnasium

nasia. At the northwest corner of the gymnasium there are the remains of an auditorium with a seating capacity of about 1,000. At the center of the northern side of the gymnasium there was a large chamber known as the Ephebion, where all of the ceremonies connected with the gymnastic activities took place. The chamber to the east of this was in Roman times reserved for the emperor, who presided over the ceremonies in the Ephebion whenever he was in Pergamum, as Hadrian did during his visit to the city in 125.

The middle gymnasium occupies a narrow terrace measuring 150 by 36 meters with a Corinthian stoa extending along the entire length of its northern side. On the western side of the terrace we see the foundations of a small prostyle temple of the Corinthian order, with four columns in front of its porch. An inscription records that the temple was dedicated to Hermes and Heracles, the gods of physical culture, with the deified emperor also being worshipped here in Roman times. Other inscriptions record the names of ephebes dating from Hellenistic to Roman times. The lower gymnasium stands on an irregularly-shaped and tapering terrace about 80 meters in length. The entrance to both this and the middle gymnasium was via a winding vaulted stairway at the eastern end of the lower terrace. Even in its ruined state this is still a very impressive structure. Professor Ekrem Akurgal, in his *Ancient Civilizations and Ruins of Turkey,* describes the stairway as "one of the oldest and most beautiful arch-and-vault constructions of the ancient Greek world."

Below the lower gymnasium an ancient street leads downward to the southwest, its paving of large andesite blocks deeply rutted by the wheels of carts and chariots. About 100 meters beyond the gymnasium the road veers to the west as it passes on the right a peristyle structure, with a Doric stoa surrounding a central courtyard measuring 20 by 13.5 meters. This two-storied structure was originally erected in the Hellenistic period and rebuilt in Roman times by a consul named Attalus. An inscription welcomes the owner's guests and bids them to join with him in enjoying the good things of life. The house has two stories, with the lower stoa in the Doric order and the upper one in the Ionic. One can still see traces of wall paintings and a well-preserved floor mosaic, all dating from the imperial Roman era.

Beyond the House of Attalus the street passes through a complex of ancient shops and houses. The most impressive of these is a peristyle structure similar to the House of Attalus. The modern building in the central courtyard of this structure houses the staff of the German Archaeological Society.

Directly across the street from this peristyle house we see the northwest side of the lower agora, erected during the reign of Eumenes II. This agora occupies an area measuring 64 by 34 meters, surrounded on all sides by two-aisled Doric stoas, each of which had shops lining its inner aisle. The stoa was in two stories except for the back of its south side, where the sloping terrain required a third story. The stone missiles piled in the courtyard were found in the arsenal of the upper city, where they would have been used by the catapaults in the fortress there. During the excavation of the agora, beginning in 1900, a superb head of Alexander the Great was discovered in the northwest corner of the courtyard. Now preserved in the Istanbul Archaeological Museum, this is one of the finest extant examples of Hellenistic sculpture. It is a copy done in the third century B.C. of the original carved by Lysippus in the second half of the fourth century B.C.

The ancient street goes around the north and east sides of the agora and then leads down to the south gate of the city. This interesting and complicated portal was erected by Eumenes II when he extended the fortifications of Pergamum to enclose the middle city.

We now return to Bergama to see the remains of the lower city, beginning with the Asclepieum, to which we are directed by a signpost on the main street of the town. Starting at the car park of the archaeological site there, we approach the Asclepieum along a splendid colonnaded way known in Roman times as the Via Tecta. The Via Tecta began at the center of the Roman city below the acropolis hill and extended for half a Roman mile to the Asclepieum, with the last stretch flanked by Corinthian stoas. This was a bazaar street lined with shops catering to the pilgrims who came to the Asclepieum, one of the most famous therapeutic shrines in the ancient Graeco-Roman world.

The cult of Asclepius seems to have spread from Epidaurus to Mysia early in the fourth century B.C., when the first sanctuary of his cult was built on this site. The Pergamene Asclepieum was extended and rebuilt at various times in the Hellenistic and Roman periods. The ruins we see today for the most part date from the first half of the second century A.D., when the shrine here reached the height of its popularity, surpassing Epidaurus as the principal healing sanctuary in the Graeco-Roman world.

The fame of the Pergamene Asclepieum during the latter Roman imperial era was largely owing to the renown of the physician Galen, who was born in Pergamum in the year A.D. 129. Galen, the greatest physician and medical writer of the Roman era, received his first training in medicine and philosophy at the Pergamene Asclepieum. Galen also served his medical internship here, where among his other duties he would have treated the wounds of the gladiators who fought at the local amphitheater. Later, after moving to Rome, Galen served as personal physician to three Roman emperors: Marcus Aurelius (r. 161-80), Lucus Verus (co-emperor, r. 161-69), and Commodus (r. 180-92). Galen's writings systematized all of the Greek anatomical and medical knowledge that had accumulated since the pioneering work of Hippocrates of Cos in the fifth century B.C. His treatises formed the basis for medical science from the Roman imperial era up to the Renaissance, when he was known as the "Prince of Physicians."

We enter the Asclepieum through what was once the propylon, the forecourt of which formed the western end of the Via Tecta. An inscription records that this was erected during the reign of Antoninus Pius (138-61) by the Pergamene historian and consul Claudius

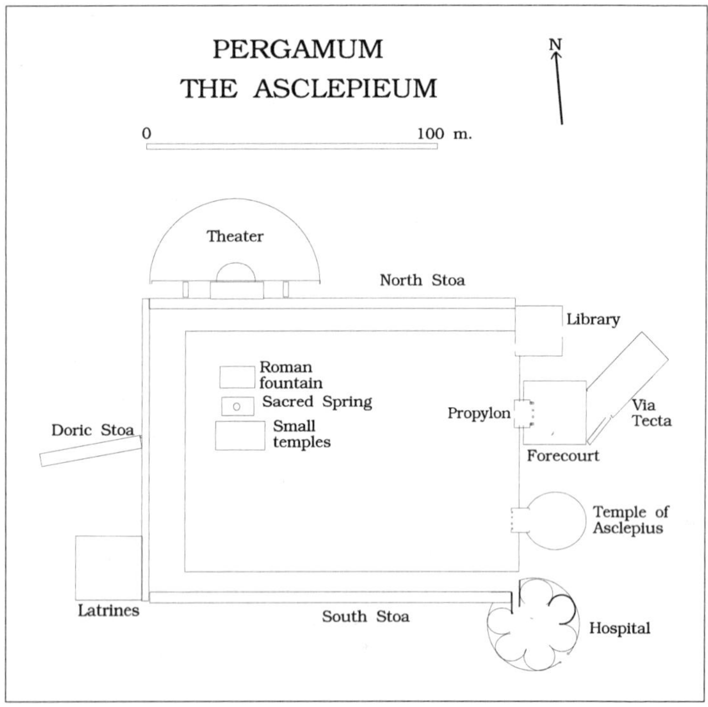

Via Tecta

Charax as a gift to the city of his birth. Here we pass into the main area of the shrine, a vast courtyard measuring 130 by 110 meters, with colonnaded stoas on all sides except the east. These stoas were originally in the Ionic order, but after an earthquake in A.D. 178 the columns at the east end of the north stoa were given Corinthian capitals. The structure at the corner of the courtyard to the right was the library, where there was also a shrine to the deified emperor. The two large circular buildings on the left inside the propylon were the principal edifices of the shrine. The building just inside the gateway was the temple of Asclepius, and the one beyond that, at the southeast corner of the shrine, was the main hospital.

An inscription records that the temple was erected ca. A.D. 150 through the generosity of the consul Lucius Rufinus. This is the most impressive building in the Asclepieum, a somewhat larger than half-size copy of the Pantheon that Hadrian had erected in Rome some two decades earlier. It originally had a dome 24 meters in diameter, and both its walls and floor were covered with marble mosaics. Around its interior there were a series of recesses, alternately round and rectangular; these contained statues of the healing deities associated with the shrine, the central one being a colossal figure of Asclepius.

The hospital was probably built soon after the temple of Asclepius. The building is circular in form, with three apses on either side flanking its two portals, one of them outside the courtyard and the other within. The most remarkable feature of the building is the vaulted passageway that leads from the hospital to the sacred spring at the center of the courtyard, a distance of some 80 meters. Known as the cryptoporticus, the tunnel was designed to shelter the patients from the elements on their way to and from the sacred spring. The treatment in the hospital stressed good diet, mud baths and bathing in the sacred spring, even in the depths of winter, hence the need for the cryptoporticus. Psychotherapy was also used for patients suffering from mental and emotional problems, and included an imaginative interpretation of dreams, eighteen centuries before Freud. One of the psychological complaints recognized by Galen was love-sickness, which he believed to be one of the main causes of insomnia. In one of his treatises he notes that "the quickening of the pulse at the name of the beloved gives the clue."

Outside the western end of the north stoa we see the restored Roman theater of the Asclepieum, which was dedicated to Asclepius and Athena Hygieia, goddess of health. The auditorium has a single diazoma and is divided into five cunei, with a seating capacity of some 3,500. There was originally a three-storied stage building, but this has vanished. The patients and their visitors were entertained here by performances of drama and music, for the Asclepieum was very much a spa in the old-fashioned European sense. But it was also a spa with very deep religious roots; in the central courtyard near the theater were several small temples, dedicated to Asclepius and other deities associated with him in his healing cult, including his daughter Hygieia. The site of one of these sanctuaries, a small temple dedicated to Asclepius, is marked by rectangular rock cuttings in the courtyard in front of the theater.

Hellenistic Stoa at West End of Asclepieum

A crack in the rock between this temple of Asclepius and the theater marks the site of the sacred spring that was the heart of the Asclepieum. Just to the north of this there is a Roman fountain, where the patients drank from the spring and bathed in its healing waters, which were probably radioactive. There is another fountain near the center of the west stoa, where patients also bathed in a rock-cut pool. A third water source was the spring that still supplies water to the pool at the center of the courtyard, near the end of the cryptoporticus. This spring was once covered by a fountain house, designed to shield the patients from the elements when they bathed and drank at the pool.

Mud baths were part of the treatment prescribed for patients at the Asclepieum. A graphic account of this treatment is given in the writings of Aelius Aristides, a distinguished orator and scholar who lived in Smyrna in the second century A.D. Aristides was a lifelong hypochondriac; his complaints brought him frequently to the Asclepieum, as he writes in his account of one of his visits to the shrine:

Northern Portico of the Asclepieum

> One summer, my stomach gave me a lot of trouble. I was suffering from thirst day and night, sweated abundantly and felt as weak as a rag: when I needed to get up it took two or three men to get me out of bed. The god [Asclepius] gave me a sign to leave Smyrna, where I was at the time, so I decided to start at once on the road to Pergamum....

Another complaint brought Aristides to the Asclepieum in midwinter, and it was then that Asclepius spoke to him in a dream and recommended that he undergo a regime of mud baths. Though it was in the dead of night and bitter cold Aristides arose at once and took the god's advice. He smeared himself with mud and ran three times around the temples in the courtyard, after which he washed himself off in the sacred fountain. He tells us that two friends started out to accompany him in this regime, but one of them turned back at once while the other was seized with a spasm and had to be carried to the hot baths to be thawed out.

Beyond the temenos of the Asclepieum to the west there are the remains of a Doric stoa. The stoa was about 100 meters in length, with a colonnade along its southern side and a row of 18 arcaded chambers along its northern side. This was undoubtedly another bazaar street, similar to the Via Tecta though much shorter.

There are three more monuments of the Roman city some 800-1,000 meters to the northeast of the Asclepieum, but since they are in a military zone they are off-limits to civilians. These are the theater, the amphitheater and the stadium. The theater is at the eastern end of the Via Tecta, with the amphitheater about 300 meters to its north and the stadium about the same distance to its northeast. All three structures date from the mid-second century A.D., when the Roman city of Pergamum reached the peak of its prosperity and population.

After leaving the Asclepieum we return to the main street of Bergama to visit the Archaeological Museum. The Bergama museum is one of the most attractive and interesting institutions of its kind in Turkey, with antiquities from Pergamum and other sites on the northern Aegean coast. The more recent finds include the sculptures and reliefs from the Marble Hall in the City Excavations in Pergamum.

The town of Bergama itself is interesting and picturesque, with a number of monuments dating from the Ottoman period, including mosques, *hans*, *hamams* and fountains, as well as a Selçuk minaret dating from the fourteenth century. The oldest Ottoman monument is the Ulu Cami, built in 1398 by Beyazit I (r. 1389-1402), just four years before his catastrophic defeat by Tamerlane at the battle of Ankara.

We leave Bergama along the same road by which we entered the town. As we do so we pass on our left an ancient tumulus known locally as Maltepe, whose tomb chamber was excavated by Wilhelm Dörpfeld when he was director of the Pergamum excavations. The tumulus is entered through a long passageway that leads into the tomb proper, a tripartite chamber dating from the late Hellenistic era. Pausanias believed that this was the tomb of Auge, mother of Telephus, the mythical founder of Pergamum. He recounts the myth of Telephus:

Sculptural Detail from Pergamum, Bergama Museum

> According to Heketaios, Herakles lay with Auge when he came to Tegea, and in the end she was caught with Herakles' child, and Aleos shut her and the boy in a chest and sent them out to sea; she landed and met Teuthras, who was a powerful man in the Kaikos plain, and he loved and married her; and today Auge's monument is at Pergamos on the Kaikos, a tumulus of earth surrounded by a stone platform and surmounted by a naked woman in bronze.

We now continue along until we come to the turnoff for İzmir, which soon brings us back to highway E87/550. There we drive southwest along the valley of the Caicus, crossing the river itself a short way beyond the Bergama exit.

Some three kilometers to the west of this bridge archaeologists have identified the site of ancient Teuthrania, the capital of the first kingdom to emerge in the Caicus valley. The ruins, which amount to little more than a few stone fragments and traces of walls and foundations, are on the slope of a very prominent hill known as Kalarga Tepesi. As the site is on the summit of a hill, and as it is accessible only by goat paths, it is rarely visited. But travelers passing by on the highway to İzmir might at least glance off to the west from this bridge over the Caicus river, for the hill of Kalarga is where the story of the illustrious Pergamene kingdom begins. As the poet known as Pseudo Scymnus wrote early in the Byzantine era, recalling the golden age of this vanished kingdom: "The glory of the kings of Pergamum, even if they are dead, shall remain ever living among us all."

CHAPTER THREE

THE AEOLIAN COAST

We now continue south along highway E87/550 towards İzmir. The first part of our drive takes us along the valley of the Caicus River, which flows into the Aegean at the head of the Çandarlı Körfezi, known in antiquity as the Elaitic Gulf. As we drive along, we pass from Mysia into the region known in antiquity as Aeolis, which was bounded on the north by the Caicus and the Elaitic Gulf, and on the south by the Hermus River and the Gulf of Smyrna, Turkish İzmir.

Aeolis took its name from the fact that the first Greeks who settled here were Aeolians, from Thessaly, Phocis, Locris and Boeotia. The Aeolians had been forced out of their homes by the Dorians, a warlike Hellenic people who came to power in Greece at the end of the second millennium B.C. The Dorians also displaced the Ionians, another Hellenic people whose homeland was principally in Attica. The Aeolians settled first in Lesbos and Tenedos and then moved on to the Aegean coast of Asia Minor. Soon afterwards the Ionians migrated to the islands of the central Aegean and the Anatolian coast south of Aeolis. The third stage of this great migration came when the Dorians themselves migrated from the Greek mainland to the islands of the southern Aegean and then to the southwestern coast of Anatolia, completing the population movement that would eventually Hellenize western Asia Minor.

According to Herodotus, the Aeolians founded a dozen cities on the Aegean coast between the Elaitic Gulf and the Gulf of Smyrna, the most notable being Smyrna. But they later lost Smyrna to the Ionians, who founded twelve cities of their own on the Aegean coast and offshore islands south of Aeolis. The Aeolians and Ionians organized themselves into two separate confederations, each of which had twelve members before Smyrna changed sides. Besides

Smyrna, Herodotus lists the Aeolian cities as: Cyme, Larisa, Neonteichos, Temnus, Cila, Notium, Aegiroessa, Pitane, Aegae, Myrina and Gryneum. The Ionian cities won great renown, but those of the Aeolians did not, and now the names of most of their settlements are known only to specialists in the history and archaeology of the northern Aegean coast of Asia Minor. The obscurity of the Aeolian cities, as compared with those of the Ionians, probably stems from the very different ways of life of the two Greek peoples who founded them. The Aeolians were mostly farmers and herdsmen, while the Ionians were seafarers and merchants who came into contact with a much broader world. While the Ionians made their indelible mark in history, sailing to the far ends of the known world and sometimes beyond, the Aeolians stayed home and simply settled for the good life on their fertile farms. As Athenaeus notes in his *Doctors at Dinner,* written in the late second century A.D., the Aeolians were much "given to wine, women and luxurious living," which is probably why they have left so few monuments on the Aeolian coast of Asia Minor.

We now turn off highway E87/550 to the right on a road signposted for Çandarlı, a drive of eleven kilometers. Çandarlı is a picturesque seaside village situated at the neck of a tongue-like peninsula that projects into the Elaitic Gulf. The village is dominated by a handsome and remarkably well-preserved Genoese castle of the late thirteenth century, with five main towers connected by curtain walls. The peninsula is the site of the ancient Aeolian city of Pitane, of which virtually nothing survives other than the fortress.

Pitane was the northernmost city in the Aeolian League. The original settlement in Pitane appears to have been far earlier than the Aeolian migration, for sherds have been found in its necropolis dating back to the third millennium B.C. The Aeolians believed that the city had been founded by one of the women warriors who held command under the legendary Amazon queen, Myrina, mentioned by Homer in *The Iliad.* At the time of the Aeolian migration the site of Pitane was already inhabited by the people known to the

Genoese Castle at Çandarlı

Archaic Statue from Pitane, Bergama Museum

Greeks as the Pelasgians. The Pelasgians evidently tried to regain the city after the Greeks settled there, for the Aeolians in Pitane were forced to seek help from the Ionians in Erythrae to drive out the natives. After the rise of Pergamum, Pitane and the other cities in the Aeolian League were absorbed into the Attalid kingdom, sharing in its prosperity and brilliant culture. The most renowned son of Pitane during the Hellenistic period was Arcesilaus, head of the Platonic Academy in Athens in the mid-third century B.C. He is credited with being the first philosopher to argue both sides of a question. (But because of his open-mindedness Arcesilaus could never bring himself to write a book, or so it was said of him in his time.) The most noteworthy incident in the history of Pitane during the Roman era occurred here in 85 B.C., the last year of the First Mithridatic War. King Mithridates himself took refuge here when the city was besieged by the rebel Roman commander Fimbria. Mithridates escaped from Pitane to Lesbos, while Fimbria, terrified of the wrath of Rome after his abortive rebellion, retired to the Asclepieum in Pergamum and committed suicide there.

Returning to highway E87/550, we turn right and resume our drive toward İzmir. As we do so we come almost immediately to within sight of the Elaitic Gulf again at the village of Kazıkbağları, whose center is only about 500 meters from the shore. This is the site of the ancient city of Elaea, which gave its name to the Elaitic Gulf. Elaea had the distinction of being the oldest Greek city on the Aeolian coast, with local legend ascribing its founding to Menestheus, leader of the Athenian contingent in Agamemnon's army at the siege of Troy. Homer mentions Menestheus in the Catalogue of Ships in Book II of *The Iliad,* where he writes: "Never on earth had there been a man like him/for the arrangement of horses and shielded fighters." According to the legend, Menestheus did not return to Athens after the Trojan War, but led part of his contingent here to form an Ionian colony.

Here too the earlier settlers appear to have been Pelasgians, who, according to Herodotus, were a non-Hellenic people living in Greece and northwestern Asia Minor, where they were displaced by the Greeks. Strabo refers to a lost history by Menecrates of Elaea in his effort to trace the origin and movements of the Pelasgians:

> That the Pelasgians were a great tribe is said also to be the testimony of history in general: Menecrates of Elaea, at any rate, in his work, On the Founding of Cities, says that the whole of what is now the Ionian Coast, beginning at Mycale, as also the neighbouring islands, were in earlier times inhabited by Pelasgians. But the Lesbians say that their people were placed under the command of Pylaeus, the man whom the poet [Homer] calls the ruler of the Pelasgians, and it is from him that the mountain in their country is called Pylaeus. The Chians, also, say that the Pelasgians from Thessaly were their founders. But the Pelasgian race, ever wandering and quick to migrate, greatly increased and then rapidly disappeared, particularly at the time of the migration of the Aeolians and Ionians to Asia.

Elaea never became a member of the Aeolian League, probably because it had been an Ionian foundation and retained its ties with Athens. During its early history Elaea was of little significance, but it achieved some importance during the Hellenistic period as the port and naval station of Pergamum, since it was situated at the mouth of the Caicus River. The ancient port has long since silted up and is now a waste of mud flats, within which part of the quay and the harbor mole are still visible. The acropolis of Elaea was on the summit of the low hill some 500 meters due west of the center of Kazıkbağları, and in the fields between this eminence and the village there are fragments of the city walls, including the remains of a gateway. This is all that is left of ancient Elaea, where in 190 B.C. the allied fleets of Rome and Pergamum anchored in the last months of the war that led to the final defeat of Antiochus III early in the following year.

We continue along the highway as it takes us around the head of the Elaitic Gulf, which is divided into two bays by a broad headland. At the beginning of the second bay we come to the village of Yenişakran, where we turn left on to a secondary road signposted for Köseler, a drive of 15 kilometers. From the end of the road at Köseler it is a 45-minute walk to the site of ancient Aegae, on an acropolis hill of the Yund Dağı, the mountainous region between the Caicus and Hermus valleys. There are no signs to point the way; it might be best to hire the *bekçi* (watchman) of the site, to guide one out from Köseler, where he is stationed.

Aegae is mentioned by both Herodotus and Strabo as being a member of the Aeolian League. Strabo notes that Aegae and Temnos, another city of the Aeolian League, "are situated in the mountainous country that lies above the territory of Cyme and that of the Phocaeans and that of the Smyrnaeans, along which flows the Hermus." Aegae was absorbed into the Pergamene kingdom in the early days of the Attalids, who endowed the city with several temples and rebuilt its defense walls in the mid-second century B.C., after it had been sacked by the Bithynians. The remote location of Aegae has preserved it to a far greater degree than the other cities along the coast of Aeolis, and thus its remains, although in ruins, are

Roman Market Building at Aegae

Restored Drawing of Roman Market Building at Aegae

much more impressive than those of any other member of the Aeolian League.

The summit of the acropolis hill is 365 meters above sea level, surrounded by a defense wall some 1.5 kilometers in length. The path leading up to the acropolis takes one through the necropolis, where a number of sarcophagi lay scattered about. It then goes around the northern side of the steep acropolis hill to the main gateway of the ancient city, a well preserved portal known locally as Demir Kapı, the Iron Gate. The most prominent structure on the acropolis is a three-storied market building on the southeast side of the plateau. It is 82 meters in length and still stands to a height of eleven meters. This dates from the Hellenistic period, though it was rebuilt in the imperial Roman era. Adjoining the market building are the ruins of the bouleuterion. At the northwest corner of the acropolis there are the remains of an Ionic temple of the second century B.C., with six columns at its ends and twelve along its sides. It is believed that the temple was originally dedicated to Apollo Chresterius, the second name of the god being a local appellation found only at Aegae. The temenos of the temple is defined by the northwestern corner of the citadel wall and on its two straight sides by two-storied stoas, the lower story Doric and the upper one Ionic. The architectural style of their structure is similar to that of the Stoa of Attalus in Athens, which has led scholars to attribute these stoas to Attalus II. Below this temenos is the theater, its cavea hollowed out of the precipitous slope of the acropolis rock, with its vaulted entrance still standing above the northeastern corner of the auditorium. About 50 meters to the north of the orchestra there are the remains of a small Doric *templum-in-antis,* with an inscription of the second century B.C. recording its dedica-

Entrance to Theater at Aegae

tion to Demeter and Kore. South of the theater a large level area was created by cutting away the hill on the east and building a large retaining wall on the west. This area was then bordered with stoas on the east, south and west sides to create a gymnasium, with a stadium to its north. The site has never been excavated; the ruins of all these structures lie tumbled all over the hillside, with only the market building remaining relatively intact. The ruins of Aegae are seldom visited, so one can contemplate its splendid ruins without the distraction of other travelers or indeed any other intrusion from the modern world. It stands isolated from time and space here on its remote hilltop in the Yund Dağı.

After this detour we return to highway E87/550 at Yenişakran, where we turn left and continue driving towards İzmir.

About a kilometer beyond Yenişakran we stop to walk down toward the shore to a little promontory called Temaşalık Burnu. This is the site of ancient Gryneum, another city of the Aeolian League. Little remains here other than a few fragmentary columns and capitals along with numerous pottery shards.

Here too the original settlement probably predated the Greek migration, for the site of Gryneum seems to have been inhabited by the Pelasgians before the Aeolians established their city. Local legend attributed the founding of the city to an Amazon named Gryne, one of Queen Myrina's lieutenants. According to the legend, Gryne was violated at this place by Apollo, who was worshipped here at a famous shrine. Strabo describes Gryneum as having "an altar of Apollo, an ancient oracle, and a costly shrine of white marble." Pausanias writes of "Gryneum, where Apollo has a most beautiful grove of fruit trees and other wild trees which are pleasant to smell and look upon." The oracular shrine here is mentioned by Virgil in Book IV of *The Aeneid,* where Aeneas tells Queen Dido of Carthage how "the oracle of Apollo at Gryneum, where he gives his divinations by lot, has insistently commanded me to make my way to Italy's noble lands." The shrine is also mentioned by Aelius Aristides, who stopped here on one of his visits to the Pergamene Asclepieum; as he writes: "On reaching Gryneum, I made my sacrifice and occupied myself in my customary way; then proceeding to Elaea, I put up there for the night, and on the following day arrived in Pergamum."

We now drive for a short way around the second bay of the Elaitic Gulf toward the promontory at its southern end, stopping where the highway crosses a little river called Güzelhisar Çayı, the Stream of the Beautiful Castle. This is the mouth of the river Pythicus, which in its upper course flows past the ancient city of Aegae. The river flows out to the sea around the southern side of the promontory, which is the site of ancient Myrina, another city of the Aeolian League.

Like Pitane, Elaea and Gryneum, Myrina was first settled long before the Aeolian migration, undoubtedly inhabited by the Pelasgians. According to local legend, the city took its name from its founder, the Amazon queen Myrina. Homer mentions the Amazon queen in Book II of *The Iliad,* where he writes of her mythical tomb outside the walls of Troy: "This men call the Hill of the Thicket, but the immortal/gods have named it the burial ground of dancing Myrina." Here and elsewhere in northwestern Asia Minor, the myth of the Amazons may be due to two prominent reliefs, both mentioned by Herodotus, that the first Greek settlers saw in the hinterland of Smyrna. In each of them a Hittite warrior is shown wearing a kilt, leading the Hellenes to imagine that these earlier people were a race of women warriors.

Virtually nothing now remains of Myrina except fragments of the walls of its citadel, which was on the low hill known as Birki Tepe, and some stones from the quay of its harbor on the northern side of the promontory. The necropolis was in the valley between Birki Tepe and the next hill to its north. On the top of the second hill to the north there is a rock-cut chamber tomb known as Intas, which is in a curious outcrop near the summit. Numerous other rock-hewn tombs are known to the local shepherds. Archaeological excavations of the necropolis and the rock tombs have unearthed a large number of interesting funerary offerings, ranging from the time of Alexander the Great to the reign of Tiberius (r. 14-37), who rebuilt Myrina after it had been destroyed in an earthquake in the year A.D. 17. The most important of these funerary objects are terracotta figurines—more than a thousand in all—similar to the famous Tanagra statuettes, including: representations of deities, humans and animals, as well as theatrical masks, grotesque and comic figures, and caricatures. There are also numerous bronze coins to be used to pay for the fare of the deceased on Charon's ferry across the river Styx into the Underworld; plates for food and clay bottles for wine to be consumed in the next world; and for women—lamps, mirrors, needles, perfume containers, jewelry and other objects of daily life, as if that would be continued in the same fashion beyond the grave. These finds are now preserved in the Istanbul Archaeological Museum and in the Louvre.

Aelius Aristides also stopped at the town of Myrina on his way to Pergamum. His lively account of his stay gives us some idea of the difficulties of travel along the Aegean coast in the imperial Roman era:

> About cock crow we reached Myrina, and there we found our men outside one of the inns, still not unpacked because, as they said, they too had found nothing open. In the porch of the inn was a pallet-bed; we spent some time carrying this up and down, but could find no comfortable place to put it. Knocking at the door was useless, as no one answered it. At long last we managed to get into the house of an acquaintance; but by bad luck the porter's fire was out, so that I entered in complete darkness, led by the hand, seeing nothing and myself invisible. By the time a fire had been procured and I was preparing to enjoy a drink in front of it, the morning star was rising and dawn had begun to break. Pride rebelled against going to bed by daylight, so I decided to make a further effort and go on to the temple of Apollo at Gryneum, where it was my habit to offer sacrifice on my journeys up and down the road.

The highway now goes along the shore of a bay that forms the southern cusp of the Elaitic Gulf, passing the small industrial town of Aliağa at the far end. After driving across the neck of the promontory that forms the southern arm of the gulf, we turn right off the highway onto a secondary road that brings us out to the sea at Namurt Köyü, a hamlet on the bay called Namurt Limanı, the Harbor of Nimrod. At the end of the road we come to the site of ancient Cyme, which Strabo called "the largest and best of the Aeolian cities."

The story of Cyme's foundation is much the same as that of the other cities to its north in the Aeolian League, in that its original settlement was probably by the Pelasgians long before the great Hellenic migration. Local legend had it that the city was named for its eponymous founder, the Amazon Cyme, presumably another of Queen Myrina's lieutenants. Aeolian Cyme, along with Chalcis and Eretria, joined together in 757 B.C. to found the city of Cumae, the first Greek colony on the Italian mainland. The Cymeans on their own later founded the city of Side on the Mediterranean coast of Asia Minor. Cyme was forced to contribute ships to the Persian fleet in 512 B.C., when Darius crossed the Bosphorus in his campaign against the Scythians, and again in 480 B.C. when Xerxes invaded Greece, the only Aeolian city to participate in these two wars. After the Greek victory at the battle of Salamis the Persian fleet returned to Asia, laying at anchor in the harbor of Cyme through the winter of 480-479 B.C.

Despite the fact that Cyme was the most active of the Aeolian cities in seafaring, the Cymaeans were mocked by the other eastern Greeks for their supposed failure to exploit their potential as a naval power. Strabo tells several stories ridiculing the stupidity of the Cymaeans, although he does note that Cyme was the birthplace of Ephorus, an orator, philosopher and inventor who flourished in the fourth century B.C. Strabo also tells us that Cyme may have been the birthplace of both Homer and Hesiod, although this is in both cases unlikely. Hesiod, in his *Works and Days*, tells us that his father was from Aeolian Cyme, and that he emigrated from there to Boeotia. One wonders why Dius left the fertile lands and pleasant weather of the Aeolian coast for the harsh clime of the Boeotian mountains, where, as Hesiod writes of his father's life: "He dwelt near Helicon in Ascre, a village wretched in winter, in summer oppressive, and not pleasant in any season."

There is little of ancient Cyme to be seen, other than the exiguous remains of the theater, an Ionic temple, the foundations of a large building of unknown identity, and the mole of its harbor.

After returning to the highway we drive on for only a short way before turning off to the right on the road that leads to the seaside towns of Yeni (New) Foça and Eski (Old) Foça, their last name a a corruption of the Greek Phocaea. Both of these towns are situated on the huge peninsula that forms the northern arm of the Gulf of İzmir. Yeni Foça is about halfway out along the north shore of the peninsula, while Eski Foça is on its northwestern coast. The road brings us first to Yeni Foça, which is set on a beautiful bay with a superb beach that is now occupied by the Club Mediterranée.

Yeni Foça is said to stand on the site of ancient Cyllene, an obscure Aeolian city about which virtually nothing is known, but this identification is doubtful. In any event, the present town of Yeni Foça is a direct descendant not of an ancient Greek city but of the late medieval Genoese colony of Foglia Nuova (New Phocaea). The history of this colony begins in 1275, when Michael VIII Palaeologus granted an imperial fief to two Genoese merchant adventurers, the brothers Benedetto and Manuele Zaccaria. They were to develop the peninsula's lucrative mines of alum, the processed salts of which were in great demand for the dyeing of cloth and also as an emetic and astringent. This fief centered on the town of Phocaea, the present Eski Foça, which in antiquity had been one of the cities of the Ionian League. When they received this fief the Zaccarias built a fortified port on the northern side of the peninsula to protect their alum mines there, and this soon developed into the town of Foglia Nuova, while the ancient city came to be called Foglia Vecchia (Old Phocaea). The Zaccaria brothers also built a fleet to protect their merchantmen from pirates. Foglia Nuova developed into one of the richest towns in the Levant, remaining a Genoese possession until 1455, when both it and Foglia Vecchia fell to the Ottoman Turks. Today there is nothing whatsoever to be seen of the Genoese town of Foglia Nuova, which has vanished under the Turkish houses of Yeni Foça.

We now continue on to Eski Foça, a pleasant town clustered around a little peninsula at the inner end of an almost landlocked harbor, nearly cut off from the Aegean by a succession of promontories and offshore islets. This is the site of ancient Phocaea, which Strabo considered to mark "the beginning of Ionia and the end of Aeolis" for mariners sailing south along the coast of Asia Minor.

Although Phocaea is on the Aeolian coast, it was Ionian in foundation and a member of the Ionian League. Phocaea appears to have been founded some two hundred years after the original Hellenic migration to Asia Minor. It was settled by colonists from the Ionian cities of Erythrae and Teos, probably in the eighth century B.C. The site was obviously chosen for its excellent harbor, the finest by far on the Aeolian coast. The Phocaeans took full advantage of their superb location, and early in their history their city emerged as one of the most active and venturesome maritime cities in the Greek world. Phocaea was one of the first Greek cities to send colonizing expeditions overseas, joining Miletus in the mid-eighth century B.C. to establish a colony on the southern shore of the Pontus (Black Sea) at Amisus (Turkish Samsun). In 654 the Phocaeans on their own founded Lampsacus on the Hellespont (Dardanelles). Around 600 B.C. they established Massalia, the present Marseilles, with colonists going on from there to found the daughter colonies of Nicaea and Antipolis, now known as Nice and Antibes. Then in 560 B.C. the Phocaeans founded Alalia on Corsica, and at the same time they established a short-lived colony on Sardinia. They even sailed out into the Atlantic and up the Iberian coast as far as Tartassus, near present-day Cadiz. Herodotus describes these voyages in Book I of his *Histories,* where he writes of the Phocaeans and their city:

> The Phocaeans were the first Greeks to make long sea-voyages; it was they who showed the way to the Adriatic, Tyrrhenia, Iberia, and

> Tartassus. They used to sail not in deep, broad-beamed merchant vessels but in fifty-oared galleys. When they went to Tartassus they made themselves agreeable to Arganthonius, the King, who had ruled the place for eighty years, and lived to be a hundred and twenty. Indeed, this person took such a fancy to them that he asked them to quit Ionia permanently and settle wherever they liked on his own land; the Phocaeans, however, refused the offer, whereupon the king, hearing that Median power was on the increase in their part of the world, gave them money to build a wall around their town. And he must have given them a good deal, for the wall at Phocaea is of pretty considerable extent, and constructed of large stone blocks well fitted together.

After the Persian king Cyrus captured Sardis in 546 B.C., he sent his general Harpagus the Mede to subdue the Greek cities on the Aegean coast, all of which surrendered immediately except Phocaea. Herodotus continues his account of the history of the Phocaeans by telling the story of the Persian siege of Phocaea and its aftermath:

> Harpagus, then, brought his troops to Phocaea, whose defenses were built in the way I have described, and began a siege, proclaiming to the Phocaeans that he would be satisfied if they consented to pull down a single tower in the fortifications and sacrifice one house. The Phocaeans, however, indignant at the thought of slavery, asked for one day in which to consider the proposal before answering; stipulating at the same time that he should withdraw his forces during their deliberations. This Harpagus consented to do, though he was perfectly aware of their intentions. So the troops were withdrawn, and the Phocaeans at once launched their galleys, put aboard their women and children and moveable property, including the statues and other sacred objects from their temples—everything in fact, except for paintings and images made of bronze or marble—and sailed for Chios. So the Persians on their return took possession of an empty town.

Herodotus then goes on to tell of how the Persians decided to go on to establish a new city in Corsica, but only after taking their revenge on the Persians:

> But before starting on their voyage, they returned to Phocaea and killed the Persian garrison left there by Harpagus. Then they tried to secure unity for their expedition by laying fearful curses upon any man who should fail to accompany it. They also dropped a lump of iron into the sea and swore never to return to Phocaea until it floated up again. But at the very beginning of the voyage to Corsica more than half of them were seized with such passionate longing to see their city and their old homes once more, that they broke their oaths and sailed back to Phocaea.

The Phocaeans who continued to Corsica soon afterwards moved to southern Italy to establish the colony of Rhegium, known today as Reggio Calabria. From there some of them sailed up the west coast of Italy to found the city of Elea, which soon became the intellectual center of Magna Graecia, the Greek cities in southern Italy and Sicily, giving rise to the Eleatic school of philosophy.

Phocaea itself revived after the return of those who did not go on to Corsica, joining the other Ionian cities in their revolt against Persian rule in 499-494 B.C. The Phocaeans defended their city against besieging Roman armies in 190 B.C. and again in 130 B.C. On the second occasion the Phocaean resistance so provoked the besiegers that the Roman Senate ordered the city to be destroyed and its people dispersed. The citizens of Massalia, Phocaea's former colony, appealed against this harsh sentence and persuaded the Senate to spare their mother city and grant clemency to its people. The heroism of the Phocaeans thus became legendary in antiquity, leading Diogenes Laertius to remark that "Phocaea is a city of moderate size, skilled in nothing but to rear brave men."

Phocaea took on a new lease of life in 1275 under the Genoese, who called it Foglia Vecchia. The city remained in the hands of the Genoese until 1455, when it fell to the Ottomans, who called it Eski Foça. Throughout most of the Ottoman period Eski Foça continued to be a seaport of some importance. But this ended with the invention of the steamboat. Today Eski Foça is little more than a fishing port and a stopping place for yachts sailing along the Aeolian coast. One must read the accounts of earlier travelers to evoke a picture of what life was like here when Eski Foça was still a port of call for ships sailing from İzmir to Athens or Istanbul. The most interest of these accounts is that of William J. Hamilton in Volume I of his *Researches in Asia Minor, Pontus and Armenia,* published in 1842. He describes his voyage from fever-stricken İzmir to Eski Foça, which he calls Fouges:

> At the end of December [1835] the kindness of Captain Mundy offered me a cruise on board the *Favourite,* and as I trusted that a month or six weeks at sea would remove all remains of fever, I accepted the proposal. We were bound in the first place for Athens; but contrary winds compelled us to put into the small harbor of Fouges, the ancient Phocaea. This place, conveniently situated near the southern entrance of the Gulf of Smyrna, was one of the most celebrated on the coast of Asia Minor, in the early days of Greek navigation, and till the fortunes of war drove its inhabitants to become the founders of Marseilles. The harbor is very snug, and protected from all winds except the west. The modern town is situated on a narrow tongue of land, extending into the little bay from the east, and corresponding with the description of it, and the two harbor Naustatamon and Lamptera, given by Livy in his account of the war with Antiochus.
>
> It now contains 1,000 houses, of which 600 are Turkish, and the remainder Greek. It is built on the peninsula and surrounded by walls, which appear to be Genoese. Some blocks of stone and marble have been let into the walls on the land side, but in general few remains of antiquity were to be seen. Within the town I saw fragments of columns, and outside the gate a large marble sarcophagus, which appeared never to have been finished....

Virtually nothing remains of ancient Phocaea except for the foundations and some architectural fragments of an Ionic temple of

Athena, discovered in 1953 by Professor Ekrem Akurgal in the garden of the local schoolhouse. The temple, whose architectural fragments are preserved in the İzmir Archaeological Museum, is dated to the second quarter of the sixth century B.C. It appears to have been rebuilt later in that same century after its destruction by the Persians. A single monument remains from the Genoese town of Foglia Vecchia—a late thirteenth century fortress on the promontory that forms the western horn of the harbor. Outside the town on a hillside to the southwest there is an ancient rock-hewn tomb known as Şeytan Hamamı, the Devil's Bath.

We leave Eski Foça on highway 250, which takes us eastward through the peninsula to link up with highway E87/550. About seven kilometers along we pass on our left an impressive rock-hewn tomb known as Taş Kule, the Stone Tower. The structure, which is 4.5 meters high, is carved out of rock in the form of a two-storied building composed of two superimposed blocks. The lower one measures 8.5 by 5.8 meters in plan, with a false door of three panels in its east face. The upper story is above the eastern part of the lower one, a rectangular block raised on a stepped platform. The tomb proper is below this in the lower block, where the real door gives entrance to an antechamber. Another door at the rear of this room on the right leads into the burial chamber itself, where the deceased was buried in a simple rectangular trough. The tomb is believed to have been built in the early fourth century B.C. for a local tyrant who ruled under the Persians.

After reaching highway E87/550 we turn right to head south for İzmir once again. After about five kilometers we see on the left a turnoff for the village of Yanık, a drive of some three kilometers. Directly above the village we see a conical hill surmounted by a great circular rock. This was the site of the citadel of Neonteichos, one of the cities of the Aeolian League. The approach to the summit from the village follows the course of the ancient road to the citadel, its surface still paved with large stone blocks. The slopes and summit of the hill are littered with an abundance of pottery shards, ranging in date from the sixth century B.C. to Byzantine times, with the majority from the fourth and third centuries B.C. Proceeding upwards, we see a number of pieces of handsome polygonal masonry, mostly in the retaining walls of terraces, as well as in a long stretch of the city's defense walls. All that remains of the citadel are a rock-hewn stairway and the stone blocks of an observation post on the summit. We can see here that Neonteichos, which means "New Fort," was primarily a fortress town. Strabo tells us it was built by the first Aeolian settlers as a base to attack the Pelasgians who were dwelling in nearby Larisa.

We return once again to highway E87/550 and continue driving towards İzmir. Some two kilometers farther along we come to Buruncuk, a village at the foot of a steep hill about 100 meters high. The summit of the hill is the site of ancient Larisa, another city of the Aeolian League.

We approach the site via the ancient road, which leads up to the summit of the hill in a long hairpin turn to bring us to the main gate of ancient Larisa on the north side of the acropolis. The acropolis was apparently first fortified ca. 500 B.C., although pottery shards have been found on the summit dating back to the seventh century B.C. Early in the fourth century B.C. the fortifications were rebuilt and extended to enclose a considerably larger area eastward along the crest of the hill, with the ruins of five of its towers still to be seen. At the westernmost corner of the acropolis excavations have unearthed the remains of a complex of peristyle chambers, identified as a palace dated ca. 330 B.C. The excavations also unearthed the foundations and some architectural fragments of two small temples, the oldest of which is an Aeolic edifice dated to the sixth century B.C. An Aeolic capital of this archaic temple is now on exhibit in the Istanbul Archaeological Museum, along with a capital of the same type from Neandria.

Larisa is the only Aeolian city mentioned in *The Iliad.* Homer refers to it in the Catalogue of the Trojans, listing the contingent from Larisa directly after those from the Hellespontine cities of the Troad:

Hippothoös led the tribes of spear-fighting Pelasgians,
they who dwelt where the soil is rich around Larisa;
Hippothoös and Pylaios, scion of Ares, led these,
sons alike of Pelasgian Lethos, son of Teutamos.

This and the reference by Strabo indicate that here too the site of the city was occupied by the Pelasgians long before the Aeolian migration. Legend has it that Larisa was named for a daughter of one of these Pelasgian kings, of whom Strabo has this bizarre tale to tell:

> Piasus...was ruler of the Pelasgians and fell in love with his daughter Larisa, and having violated her, paid the penalty for his outrage; for having observed him leaning over a cask of wine, she seized him by the legs, raised him, and plunged him into the cask. Such were the ancient accounts.

A short way beyond Buruncuk the highway crosses the Gediz

Aeolic Capital from Larisa, Istanbul Archaeological Museum

Çayı, the River Hermus of the Greeks. The Hermus was in antiquity the boundary between Aeolis and Ionia, flowing into the Aegean near Phocaea. But in the medieval era the Hermus changed its course and flowed south into the Gulf of Smyrna, where over the centuries it formed an alluvial delta that by late Ottoman times threatened to block İzmir's harbor. The Hermus was diverted back into its original channel in 1886, by which time its silt had caused the coastline to advance a considerable distance, most notably at Menemen, a former coastal town now some 20 kilometers inland.

We pass Menemen as the highway curves inland through the alluvial plain of the Hermus, and soon afterwards İzmir comes into view, its tiered houses stretching for miles along the hills around the inner end of the gulf that bears its name.

Harbor of İzmir, with Acropolis in Background, Allom Print

CHAPTER FOUR

İZMİR

İzmir, the Greek Smyrna, is the third largest city in Turkey after Istanbul and Ankara. It is far and away the most important port on the Aegean coast of Turkey, located at the head of the Gulf of İzmir, one of the best natural harbors in the Levant. The city has now spread out for miles around the head of the gulf on both sides of its historic center, the area under Kadifekale, the acropolis hill known to the Greeks as Mt. Pagus. This is the oldest quarter of İzmir, the site of its famous Bazaar and of its historic monuments. But despite its antiquity this is not where the city had its beginnings.

Archaeological excavations in 1948-51 by Professors John M. Cook and Ekrem Akurgal showed the original site of Smyrna was at Bayrakli, at the northeast corner of the gulf some two miles from the city center. The excavations indicate that the site at Bayraklı was inhabited as early as the first half of the third millennium B.C., the oldest strata of the settlement being contemporary with Troy 1 and 2. Virtually nothing is known of the original inhabitants of Smyrna. Strabo writes that ancient authorities attributed the founding of Smyrna to the Amazons. He also says that when the first Greeks arrived they found the place occupied by the Lelegians, another non-Hellenic people who inhabited western Anatolia before the migration of the Aeolians and Ionians. The excavations at Bayraklı revealed that the earliest Hellenic settlers arrived here in the tenth century B.C., as evidenced by the large quantities of proto-geometric pottery of that period unearthed in the dig. These colonists were presumably Aeolian Greeks, since Smyrna was originally one of the cities of the Aeolian League. The excavations also unearthed houses dating from the ninth to the seventh century B.C., as well as an archaic temple of Athena, originally built ca. 640 B.C., which Professor Akurgal describes as "the earliest and finest building of the eastern Greek world in Asia Minor." The temple would have been erected by the Ionians, who in the second half of the eighth century B.C. seized control of Smyrna from the Aeolians. According to Herodotus, this coup was carried out by a group of exiles from the Ionian city of Colophon, as he tells the story in Book I of his *Histories:*

> The Aeolians lost Smyrna by treachery. They had received into the town some men from Colophon, who had been defeated by the rival faction and expelled; the fugitives watched their chance and, when the people of Smyrna were celebrating a festival of Dionysus outside the walls, shut the gates and got possession of the town. The Aeolians of the other states came to their help, and terms were agreed to whereby the Ionians should surrender all moveable property but keep possession of the town. The people of Smyrna were then distributed amongst the other eleven Aeolian towns, where they were given civic rights.

Around 665 B.C. King Gyges of Lydia invaded the territory of the Ionians, putting Smyrna under siege, but the townspeople fought off the invaders. The Lydians returned in 600 B.C., when King Alyattes invaded Ionia and took Smyrna, destroying the city and dispersing the survivors, some of whom took refuge in the Ionian city of Clazomenae. During the two decades that followed some of the Smyrnaeans returned to the ruined city and rebuilt their houses. The excavations at Bayraklı indicate that by 500 B.C. they had restored the temple of Athena. But the archaic city of Smyrna never again recovered its former stature, and during the classical period it was little more than a collection of villages at the northeastern corner of the gulf. Then the original site was abandoned altogether at the beginning of the Hellenistic period, when a new city was built under Mt. Pagus.

The founding of the new city of Smyrna was attributed to Alexander the Great, according to Pausanias and other ancient sources. As Pausanias tells the tale, Alexander was out hunting on Mt. Pagus when he fell asleep under a plane tree sacred to the Vengeances, the goddesses of divine fate and retribution. The god-

Camel Caravan Crossing Ottoman Bridge, with Acropolis of İzmir in Background, Allom Print

desses appeared to him in a dream and commanded him to build a new city on the site and to resettle the Smyrnaeans there. When Alexander's dream was reported to the Smyrnaeans they sent a delegation to the oracle of Apollo at Claros, who responded with this cryptic couplet: "Three and four times happy shall these men be hereafter/Who shall dwell on Pagus beyond the sacred Meles." The oracle was here referring to the River Meles, which flows into the head of the gulf north of Mt. Pagus. The Smyrnaeans thus accepted the oracle's advice and abandoned the site at Bayraklı, building a new city south of the Meles on the seaward slope of Mt. Pagus, or so the story goes.

Putting the story in historical perspective, Alexander may in fact have made a brief visit to Smyrna in the spring of 334 B.C., perhaps on his way from Sardis to Ephesus. But even if Alexander did decide to relocate and rebuild Smyrna then, there would have been no time for him to do so on his rapid campaign, and the plan could only have been carried out after his death in 323 B.C. by his successors. The foundation of the new city on Mt. Pagus may have been begun by Antigonus before his death in 301 B.C., but in any event the project was completed by Lysimachus, probably after his conquest of Ephesus in 295 B.C. The climax of this resettlement came in 288 B.C., when Smyrna was made the thirteenth member of the newly revived Panionic League, the confederation of the Ionian cities originally founded in the archaic period.

The most detailed description of the Graeco-Roman city on the slope of Mt. Pagus is that given by Aelius Aristides, who was born in Mysia ca. A.D. 117 and died in 181, having lived much of his life in Smyrna. One of the edifices mentioned by Aristides in his description of Smyrna is a temple known as "Dionysus Before the City," which is believed to have stood on a hill near the southern gate, from where a road led to Ephesus. This would have been the shrine of "Dionysus outside the walls" mentioned by Herodotus in his story of the Ionian capture of Smyrna. Another incident associated with this shrine occurred in 244 B.C., when Smyrna was attacked by a fleet from Chios. On that day the entire population of Smyrna had gone out to celebrate the festival of Dionysus at the god's shrine outside the walls, when some of them spotted the Chian triremes sailing up the gulf towards the city. After the alarm was given the men of Smyrna rushed down to the shore to repel the Chians, defeating them and capturing some of their ships, after which they returned in triumph to the temple of Dionysus to continue the festival. The victory was commemorated throughout the remainder of antiquity at the annual festival of Dionysus. A group of ephebes carried one of the captured Chian triremes to the wine god's temple outside the walls, the high priest of the cult acting as helmsman.

Another sanctuary in Smyrna mentioned by Aristides and other ancient sources is the Homerium, a heroon dedicated to Homer. There was a strong tradition among writers in antiquity that Homer was born in Smyrna, by the banks of the river Meles, though later he dwelt in other places, most notably Chios. Pausanias writes that "Smyrna has the river Meles with the finest water, and a cave with a spring where they say Homer wrote his poetry." Aristides gives a description of the course of the Meles through Smyrna that has led a number of scholars to identify it with the Halkpınar Suyu, recently renamed the Melez Çayı, a stream that rises from a spring-fed pool within the grounds of the İzmir water supply station. This pool is known popularly as "Diana's Baths," because of the discovery there of a statue of Artemis, the Roman Diana. Beneath the tree-shaded waters of the pool one can see several Ionic column bases and other ancient architectural fragments, possibly the remnants of a sanctuary of Artemis. Perhaps this is the pool referred to in one of the Homeric Hymns to Artemis, where the divine huntress "having washed her horses in deep-reeded Meles, drove swiftly through Smyrna to Claros deep in vines." An inscription found in the spring, now built into Burnabat Camii, reads: "I sing the praises of the Meles, my saviour, now that every plague and evil has ceased." This is believed to refer to a plague that ravaged the city in the years A.D. 165-68, during the reign of Marcus Aurelius. The curative waters of the spring seem to have been credited with ending the epidemic.

The best view of the historic center of the city is from Kadifekale, the ancient fortress on the summit of Mt. Pagus. The summit is to a large extent surrounded by the walls and towers of Kadifekale, the Velvet Castle, still formidable looking even in its ruins. The citadel on Mt. Pagus was the focal point of the city's defenses, with two lines of massive walls leading down from there to the shore. The seaward walls have vanished, and all that remains of the fortifications is the citadel on Mt. Pagus. Even there only the foundations and perhaps a few of the lower courses date from the time of Lysimachus, with the remainder owing to successive reconstructions by the Romans, Byzantines and Ottoman Turks.

Hellenistic Smyrna existed as an independent city from the time of its foundation by Lysimachus until 129 B.C., when it was included in the Roman Province of Asia. Then in 27 B.C., when Octavian became Augustus, Smyrna was made part of a new Roman federation known as the League of Asia, governed by a proconsul sent out annually from Rome. Smyrna enjoyed three centuries of peace and prosperity under the mantle of the *pax Romana,* but then in A.D. 178 the city was devastated by the worst earthquake in its history. Aristides had left Smyrna a few days before, by divine guidance, he said, and when he learned of the catastrophe he wrote to Marcus Aurelius. The emperor wept when he read the letter and gave orders for the work of reconstruction to begin at once. Within three years Smyrna had been completely restored. The Smyrnaeans were deeply grateful for this help, and in commemoration they erected statues of Marcus Aurelius and Aristides in the rebuilt theater.

By then there were already a substantial number of Christians living in Smyrna. Smyrna was one of the Seven Churches of Revelation. The Christian community in the city received this cryptic message from St. John the Evangelist:

> I know thy works and tribulations, and poverty (but thou art rich), and I know the blasphemy of them which say they are Jews, and are not, but are the Smyrna synagogue of Satan. Fear none of these things which thou shall suffer: behold the devil shall cast some of you into prison, that we may be tried: and ye shall have tribulation ten days: be thou faithful unto death, and I will give thee a crown of life. He that hath an ear, let him hear what the spirit saith unto the churches: he that overcomes shall not be hurt by the second death.

The first bishop of Smyrna was St. Polycarp, who is said to have been consecrated by St. John the Apostle in the last years of the first Christian century. Bishop Eirenaios, writing ca. 190, remembered Polycarp well from the days of his youth in Smyrna, reminiscing of "how he had told me of his association with John and the rest who had seen the Lord: and as he remembered their words, and what he had heard from them about the Lord and about His deeds and power and about His teachings." Eirenaios goes on to tell of how "Polycarp used to narrate everything in conformity with the Scriptures—as one who had received the story from the eyewitness of the life of the world." Polycarp served as Bishop of Smyrna for more than half a century, leading the Christian community here until 22 February 153, when he suffered martyrdom for his faith. He was burned at the stake in the stadium on orders of the Roman proconsul, L. Statius Quadratus.

Despite further persecution, the Christian community in Smyrna continued to grow in numbers throughout the late Roman era, and when Constantine the Great convened the first ecumenical council of the church at Nicaea in 325 the Smyrnaeans were represented by their bishop. During the sixth century the city was elevated to the level of a metropolis in the Greek Orthodox Church. Smyrna retained the title of metropolis throughout the Byzantine and Ottoman periods, though the city changed hands repeatedly in the course of its turbulent history during those eras. The lower city of Smyrna was overrun during the first two Arab invasions of Asia Minor, in 654 and 674-78. On both occasions the citadel on Mt. Pagus held out until the invaders, the dreaded Saracens, had gone. The citadel was captured in 1078 by the Selçuks under Prince Süleyman. Smyrna then remained in the hands of the Turks until it was recaptured by the Byzantines in 1097, at the beginning of the First Crusade.

A new era in the history of the city began in 1261, when Michael VIII Palaeologus (r. 1259-82) entered into an alliance with the Genoese, formalized in the Treaty of Nymphaeum. By the terms of the treaty, the emperor granted the Genoese extensive concessions in the Byzantine Empire, including full control of Smyrna, "a city fit for commercial use, having a good port and abounding in all goods." The Genoese retained Smyrna until 1310, when the citadel was taken from them by Umur Bey, Emir of Aydın, which was then the capital of a Türkmen *beylik* in western Asia Minor. Pope Clement VI then appointed Martino Zaccaria as captain of a flotilla of four papal galleys, which he led into the Gulf of Smyrna in December 1344 to recapture the Castle of St. Peter, the city's principal maritime fortress. This allowed him to take the lower city of Smyrna, while Umur Bey held out in the citadel. Then on 7 January of the new year, when the Roman Catholic archbishop of Smyrna was celebrating a thanksgiving mass in the cathedral, a group of armed Turks broke in and captured Zaccaria, bringing his severed head back to Umur Bey as a trophy of revenge. The Türkmen of the Aydın *beylik* continued to hold the citadel until the beginning of the fifteenth century, while the Christians remained in control of the Castle of St. Peter and the lower town. Thus it came to be that the citadel was known to the Turks as "Muslim İzmir," while the lower town was called "Gâvur (Infidel) İzmir." During the mid-fourteenth century the Castle of St. Peter and the lower town came under the control of the Knights of St. John, whose headquarters was then on Rhodes. The knights held their part of Smyrna until December 1402, when Tamerlane captured the city after a two-week siege, driving the Christian survivors from the lower city. Shortly afterwards Tamerlane returned to the East, leaving full control of İzmir to the Emir of Aydın. But then a rival Turkish chieftain named Cüneyt Bey rebelled and captured the city along with considerable territory in its hinterland. Smyrna remained in Cüneyt's hands until 1415, when the city was captured by the Ottoman Turks under Mehmet I (r. 1413-21). Cüneyt managed to regain control of İzmir in 1422, but two years later he was captured and executed by Murat II (r. 1421-51). İzmir then became a permanent part of the Ottoman Empire, with the Turks defeating an attempt by the Venetians to capture the city in 1473.

When Murat II regained İzmir it was in ruins and virtually abandoned, but the rise of the Ottoman Empire revived the city's fortunes, and soon it became Turkey's second most important port after Istanbul. During the reign of Süleyman the Magnificent (r. 1520-66) the Turks began granting commercial concessions to European powers in order to develop the foreign trade of the Ottoman Empire. Murat III (r. 1574-95) wrote to Queen Elizabeth I in encouragement of this trade, assuring her that he had signed a firman, or imperial directive, which safeguarded any of her representatives "as shall resort hither by sea from the realm of England," who "may lawfully come to our imperial dominions, and surely return home again, and no man shall dare to molest or trouble them." The

Sultan also informed the Queen that the English would have the same commercial privileges as "our familiars and confederates, the French, Venetians, Polonians, and the King of Germany, with divers other neighbors about us," and they would have the right to "use and trade all kinds of merchandise as any other Christians, without any let or disturbance of any." This led to the incorporation of a group of English merchant adventurers called the Levant Company, also called the "Company of Turkey Merchants," who in September 1581 were given a seven-year charter by the Sultan which enabled them to set up trading stations in İzmir and Istanbul. The principal products exported from Turkey by the English and other foreign merchants in Turkey were figs, currants, carpets and coffee, the latter commodity being introduced to Europe for the first time through this trade. Thus Smyrna and its hinterland became very prosperous, and in the first half of the eighteenth century the population rose to around 100,000, as high as it had been in the imperial Roman era. The English antiquarian Richard Pococke, who visited İzmir in 1739, estimated the population to include 84,000 Turks, 8,000 Greeks, 6,000 Jews and 2,000 Armenians. Besides these there were probably several hundred European merchants, who were known locally as "factors." The most numerous and influential factors were those of the Levant Company, who were supported by an English consul appointed by the Crown. Richard Chandler who first visited the city in 1764, gives a vivid description of the rich ethnic mixture in Infidel İzmir, as he writes:

> Smyrna continues a large and flourishing city. The bay, besides numerous small craft, is daily frequented by ships of burden from the chief ports of Europe, and the factors, who are a respectable body, at once live in affluence and acquire fortunes. The conflux at Smyrna of various nations, differing in dress, in manners, in language, and in religion, is very considerable. The Turks occupy by far the greater part of the town. The other tribes live in separate quarters. The protestants and Roman catholics have their chapels, the Jews a synagogue or two; the Armenians a large and handsome church, with a

Street Scene in Ottoman Smyrna (İzmir), Allom Print

burying ground by it. The Greeks, before the fire, had two churches...

Chandler then goes on to write of how the European merchants generally chose their wives from the Christian minorities, particularly the Greeks, whose colorful costumes contrasted dramatically with those of the Turkish women of İzmir.

> The factors, and other Europeans settled at Smyrna, generally intermarry with the Greeks, or with natives of the same religion. Their ladies wear the oriental dress, consisting of large trowsers or breeches, which reach to the ancle; long vests of rich silk, or of velvet, lined in winter with costly furs; and around their waist an embroidered zone, with clasps of silver or gold. Their hair is plaited, and descends down the back, often in great profusion. The girls have sometimes about twenty thick tresses, besides two or three encircling the head, as a coronet, and set off with flowers, and plumes of feathers, pearls, or jewels. They commonly stain it of a chestnut color, which is the most desired. Their apparel and carriage are alike antique. It is remarkable that the trowsers are mentioned in a fragment by Sappho. The habit is light, loose, and cool, adapted to the climate. When they visit each other they put over their heads a thin transparent veil of muslin, with a border of gold tissue. A janizary walks before, and two or more handmaidens follow them through the streets. When assembled, they are seen reclining in various attitudes, or sitting cross-legged on a sofa. Girls of inferior rank from the islands, especially Tinos, abound; and are many of them as beautiful in person, as picturesque in appearance. They excel in a glow of color, which seems the effect of a warm sun, ripening the human body as it were into an uncommon perfection. The women of the Turks, and of some other nations, are kept carefully concealed; and when they go out, are wrapped in white linen, wear boots, and have their faces muffled.

The beauty of the city's setting and its fine climate are described by William J. Hamilton, who first landed in İzmir on 31 October 1835:

> After another stormy night we entered the Gulf of Smyrna, at 6 A.M., passing under the bold bluff headland of Cape Karabournou (Black Nose). As we advanced we were struck with the beauty of the mountain scenery on the southern shore. Steep and wooded hills rise abruptly from the sea, covered with evergreens and wild pear trees; the latter when in bloom, as I afterwards saw them in the spring, giving a gay appearance to the mountain side. Higher up the gulf the mountain range attains an elevation of nearly 3000 feet in two remarkable hills, which have received the appellation of the Two Brothers, and form a conspicuous object from Smyrna, where their clear or clouded appearance is looked upon as a certain prognostic of fine or foul weather....But Smyrna must be seen to be understood; the soft Ionian climate must be felt before it can be appreciated; and with the change which has of late taken place in the Turkish character, a residence in Smyrna or its neighbourhood would be as free from alarms as any part of Italy or Spain: indeed, I might say, much more so. There is an exquisite softness in the air of this climate at the commencement of spring, when the ground is enamelled with flowers, of which no description can convey an idea. But I must not anticipate; we are still in the middle of winter; and a most severe one it proves to be.

Hamilton then goes on to describe the Bazaar of İzmir, surpassed in Turkey only by the famous Covered Market in Istanbul, which in his time it rivalled not only in the number and variety of objects sold there but also in the ethnic diversity of those who frequented it; as he writes:

> In modern Smyrna, the objects most deserving of attention are the bazaars, which, though inferior to those of Constantinople, are in some respects more remarkable. Goods of different kinds are sold in different parts, arranged in wooden booths spread over a large extent of ground. The narrow road or path between them is covered in, and sometimes boarded under foot. At night they are regularly locked up and guarded by watchmen. One long row of booths is occupied by the sellers of dried fruits, where baskets of raisins, figs, dates, apricots

and plums are arranged in inviting piles; whilst a neighbouring gallery is occupied by shops, solely devoted to the manufacture of wooden drums or boxes in which the figs of Smyrna are sent to Europe. In another part are the bazaars for ancient arms, matchlocks, yataghans, and pistols, with other curiosities, and objects of *virtu.* Pipes are sold in another quarter, and one gallery, called the English bazaar, is occupied by cotton goods, and printed calicoes chiefly from Manchester.

But perhaps the most striking object there is the great variety of curious and gay costumes, various even among the different classes of Turks, but still more from the heterogenous nations that swarm and congregate in this quarter. The grave and stately Turkish merchant or shopkeeper, in his ample robes, and squatting on his shop-board, contrasts with the strong, active, and almost gigantic hamal, or porter, bending beneath a burden which it seems scarcely possible for the human back to sustain, though I am told that it is not unusual for them to carry a weight of twelve to fourteen hundred cwt. Their dress is as simple as that of the other is ostentatious, with bare legs and white drawers, and a wisp of cotton cloth rolled around their dirty fez or red skull-cap. Again, the Xebeque from the mountains, and the banks of the Maeander, with bare legs and white drawers fitting tight to his thighs, but made preposterously loose behind, with his high and gaudy turban bedecked with tassles and fringes, is a very different being from the Euruque or Turcoman, clad in sombre brown tramping along in heavy-shod iron boots, and driving along on his camels and asses laden with charcoal for sale. Then the Armenians and Levantines, with their huge kalpaks and flowing robes, their dark complexions, and clean-shaved chins, are as different from the...fair-haired Jews, with bare foreheads, long-pointed beards, and rather open necks, as anything can well be imagined....Again, what a striking difference we see between the proud chavase with his splendid arms, his dagger, pistols, and silver-mounted yataghan, and the bandy-legged half-starved tactico (regular infantry soldier), with his ugly, useless fez and blue tassel, looking half angry and half-ashamed of his ill-made and un-mahometan dress! Hard by us a long chain of Turkish women, silently shuffling along in their yellow slippers, whose spectral dress forms a

> striking variety to the party-coloured figures by which they are surrounded. Their faces are invisible, being concealed by a black silk mask, which strangely clashes with the white shroud or cloak thrown over their heads, and almost envelopes their body in its ample folds. It is rare indeed that any other part of their dress can be seen but the hem of a robe or the tip of a yellow boot.

İzmir continued to be a multi-ethnic city up until the Graeco-Turkish War that followed World War I. This conflict began when the Greek army landed in İzmir on 15 May 1919, after which they advanced into western Asia Minor. The Greek claim was legitimized on 10 August 1920 by the Treaty of Sevres, which empowered Greece to occupy and administer İzmir and the surrounding region for a period of five years. The Greek claim to western Asia Minor was violently opposed by the Nationalist movement led by Mustafa Kemal Pasha, later to be known as Atatürk, who strove to create a new Turkish nation out of the ashes of the Ottoman Empire. The Nationalist Turkish forces ultimately defeated the Greek army in the ensuing war over the next two years, and at the beginning of September 1922 Greece evacuated all of its forces from Asia Minor, most of them leaving from İzmir. The Turkish army, led by Mustafa Kemal Pasha, triumphantly entered İzmir on 9 September of that year. Four days later, after widespread riots, the city was destroyed by a great fire in which thousands died, most of them Greek. Most of the surviving Greeks then fled from İzmir and the surrounding region aboard whatever shipping they could find, with many more losing their lives in the process. Then in 1923 the remaining Greek population in Asia Minor was deported in the exchange of minorities agreed to in the Treaty of Lausanne, which ended the Graeco-Turkish War. The Anatolian Greeks were replaced by Turkish refugees from Greece, mostly from Crete and the Aegean isles, ending another chapter in the age-old conflict between East and West that forms the theme of *The Histories* of Herodotus. As he writes in the opening sentence of his work: "Herodotus of Halicarnassus, his Researches are here set down to preserve the memory of the past by putting on record the astonishing achievements both of our own and other peoples; and more particularly, to show how they came into conflict."

The scars of the great fire of 1922 have long since healed in İzmir, which is now for the most part a modern city, with only part of its old Turkish and Jewish quarters surviving from the Levantine town of late Ottoman times. The little that is left of old Smyrna has been almost entirely engulfed by the enormous amount of new construction that has taken place in the last quarter century. During this time İzmir has been the fastest-growing city in Turkey, its population now over three million. And so Levantine Smyrna is now just a fading memory, and only a few fragmentary ruins remain from the Graeco-Roman city that came into being through Alexander's dream.

The principal archaeological site remaining from Graeco-Roman Smyrna is the Agora, which is about midway between Kadifekale and the port. This market square was originally constructed in the mid-second century A.D., and was then destroyed in the great earthquake of 178. Shortly afterwards it was restored by the Empress Faustina II, wife of Marcus Aurelius. The Agora consisted of a central courtyard measuring 120 by 80 meters, surrounded on all sides by Corinthian stoas, of which only those on the north and west sides have been evacuated. Beneath the north stoa there is a splendid vaulted basement, above which there was an arcade of shops that opened out into a Roman market street.

Some of the sculptures that once adorned the Agora are now in the new İzmir Archaeological Museum, which is on the road that winds uphill from the southern end of the port. The most notable of these are statues of Poseidon and Demeter, the principal figures in a beautiful and well-preserved group dating from the imperial Roman era, discovered when the Agora was excavated in 1931-32. These statues symbolized the two principal sources of ancient Smyrna's wealth, for Poseidon was god of the sea and Demeter goddess of agriculture.

The other exhibits in the museum represent many of the archaeological sites along the Aegean coast of Turkey, including some other antiquities from ancient Smyrna. Among the latter there are some interesting architectural fragments from the archaic temple of Athena at Bayraklı, including an Aeolic capital of a type quite different from those found at Neandria and Larisa. The most spectacular exhibit in the museum, located in the basement gallery, is the head and forearm of a colossal marble statue of Domitian (r. 81-96). It is part of a cult figure of the Emperor which was in the temple dedicated to him in Ephesus.

The seaside square near the southern end of the port is known as Konak Meydanı. The principal landmark in the square is the Clock Tower, a neo-Moorish structure erected in 1901. Directly across the square from the tower we see Konak Camii, a pretty little octagonal mosque dating from 1794, its exterior revetted in tiles.

The main avenue leading into the center of the city from Konak Meydanı is Anafartalar Caddesi, better known by its old name of Kemeraltı (Under the Arches). This leads to the old Turkish quarter of Ottoman Smyrna, as one can see from the number of minarets projecting skywards from this labyrinth, which is almost entirely taken up with İzmir's renowned Bazaar. The oldest of these mosques are Hisar Camii (1598), Şadırvanaltı Camii (1636-37), Başdurak Camii (1652, restored in 1774), Kestane Pazarı Camii (mid-seventeenth century), Ali Ağa Camii (1671-72), and Hacı Mehmet Ağa Camii (1672). This last edifice is also known as Kemeraltı Camii, giving its name to the main street of the market quarter, whose most colorful stretch begins literally under the arches of the mosque's arcaded courtyard. Here one enters the Bazaar, which extends almost the entire length of Kemeraltı. The oldest part of the Bazaar is at the western end of Kemeraltı, around Hisar Camii, the Mosque of the Fortress. The narrow, winding streets that lead off from the little square around Hisar Camii are flanked by the oldest and most fascinating Ottoman buildings in İzmir, the *han*s, huge commercial structures that originally served as inner-city caravansarais. The finest of these is the Kızlarağası Hanı; this was originally built in the second quarter of the seventeenth century by Beşir Ağa, Chief Black Eunuch during the reign of Mahmut I (r. 1730-54). These *hans* were particularly important in the commercial life of Ottoman İzmir, which was the terminus of the main east-west caravan route in Anatolia. Chandler writes of the *hans* of the Bazaar in his description of the Ottoman buildings of İzmir:

> The principal buildings in Smyrna are the mosques, the public baths, the bezesten or market, and the khans or inns. Some of these are very ample and noble edifices. The khans have in general a quadrangular or square area, and sometimes a fountain in the middle. The upper story consists of an open gallery, with a range of apartments, and often a small mosque, or place of worship, for the use of the devout mussulmen. Below are the camels with their burdens, and the mules, or horses. A servant dusts the floor of a vacant chamber when you arrive, and spreading a mat, which is all the furniture, leaves you in possession. The gates are shut about sunset, and a trifling gratuity is expected by the keeper at your departure....

Roman Agora in İzmir

Statues of Poseidon and Demeter from Roman Agora, İzmir Archaeological Museum

The old Jewish quarter is near the western end of Kemeraltı, where the gold merchants have their shops. In times past most of these gold merchants were Sephardic Jews. Only a few continue to do business in the Bazaar, as the size of the Jewish community in İzmir has much diminished in the past quarter-century. De La Motraye, a French traveler who visited İzmir in 1699, noted that there were eight synagogues in the city, along with nineteen mosques, two Greek churches, and one Armenian church. Today there are eleven synagogues in İzmir, all of them in excellent repair. The oldest of these is the Etz-Ha-Haim Synagogue, which was already in existence by the year 1300. This synagogue was used by the first Sephardic Jews who came to the Ottoman Empire in 1492 at the invitation of Beyazit II (r. 1481-1512). It is famous as the site of the supposed miracle performed in 1666 by Shabbetai Sevi, the famous False Messiah, who was born in the Jewish quarter of İzmir in 1626. Many thousands of Jews all over the Ottoman Empire and in eastern Europe were led by this miracle to believe that Shabbetai was the long-awaited Messiah. The disturbances aroused by the news of this new religious leader led Mehmet IV (r. 1648-87) to order the arrest of Shabbetai, who later that year was brought before the Sultan in his court at Edirne. There, threatened with execution, Shabbetai saved his life by converting to Islam, after which he convinced many of his followers to become Muslims. Thus arose the strange and secret cult known to the Turks as Dönme (Turncoats)—Jews who converted to Islam through their reverence for Shabbetai Sevi, who led them to believe that he would one day return as their Messiah and lead them to their just reward in the next world. The sect is still in existence, principally in Istanbul and İzmir, though only a few of the older Dönme continue to await the second coming of their lost messiah.

The focal point of the modern city is Kültürpark, the site of the İzmir International Trade Fair, held annually in late August and early September. The Fairgrounds is the city's largest park, and its outdoor cafés make it a favorite gathering place in good weather. The park has a Gallery of Painting and Sculpture, in which both

Turkish and foreign artists are represented, and also a Museum of Turkish Art, which has changing exhibitions of objects on loan from the archaeological museums in İzmir and Istanbul.

Modern İzmir's most attractive feature is the Kordon, a seaside promenade that stretches for some four kilometers north from the maritime passenger terminal in the port. The main seaside square along the Kordon is Cumhuriyet Meydanı, where an equestrian statue of Atatürk commemorates his triumphal entry into İzmir at the head of the Turkish nationalist forces on 9 September 1922.

There are numerous cafés and restaurants along the Kordon, all of them with views of the surounding hills and mountains. The highest of the peaks around the head of the gulf is Kızıldağ, the Red Mountain, which rises to an elevation of 1,067 meters some twenty-five kilometers to the west along the southern shore of the gulf. The most prominent feature of Kızıldağ is a bifurcated rocky peak known as the Two Brothers, which rises 883 meters above sea level just above the shore highway leading out along the peninsula west of İzmir. The Two Brothers are carefully watched by the people of İzmir, as Hamilton noted more than a century-and-a-half ago, because if clouds gather around them, particularly at sunset, then the next day is sure to bring rain. Those watching from the cafes along İzmir's waterfront mark sunset as the time when the sun falls behind the silhouette of the Two Brothers, its refracted light casting a changing palette of pastels over the gulf, as twilight begins to shroud the city with its sadness. The Greek poet George Seferiades, winner of the Nobel Prize for literature in 1963, was born within sight of the Two Brothers, and he mentions them in one of his last poems, catching the mood of sunset and twilight in İzmir: "[T]he sun sets below the rock of the Two Brothers./The twilight spreads over the sky and sea like the colors of an inexhaustible love."

CHAPTER FIVE

LYDIA: SARDIS

Our present itinerary will take us on a round trip from İzmir to Sardis, the ancient capital of Lydia, stopping enroute to see monuments from the Hittite, Lydian, Graeco-Roman, *beylik* and Ottoman periods.

We head out from İzmir on highway 565, which takes us northeast to Manisa, a drive of 43 kilometers. Some seven kilometers from the center of İzmir, we pass through Bornova, a garden suburb that in Ottoman times was the residence of many of the wealthy English merchants of Smyrna, a few of whose descendants continue to live there today.

After passing Bornova the highway crosses the plain of İzmir and begins to climb, going over the Sabuncu Pass at an altitude of 707 meters. On our left is Yamanlar Dağı, whose highest peak is at 981 meters, and on our right is Manisa Dağı, the ancient Mt. Sipylus, whose summit is 1,493 meters above sea level.

Both of these mountains have legendary associations with the myth of Tantalus, said to be a son of Zeus and a daughter of Cronus named Pluto. Tantalus married a daughter of Atlas, the Pleiad Dione, who bore him several children, the most notable being their daughter Niobe and their son Pelops. Tantalus was extremely rich and built a city on Mt. Sipylus, where he entertained the gods. But he abused the friendship of his divine guests, stealing nectar and ambrosia from their table and revealing their secrets to men. At one of his feasts he served up to the gods the butchered body of his son Pelops, who was later restored to life and escaped to the Peloponnesus, which is named for him. The gods punished Pelops by destroying his city in an earthquake, after which they confined him to a cave under Mt. Sipylus. There he was condemned to an eternity of thirst and starvation, with fresh water and abundant fruit always just beyond his reach, "tantalizing" him, to use the word that derived from his name and fate. Homer describes the fate of Tantalus in Book XI of *The Odyssey,* where Odysseus tells of those whom he saw on his visit to the Underworld:

> And I saw Tantalos, also, suffering hard pains,
> standing in lake water that came up to his chin, and thirsty
> as he was, he tried to drink, but could capture nothing;
> for every time the old man tried to drink, stooped over,
> the water would drain away and disappear, and the black earth
> showed at his feet, and the divinity drained it away. Over
> his head trees with lofty branches had fruit like a shower
> descending,
> pear trees and pomegranate trees and apple trees with fruit
> shining,
> and figs that were sweet and olives ripened well, but each time
> the old man would straighten up and reach up with his hands for
> them,
> the wind would toss them away to the cloud overhanging,...

Travelers in times past identified a number of natural features on Mt. Sipylus and Yamanlar Dağı with Tantalus and his family. As Pausanias writes: "Some traces of the life of Pelops and of Tantalos are still left in our country today; the lake named after him and his by no means inglorious grave, and Pelop's throne, on the mountain top at Sipylos..."

Manisa is situated in the valley of the Hermus at the foot of Mt. Sipylus, which rises above the town to the south. Manisa derives from Magnesia ad Sipylum, the ancient city on this site, its second name distinguishing it from Magnesia ad Maeandrum, which was located some distance to the south on the Maeander river. According to tradition, both of these cities were founded by settlers from Magnesia in northeastern Greece, the so-called Magnetes, who are supposed to have stayed on in Asia Minor after fighting in Agamemnon's army at the siege of Troy. Magnesia ad Sipylum is first mentioned by the historian Hellanicus of Lesbos, a contemporary of Herodotus, whose life spanned most of the fifth century B.C. Like most of the other Greek cities in western Asia Minor, it was a pawn during the wars of the Diadochi, and then early in the second century B.C. it was absorbed by Pergamum.

The city gave its name to the historic battle of Magnesia, which was fought north of the Hermus one rainy morning in early January 189 B.C., when the Pergamenes and their Roman allies defeated the forces of Antiochus III, ending forever Seleucid rule in Asia Minor. The Seleucid forces in the battle were commanded by Hannibal, whose elephants were left dead in their hundreds upon the battlefield, a sight that so distressed Antiochus that he decided to sue for peace, never again going to war.

After the end of the Pergamene kingdom Magnesia ad Sipylum became part of the Roman Province of Asia in 129 B.C. It continued to be an important city under the Byzantines, and in 1222 John III Vatatzes (r. 1222-54) temporarily moved his capital here from Nicaea in order to pursue a campaign against the Latins in Asia Minor and the Aegean. The ruined citadel on the acropolis hill known as Sandık Tepesi is entirely Byzantine in construction. The lower walls were erected by John III, while those on the summit date from the eighth century A.D., probably erected on the foundations of the ancient fortress there.

The city was captured from the Byzantines in 1313 by the Türkmen Emir Saruhan, who gave his name to the *beylik* that he founded with its capital at Manisa, as it was known to the Turks. Manisa was conquered by Beyazit I in 1390, but after the Ottoman defeat at Ankara in 1402 Tamerlane restored the city and the rest of the *beylik* to the Emir of Saruhan. The *beylik* was recaptured by Mehmet I in 1415, after which it became a permanent part of the Ottoman Empire. Thereafter Manisa was one of the most important provincial capitals in Anatolia, and several of the royal Ottoman princes served here in turn as governor before succeeding to the throne, including the future Sultan Mehmet II (r.1451-81), the conqueror of Constantinople. Consequently, Manisa is endowed with a number of fine mosques and other pious foundations built by the Ottoman royal family, in addition to those erected earlier by the Saruhan emirs.

The principal Saruhan monument in Manisa is at the southern end of the town at the foot of the acropolis hill. This is the Ulu Cami, built in 1376 by the Saruhan Emir İshak Bey, whose *türbe* and *medrese* are attached to the western side of the mosque and its courtyard. The mosque itself is preceded by a *şadırvan* court measuring 29.90 by 15.30 meters, with the minaret rising from the northwest corner of the courtyard. The central area around the octagonal şadirvan is surrounded on three sides by a portico of nineteen units covered by low domical vaults, with seven bays along the north and three pairs of two each on the sides. Many of the columns and capitals in the courtyard and within the mosque and *medrese* are late Roman or early Byzantine, as are other architectural elements, all of them undoubtedly taken from earlier buildings of Magnesia ad Sipylum. The prayer hall, which measures 29.90 by 15.30 meters, has the same number and arrangement of bays as the courtyard. The area in front of the mihrab—the niche indicating the kible, the direction of Mecca—is covered by a dome 10.80 meters in diameter. The dome rests on four pendentives above the diagonals of the octagonal base formed by the kible wall and six free-standing piers. The carved wooden mimber, or pulpit, is a particularly fine work in the Selçuk style.

A vaulted passage leads from the west side of the courtyard into the attached *medrese*, or theological school, which can also be entered from outside by a gateway located in the central axis of the building. On the left side of the passage leading in from the courtyard is the entrance to the domed *türbe*, or tomb, of İshak Bey, who died in 1388. The *türbe* door is flanked by two pairs of double "knotted" columns of a red and yellow breccia. They are undoubtedly Byzantine in origin, as is the fluted column on the left at the entrance from the passage into the central courtyard of the two-storied *medrese*. The south side of the courtyard opens into the main *eyvan*, or vaulted chamber (*eyvan*s are sometimes domed). This is flanked by two other vaulted chambers, the western one having collapsed. The student cells open off the west side of the courtyard in two stories.

One block to the east of the Ulu Cami we see the Muradiye Camii. This is the most splendid of all the mosques in Manisa, built in 1583-86 for Murat III, who served here as provincial governor before becoming sultan in 1574. The mosque was designed by Sinan, but the actual construction was carried out by the architect Mehmet Ağa, who would later build the famous Blue Mosque in Istanbul. The Muradiye is preceded by a five-bay portico carried by two columns of Proconnesian marble and four of granite, with the two fluted minarets rising from the corners of the building behind the porch. On each side of the building there is an arcade with a shed roof carried on four square marble piers.

The square central area of the prayer hall is covered by a dome eleven meters in diameter resting on spherical pendentives. Around the central square are grouped three abutting rectangular bays, one forming the mihrab apse and the other two flanking the main prayer room, all of them covered by vaults in the form of three planes meeting in groins. The mihrab niche is splendidly decorated with stalactite carvings and the mimber is a fine work in gilded and painted marble. The royal lodge is the gallery in the southeast corner, resting on ogive arches supported by two marble columns and the walls, the carved and painted ceiling beneath it being one of the finest works of its kind in Turkey. There is also a gallery over the main entrance resting on multifoliate arches carried on four square piers, as well as two smaller galleries over the northeast and northwest doors.

The *külliye*, or pious foundation, of the Muradiye also included an *imaret*, or soup kitchen, and two *medrese*s, one of which shared the courtyard of the mosque. The *medrese* around the courtyard of the mosque has vanished, but the other one survives, along with the *imaret*. The surviving *medrese*, which is just to the east of the mosque, now serves as the Manisa Ethnographical Museum. The *imaret*, the next building to the east, houses the Archaeological Museum. The Archaeological Museum has antiquities from various sites in Lydia, most notably Sardis, and also sculptures from Magnesia ad Sipylum dating from the Roman and Byzantine periods.

Across the intersection to the northwest of the Muradiye we see Sultan Camii, another of the imperial Ottoman mosques of Manisa. Tis was built in 1522 by Süleyman the Magnificent in honor of his mother, the Valide Sultan (Queen Mother) Hazize Hatun, a wife of Selim I (r. 1512-20). The mosque is preceded by a five-bay porch supported by tall columns with stalactite capitals. The two minarets rise from the northeast and northwest corners of the building. The entrance to the mosque is flanked by two prayer niches with exceptionally fine frames of moulded stucco. The central area of the prayer room is covered by a dome with an octagonal drum resting on a square base in the center, with two bays on either side covered by smaller and lower domes. The *külliye* also includes a *medrese,* a *hamam*, and a *darüşşifa,* or hospital, which included a *tımarhane,* or insane asylum.

We now walk northeast from Sultan Camii along Çarşı Bulvarı, at the far end of which we pass on our right the old Manisa Bazaar. Then at the next intersection we come to the Hatuniye

View of Manisa, Allom Print

Camii, the third of Manisa's imperial Ottoman mosques.

This imposing mosque was built in 1488 by Beyazit II for his mother, the Valide Sultan Hüsnü Şah Hatun, a wife of Mehmet II. The mosque is preceded by a five-bay porch supported by columns with Byzantine capitals. The minaret, which rises from the northwest corner of the mosque, has a shaft with decorative brickwork in zigzag flutes. The central area of the prayer hall is covered by a dome on Turkish triangles, with two bays each to east and west covered by smaller and lower cupolas.

The oldest dated Islamic structure in Manisa is İlyas Bey Mescidi, a small mosque built in 1362 by the father of İshak Bey. The mosque is preceded by a two-domed portico closed in with side walls, with the prayer room covered by a dome on squinches.

Besides the three imperial foundations, there are eleven other Ottoman mosques in Manisa, all of them dating from the second half of the fifteenth century. Those dated by inscriptions are Çeşnigir Camii (1474), Hoca Yahya Camii (1474), Sinan Bey Camii (1474), Attar Hoca Camii (1480), İvaz Paşa Camii (1484), and Göktaşlı Cami (1493). The others are Nişancı Paşa Camii, Çatal Camii, Aynı Ali Camii, Emir Hıdır Camii, and Serabat Camii. Only the minaret and one wall of the latter mosque remain standing today.

We now proceed by taking the road below the citadel, continuing past Ulu Cami until we come to the turn downward. There above us we see a curious rock formation about twenty meters high at the entrance to a gorge where a stream flows down from Mt. Sipylus. This rock has been identified as the figure of the "weeping Niobe," which is mentioned by several ancient writers, including Homer, Sophocles, Ovid and Pausanias. Pausanias apparently lived in the region at one time, and he gives a description of the rock formation that is still accurate today: "I myself have seen Niobe when I was climbing up the mountains to Sipylos. Niobe from up close is a rock and a stream, and nothing like a woman grieving or otherwise; but if you go farther you seem to see a woman downcast and in tears." According to the myth, Niobe had six sons and six daughters. All of them were killed by Apollo and Artemis, the twin offspring of Leto, who were angered at Niobe for having mocked their mother because she had only two children, while she herself had a dozen. Homer tells the story in Book XXIV of *The Iliad,* where Achilles is trying to persuade Priam to eat while the old king is grieving over the body of his dead son Hector:

> For even Niobe, she of the lovely tresses, remembered
> to eat, whose twelve children were destroyed in her palace,
> six daughters and six sons in the pride of their youth, whom Apollo
> killed with arrows from his silver bow, being angered
> with Niobe, and shaft-showering Artemis killed the daughters;
> because Niobe likened herself to Leto of the fair-colouring
> and said Leto had borne only two, she herself had borne many;
> but the two, though they were only two, destroyed all those others.
> Nine days long they lay in their blood, nor was there anyone
> to bury them, for the son of Kronos made stones out of
> the people; but on the tenth day the Uranian gods buried them.
> But she remembered to eat when she was worn out with weeping.
> And now somewhere among the rocks, in the lonely mountains in
> Sipylos, where they say is the resting place of the goddesses
> who are nymphs, and dance beside the waters of Acheloios,
> there, stone still, she broods on the sorrows the gods gave her.

We now leave Manisa on highway 250, which takes us eastwards along the northern flanks of Mt. Sipylus. About six kilometers out of Manisa we stop at a place called Akpınar, where high above the road on the right we find a relief known as Taş Suret, the Stone Figure. The carving is more than ten meters high, and though it is badly eroded it is still possible to make out the form of a female figure seated upon a throne. Scholars have for long suggested that the Taş Suret is a work of the Hittites, probably dating from the fourteenth century B.C. This has now been substantiated by an inscription on the relief, which has been shown to be in the Hittite language, though the date is undetermined. The Taş Suret is undoubtedly the figure on Mt. Sipylus that Pausanias describes as being "the most ancient of all statues of the Mother of the Gods." This fertility goddess was the one that Anatolian people of the Bronze Age, including the Hittites, worshipped as the Great Earth Mother, while in the archaic period the Phrygians revered her as Kubaba, the Lydians as Cybele, and the Greeks as Artemis. She was worshipped as a mountain goddess under different names in various places: on Mt. Ida in the Troad she was called the Idaean Mother; at Cyzicus she was Dindymene, Mother of the Gods; and here on Mt. Sipylus she was called the Sipylene Mother.

We now turn back toward Manisa and go as far as the turnoff for highway 565, where we turn right and head northeastward toward Akhisar, a drive of 44 kilometers. We then take the first turnoff for Akhisar, which is at the junction of highways 565 and 500, the latter road signposted for Salihli.

Akhisar is on the site of an ancient city known originally as Pelopia, according to Pliny the Younger. During the wars of the Diadochi, following the death of Alexander, the city was refounded by Lysimachus, who renamed it Thyatira. Thyatira became part of the Pergamene kingdom after the battle of Magnesia in 189 B.C., and then it came under Roman rule in 129 B.C. after the establishment of the province of Asia. Hadrian visited Thyatira in A.D. 124, and Caracalla (r. 211-17) stayed here for a time as well, endowing a number of buildings and receiving the title of "Benefactor of the City."

Christianity came early to Thyatira, which was one of the Seven Churches of Revelation. But apparently some of the Thyatirans still worshipped the older gods of Anatolia, for the Evangelist's letter to the Christian community there warns them against a "Jezebel," whom the German scholar Schürer believes to have been "a prophetess and priestess of the temple of a Chaldaean Sibyl in Thyatira, where a mixture of pagan rites with Jewish ideas was practised." As we read in *Revelation* 2:18-29:

Write to the angel of the church in Thyatira and say, "Here is the

> message of the Son of God who has eyes like a burning flame and feet like burnished bronze: I know all about you and how charitable you are; I know your faith and devotion and how much you put up with, and I know how you are still making progress. Nevertheless, I have a complaint to make: you are encouraging the woman Jezebel who claims to be a prophetess, and by her teaching she is luring my servants away to commit the adultery of eating food which has been sacrificed to idols. I have given her time to reform, but she is not willing to change her adulterous life. Now I am consigning her to bed, and all her partners in adultery to troubles that will test them severely, unless they repent of their practices; and I will see that her children die, so that all the churches realise that it is I who search heart and loins and give each of you what your behaviour deserves. But on the rest of you in Thyatira, all of you who have not accepted this teaching or learnt the secrets of Satan, as they are called, I am not laying any special duty; but hold firmly on to what you already have until I come. To those who prove victorious, and keep working with me until the end, I will give the authority over the pagans which I myself have been given by my Father, to rule them with an iron sceptre and shatter them like earthenware. And I will give him the Morning Star. If anyone has ears to hear, let him listen to what the Spirit is saying to the churches."

The only structures that remain from ancient Thyatira are a basilica and a portico, both of the late Roman era, which were excavated in the Tepemezarlığı quarter in the late 1960s. The ruins cover a square area about 35 meters on a side, with column bases and drums and both Ionic and Corinthian capitals arrayed around the site along with other architectural fragments.

After looking at the basilica we head south from Akhisar on highway 555, headed for Salihli, a drive of 62 kilometers. Some 20 kilometers out of Akhisar we pass the village of Gölmarmara, and soon afterwards we come within site of the lake for which it is named, Marmara Gölü, known in antiquity as the Gygaean Lake. South of the lake we come to the region known as Bin Tepe, the

View of Thyatira, Allom Print

Thousand Hills, which takes its name from the huge tumuli that rise up above the plain, the burial mounds of the ancient Lydian kings and nobility.

Excavations in the Bin Tepe area have unearthed evidence of human occupation going back to ca. 2500 B.C., though the oldest settlement at nearby Sardis, capital of the Lydian kingdom, date back to no earlier than ca. 1500 B.C. Hittite tablets record that their king Tudhaliyas IV (r. 1250-1220 B.C.) led several campaigns in western Anatolia against a nation called the Assuwa, who are believed to be the ancient Sardian tribe known as the Asias. According to Herodotus, the continent of Asia was named after them. These are the same people whom Homer calls the Maeonians. They fought as allies of King Priam in the defense of Troy, coming from "the Gygaean Lake beneath Mount Tmolus." Hittite archives of the same period also refer to a powerful seafaring people known as the Akhiyawa, now generally identified as the Achaians. Shards of imported Mycenaean pottery of the thirteenth century B.C. found at Sardis do indicate a possible Greek conquest of the Lycian capital at about the same time as the fall of

Homeric Troy. Other sherds found at Sardis indicate that the site was occupied by an Hellenic people during the period 1200-900 B.C. and perhaps for another two centuries after that. This would support Greek tradition, which held that the first Hellenes to rule at Sardis were the Heraclidae, the self-proclaimed sons of Heracles, who supplanted a native dynasty that had originated before the Trojan War in the time of the Maeonians.

According to Herodotus, the Heraclidae "reigned for twenty-two generations, a period in all of five hundred and five years, son succeeding father right down the line to Candaules, son of Myrsus." The dynasty of the Heraclidae reigned at Sardis until ca. 685 B.C., when they were succeeded by the Mermnadae, descendants of a Lydian chieftain named Mermnad. The first of the Mermnadae was Gyges, who seized power from Candaules, the last of the Heraclidae, a story told by Herodotus in Book I of his *Histories.* The most prominent of the tumuli at Bin Tepe have been traditionally identified as the tombs of Gyges and two of his successors, Ardys and Alyattes. The largest of these is the so-called Tomb of Alyattes, which is 355 meters in diameter and 73 meters high, with the royal burial chamber presumably somewhere at the core of the mound, though it still eludes the excavators. Herodotus considered this tumulus to be "the greatest work of human hands in the world, apart from the Egyptian and the Babylonian," and he describes its construction in Book I of his *Histories:*

> The base of this monument is built of huge stone blocks; the rest of it is a mound of earth. It was raised by the joint labour of the tradesmen, craftsmen, and prostitutes, and on the top of it there survived to my own day five stone pillars with inscriptions cut in them to show the amount of work done by each class. Calculation revealed that the prostitutes share was the largest. Working-class girls in Lydia prostitute themselves without exception to collect money for their dowries, and continue the practice until they marry. They choose their own husband. The circumference of the tomb is nearly three-quarters of a mile, and its breadth about three hundred yards.

> Near it is a large lake, the lake of Gyges [the Gygaean Lake], said by the Lydians to be never dry....

Hamilton was one of the first foreign travelers to explore the Bin Tepe area, whose appearance has changed little since his time, though one no longer sees the ruined Türkmen villages that he mentions. As he writes in his journal for 12 April 1836, referring to King Alyattes as Halyattes:

> The vegetation on these plains was very luxuriant: for some way we passed through thickets of tamarisk, and heard the nightingale for the first time this year. After three hours march due west the tumulus of Halyattes formed a conspicuous object in the view, and rose considerably above the smaller tombs by which it is surrounded. The mass of tumuli, of which we counted upwards of sixty, evidently a Necropolis of the ancient Lydian kings, is called Bin Tepeh (the thousand hills) by the Turks. We passed several villages this day, mostly in a ruined state, deserted by their Turcoman inhabitants, who were encamped upon the plain tending their flocks and herds, while thousands of storks were building their nests upon the walls and damaged trees in the neighbourhood; we also observed other rare birds upon this plain, several gray Numidian cranes, and ducks of a beautiful red and brown color,
>
> At 10h. 30 m. we began ascending, in a north-westerly direction, the low ridge of limestone hills on which the tumuli are situated, leaving the Gygaean lake on our right, filling up that part of the plain which stretches away to the north. On reaching the summit of the ridge we had at our feet the whole extent of the unruffled lake, the marshy bank skirted with reeds and rushes, surrounded by hills on every side, except to the S.E., where it opens to the Hermus, in which direction its superfluous waters escape, and to the N., where the hills appear to sink away altogether.
>
> One mile S. of this spot we reached the principal tumulus, generally designated as the tomb of Halyattes. It took us about ten minutes to ride round its base, which would give it a circumference of nearly

half a mile. Towards the north it consists of the natural rock, a white horizontally stratified earthy limestone, cut away so as to appear as part of the structure. The upper structure is sand and gravel, apparently brought from the bed of the Hermus. Several deep ravines have been worn away by time and weather in its sides, particularly on that to the south; we followed one of these, as affording a better footing than the smooth grass, as we ascended to the summit. Here we found the remains of a foundation nearly eighteen feet square, on the north of which was a huge circular stone ten feet in diameter, with a flat bottom and a raised ledge or lip, evidently placed there as an ornament on the apex of the tumulus. Herodotus says that phalli were erected upon the summit of some of these tumuli, of which this may be one.... In consequence of the ground sloping to the south, this tumulus appears much higher when viewed from the side of Sardis than from any other. It rises at an angle of 22 degrees, and is a conspicuous object on all sides.

We now continue on to Salihli, where we turn right on highway E96/300. The highway take us westward along the south side of the Hermus valley, a fertile plain that Homer refers to in *The Iliad* as "lovely Maeonia." As we cross the plain the eroded acropolis hill of Sardis comes into view on the western ramparts of Boz Dağları, the Gray Mountains, the range known in antiquity as Mt. Tmolus. Chandler, as he passed this way in 1765, on his way eastward from the site of Philadelphia to that of Sardis, wrote:

We set out at nine in the morning from Philadelphia for Sardes, distant twenty-eight miles, according to the Antonine Itinerary. The way is by the foot of mount Tmolus, which was on our left; consisting of uneven, separate, sandy hills, in a row, green and pleasant, once clothed with vines, but now neglected. Behind them was a high ridge covered with snow. The plain, beside the Hermus, which divides it, is well watered by rills from the slopes. It is wide, beautiful and cultivated; but has few villages, being possessed by the Turcomans, who, in this region, were reputed thieves, but not given to bloodshed. Their

> booths and cattle were innumerable....We travelled three hours and a half north-westward, and as long westward. We met numerous caravans, chiefly of mules, on the road; or saw them by its side feeding on the green pasture, their burdens lying on the ground; the passengers sitting in groups, eating or sleeping on the grass. We pitched our tent about sunset, and the next day, after riding two hours in the same direction, arrived at Sardes, now called Sart.

Some eight kilometers from Salihli we approach the village of Sartmustafa, as it is now called. This is the site of ancient Sardis, some of whose restored edifices we now see in the archaeological site to the right of the road just before the village center on the Ecelkapız Çayı, the river Pactolus of antiquity.

The village is on the site of the business center of Roman Sardis, which was astride the Persian Royal Road at the point where it crossed the Pactolus. The acropolis of the ancient city is about one Roman mile to the southeast—as the eagle flies, with the theater and stadium below it to the north near the highway. The temple of Artemis is to its east near the Pactolus. A road leads from Sarmustafa south along the east bank of the Pactolus; after about 1.5 kilometers it brings us to a car park near the temple of Artemis. Here we will begin our tour of "golden Sardis," the capital of ancient Lydia.

Lydia emerged as the dominant power in western Anatolia under King Gyges (r. ca. 685-652 B.C.), the first of the Mermnadae dynasty. By that time the Phrygian kingdom, which had previously controlled the region, had been destroyed by the Cimmerians, who had also overrun Sardis in the mid-eighth century B.C. The rise of Lydia was stimulated by the economic policy of Gyges, who exploited the gold that was washed down from Mt. Tmolus by the Pactolus, minting it for the world's first coins. The invention of coinage further added to the already considerable wealth of the Lydians. It allowed them to develop their widespread trade, which extended from central Anatolia to the Aegean coast. All of it passed through Sardis, making it the richest city of its time.

Gyges expanded the bounds of his kingdom westward by attacking the Ionian cities along the Aegean coast, an aggressive policy that was followed by his first three successors: Ardys (r. 651-625 B.C.), Sadyattes (r. 625-610 B.C.) and Alyattes (r. 609-560 B.C.). Herodotus, in Book I of his *Histories,* describes the annual campaigns that Alyattes conducted against Miletus, the greatest maritime power in the Ionian League:

> Alyattes carried on the war which he had taken over from his father [Sadyattes], against the Milesians. His custom each year was to invade Milesian territory when the crops were ripe, marching in to the music of pipes, harps, and treble and tenor oboes. On arrival he never destroyed or burned the houses in the country, or pulled their doors off, but left them unmolested. He would merely destroy the trees and crops and then retire. The reason for this was the Milesian command of the sea, which made it useless for his army to attempt a regular siege; and he refrained from demolishing houses in order that the Milesians, having somewhere to live, might continue to work the land and sow their seed, with the result that he himself would have something to plunder each time he invaded their country.

Alyattes was succeeded by his son Croesus (r. 560-546 B.C.), the last of the Mermnadae, under whom the Lydian kingdom reached the pinnacle of its greatness. Early on in his reign Croesus abandoned the aggressive Lydian policy toward the Asian Greeks, and instead he signed a treaty of peace with the Ionian League. The terms agreed to were very lenient for the Ionians, requiring them to pay an annual tribute to Croesus and to supply troops to his army when he was on campaign. Croesus was very generous to the Greeks, sending fabulous treasures to the shrine of Apollo at Delphi and helping the Ephesians restore their famous temple of Artemis.

The golden age of Lydia came to an end in 546 B.C., when Croesus made the mistake of attacking King Cyrus of Persia, who decisively defeated him and then captured Sardis after a two-week siege. This was the end of the Lydian kingdom, and Croesus died soon afterwards as a prisoner of Cyrus. Cyrus then sent Harpagus the Mede to subdue the Greek cities on the Aegean coast, after which his general went on to conqueror Caria, the southwestern

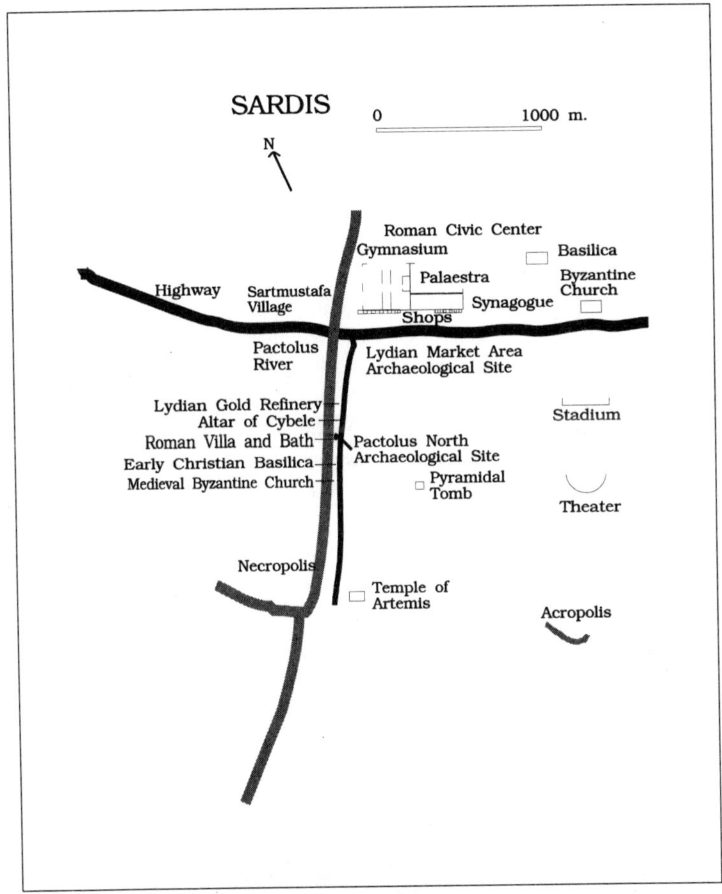

part of Asia Minor. Thus Cyrus added the whole of western Asia Minor to the Persian realm, ruling the Greek cities through satraps, or local tyrants, in Sardis and Dascylium. The prosperity of Sardis continued under their new rulers, for the city was located on the Royal Road that the Persians built to link western Asia Minor with their capital at Susa.

The Asian Greeks, aided by Athens, rebelled in 499 B.C., attacking Sardis and setting fire to the city. Herodotus writes of this in Book V of his *Histories,* where he describes how the Ionians and their Athenian allies attacked Sardis, whose defenders were led by Prince Artaphernes, a half-brother of King Darius:

> The [Ionian] fleet sailed for Ephesus, where the ships were left at Coressus in Ephesian territory; the troops, a strong force, then began their march up-country, with Ephesian guides. They followed the course of the Cayster, crossed the ridge of Tmolus, and came down upon Sardis, which they took without opposition, except for the central stronghold of the town, which was defended by Artaphernes in person, with a considerable force. But they were prevented from sacking the place after its capture by the fact that most of the houses in Sardis were constructed of reeds, reed-thatch being used even on the few houses which were built of brick. One house was set alight

View of the Acropolis at Sardis, Allom Print

Temple of Artemis at Sardis

by a soldier, and the flames rapidly spread until the whole town was ablaze. The outlying parts were all burning, so the native Lydians and the Persians as were there, caught in a ring of fire and unable to get clear of the town, poured into the market square on either side of the Pactolus, where they were forced to stand on their defense. The Pactolus is the river which brings the gold dust down from Tmolus. It flows through the market at Sardis, and then joins the Hermus, which, in its turn, flows into the sea. The Ionians, seeing some of the enemy defending themselves, and others approaching in large numbers, then became alarmed, and withdrew to Tmolus; and thence, just before nightfall, they marched off to rejoin their ships. In the conflagration at Sardis, a temple of Cybele, a goddess worshipped in that part of the world, was destroyed, and the Persians later made this a pretext for their burning of Greek temples.

The Persians counter-attacked and defeated the Ionians at Ephesus. Thus began the Ionian Revolt, which dragged on for five years and eventually involved all of the Greek cities in northwestern Asia Minor. The Persians eventually crushed the revolt, ending the campaign when their Phoenician fleet destroyed the Ionian navy at the battle of Lade in 494 B.C. Western Asia Minor then remained under Persian rule until 334 B.C., when Alexander the Great freed the Greek cities along the Aegean coast soon after his victory at the Granicus, occupying Dascylium and Sardis without a struggle. Arrian, in his work on *The Campaigns of Alexander,* written in the mid-second century A.D., describes Alexander's visit to Sardis immediately after his capture of the city:

> While he was in Sardis he went up into the acropolis, where the Persian garrison was stationed, and saw at a glance that this fortress, built as it was on a lofty and precipitous hill and defended by a triple wall, was an extremely strong position.
>
> It occurred to him to build here a temple and altar in honor of Olympian Zeus, and while he was considering the best site a summer storm, breaking suddenly with violent thunder and a fall of rain over the palace of the Lydian kings, persuaded him that Zeus himself had indicated the spot where his temple should be raised; so he gave his orders accordingly.

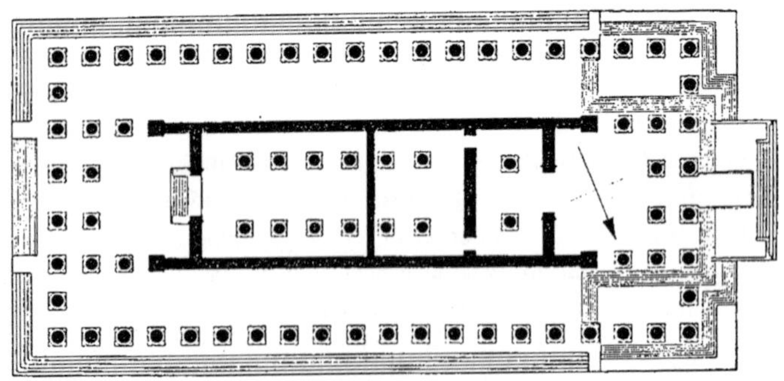

Plan of the Temple of Artemis at Sardis

After Alexander's death in 323 B.C. Lydia became part of the Seleucid kingdom, and following the battle of Magnesia in 189 B.C. it was awarded to Pergamum. In 129 B.C., after the end of the Pergamene kingdom, Sardis became part of the Roman province of Asia. Sardis remained as prosperous under Roman rule as it had been under the Persians, as much of the trade of Asia Minor continued to pass through the city along the Royal Road. Along with the other cities of western Asia Minor, Sardis reached its peak under the Romans in the second century A.D., when its population exceeded 100,000. During the reign of Diocletian (r. 284-305) Sardis became capital of the Roman province of Lydia, retaining that distinction up until the reorganization of Asia Minor in the medieval Byzantine era.

During the early Byzantine period Sardis became an important center of Christianity, another of the Seven Churches of Revelation, its first bishop being St. Clement. As we read in *Revelation* 3:1-6:

> Write to the angel of the church in Sardis and say, "Here is the message of the one who holds the seven spirits of God and the seven stars: I know all about you: how you are reputed to be alive and yet are dead. Wake up; revive what little you have left: it is dying fast. So far I have failed to notice anything in the way you live that my God could possibly call perfect, and yet do you remember how eager you were when you first heard the message? Hold on to that. Repent. If you do not wake up I will come to you like a thief, without telling you at what hour to expect me. There are a few in Sardis, it is true, who have kept their robes from being dirtied, and they are fit to come with me, dressed in white. Those who prove victorious will be dressed, like these, in white robes; I shall not blot their names out of the book of life, but acknowledge their names in the presence of my Father and his angels. If anyone has ears to hear, let him listen to what the Spirit is saying to the churches."

Sardis was still a considerable city during the early centuries of the Byzantine era, but then in 616 it was utterly destroyed by the

Sassanid Persian king Chosroes II in his invasion of Asia Minor. Sardis never fully recovered from this catastrophe, and thenceforth it was reduced to the status of a provincial town, having lost forever its ancient splendor. During the remainder of the Byzantine period Sardis almost disappears from the pages of history, mentioned only in passing by an occasional chronicler. Then in 1425 it became part of the Ottoman Empire, diminished to the status of a kaza, a mere administrative center in the province of Aydın. When Chandler visited Sardis in 1765 he reported that it had degenerated to a "miserable village" surrounded by the ruins of its illustrious past, its most conspicuous monument being the edifice now identified as the temple of Artemis.

Opposite the car park near the temple we see the headquarters of the Harvard-Cornell Expedition, the archaeological team that is excavating Sardis. The first systematic excavation of Sardis, focusing on the temple here by the Pactolus, was carried out in 1910-14 by the Princeton Expedition, headed by H. C. Butler. Nothing further was done until 1958, when the Harvard-Cornell Exploration project was begun under the direction of George M. A. Hanfmann, with the excavations continuing annually to the present day. The early excavators assumed that they were unearthing the temple of Cybele mentioned by Herodotus and other ancient writers, but inscriptions were soon discovered indicating that it was actually a temple of Artemis. Archaeologists have since discovered a shrine of Cybele elsewhere in the excavations, and thus it appears that both goddesses were worshipped in Sardis. But an historian of ancient religion would say that they were both different forms of the same deity, the great fertility goddess of Anatolia.

The original shrine of Artemis on this site was a large sandstone altar dating from the end of the fifth century B.C., located just to the west of the present temple on its longitudinal axis. Early in the third century B.C., under the Seleucids, construction began on the first phase of a west-facing Ionic temple dedicated to Artemis, with the edifice incorporating the earlier altar at its western end. This temple was a long and narrow structure with a pronaos one-third the length of the inner sanctuary, and with a very shallow opisthodomos. The cella of the temple was covered with a roof, supported by the outer walls and an internal colonnade in two rows. During the second building phase, which took place ca. 175-150 B.C., work was begun on the erection of a peristasis, or peripheral colonnade, with eight columns on each of the ends and twenty to a side. During that period only twelve columns of the peripteral colonnade were erected at the east end of the temple, as well as six more in the rear porch. The third phase of construction took place during the years A.D. 136-61, the reign of Antoninus Pius, when the peripteral colonnade was completed except for seven columns in the west front. During this final phase of construction the cella was divided into two halves by a cross wall, with the western half of the sanctuary still sacred to Artemis, but with the eastern chamber now dedicated to the late empress Faustina, who was deified after her death in 141. The Harvard-Cornell team has now cleared the temple and its immediate vicinity, establishing the plan of the edifice in its various stages of construction. A number of column drums have been erected and two of the columns still stand to their full height, capped with their superb Ionic capitals, an impressive sight when viewed against the background of the acropolis hill on its jagged spur of Mt. Tmolus.

Beside the southeast corner of the temple we see the remains of a small Byzantine chapel of the fourth century known as Church M. This is one of five Byzantine churches unearthed on the archaeological site. Those who built Church M next to the temple of Artemis were aware that the earlier sanctuary was a sacred place of great antiquity, and they took pains to exorcise the evil spirits that they believed inhabited it. As Clive Foss writes in his *Byzantine and Ottoman Sardis:* "Crosses were carved on the temple of Artemis to nullify the power of the demons who, it was believed, dwelt in the material of pagan edifices."

The acropolis hill rises to a peak some 1,500 meters east of the temple. The last part of the ascent is via a narrow and vertiginous path, where one is reminded of the account that Herodotus gives of the difficulties that the Persians had here in their siege of Sardis in 546 B.C., writing that their final assault was made on "a section of the central stronghold so precipitous as to be almost inaccessible." There are remains of a Lydian defense wall on the acropolis dating back to at least the sixth century B.C., though most of the fortifications one sees there today are Byzantine works of the sixth or seventh century A.D. One of the lower terraces of the hill is riddled with underground tombs of the Roman period. One of these is the grave of a Roman named Flavius Chrysanthios, who decorated his tomb with garlands of flowers and a dedicatory inscription; another is painted with a gorgeous depiction of a peacock, symbol of eternal life, along with bowls of fruit and flowers. The ruins on the summit of the acropolis hill also include the foundations of a palace of the archaic period, undoubtedly the imperial residence of the kings of the Mermnadae dynasty. The summit commands a panoramic view of the entire archaeological site, most of which is spread out along the east bank of the Pactolus and on both sides of the highway east of the village of Sartmustafa. Hamilton's description of the view reveals that the scene has suffered little change since his day; as he writes:

> The view from this lofty summit was truly magnificent: to the north the Hermus, winding through its rich plain, was backed by distant hills and the broad expanse of the Gygaean lake; still farther to the west were the tumuli of the Lydian kings; while the continuation of the broken and rugged line of sand hills which skirt the base of Mount Tmolus was prolonged to the east and west of the spot on which we stood. To the south were the snow-capped peaks of Mount Tmolus; while the deep intermediate space was broken into many hills and dales, either cultivated or covered with flourishing brushwood.

Returning to the temple of Artemis, we now head back along the river road toward the village. The main necropolis of ancient Sardis was across the river from the temple, where we see a number of rock-hewn tombs ranging from the sixth century B.C. to the Roman era. There are also burials on the east side of the river. About halfway along the road, where it descends to cross a ravine, a path leads off to the right to the so-called Pyramid Tomb, which is halfway up the side of the gorge at a height of some 300 meters. Professor Hanfmann believed this to be the tomb of the Persian nobleman Abradates and his wife Pantheia. The identification is based on Xenophon's account of the Persian siege of Sardis in 546 B.C., when Abradates was killed in action and Pantheia committed suicide over his body, which so moved King Cyrus that he built a mausoleum for them high on the hillside above the Pactolus.

We now come to the part of the archaeological site known as Pactolus North. Between the river and the road here archaeologists have uncovered an early Christian basilica and a Byzantine church of the medieval era (known as Churches E and EA, respectively), as well as a late Roman villa and bath, a Lydian gold refinery, and an altar of Cybele. The refinery and the altar are dated to the mid-sixth century B.C., perhaps to the reign of Croesus. The dedication of a shrine to Cybele here is a testimony to her role as a mountain goddess, the protectress of the Lydian gold sources on Mt. Tmolus, washed down to the Sardian plain by the Pactolus. The earliest reference to a sanctuary of Cybele in Sardis is by the lyric poet Alcman, who flourished in the second half of the seventh century B.C. Alcman may have been born in Sardis, though he was raised in Sparta, as he says proudly in one of his surviving fragments:

> Ancient Sardis, abode of my fathers, had I been reared in you I should have been a maund-bearer unto Cybele or beaten tambours as one of her gilded eunuches; but instead my name is Alcman and my home Sparta, town of prize tripods, and the lore I know is of the Muses of Helicon, who have made me a greater king even than Gyges, son of Dascylus.

We now pass through the village to visit the part of the archaeological site across the highway to its east, where the excavations have unearthed an enormous Roman civic center. This was begun after a catastrophic earthquake in the year A.D. 17. Some of its most monumental structures were not completed for another two centuries, remaining in continual use from then on into the medieval Byzantine era. The eastern half of the complex was designed as a gymnasium, with the western half comprising its associated baths and athletic facilities. The central area of this complex, the Marble Court, has now been reconstructed. Its most impressive feature is the monumental two-storied arcade adorning the eastern propylon of the courtyard, where one passes from the palaestra, or exercise area, into the baths. An inscription over the columns records that this edifice was dedicated in A.D. 211-12 to Julia Domna, wife of the Emperor Septimius Severus (r. 193-211) and their sons Caracalla (r. 211-17) and Geta (r. 211-12). The Corinthian capitals of the columns have heads of gods, fauns and satyrs peering out from among the acanthus leaves, a delightful feature found in no other Graeco-Roman building in Asia Minor. The Marble Court is an outstanding example of the Roman baroque style of architecture, which was beginning to appear in the early third century A.D. Most of the eastern half of the court was taken up with the palaestra. This huge colonnaded court, which has also been reconstructed, has a long suite of rooms at its southern end that apparently served as dressing chambers or lecture halls.

One particularly interesting discovery made by the Harvard-Cornell Expedition is the ancient Sardis synagogue, which in late Roman times occupied the long apsidal area in the gymnasium south of the palaestra. This is the largest ancient synagogue known, and its size and grandeur are evidence of the prosperity and eminence of the Jewish community in Roman Sardis. The building dates from the period A.D. 220-50, and it appears to have been erected as part of the gymnasium, only to be converted into a synagogue somewhat later. Evidence of a much earlier synagogue is given by the Jewish historian Josephus, writing in the latter half of the first century A.D. He quotes decrees of both Julius Caesar and Augustus guaranteeing the Jews of Sardis the right, which apparently they had long enjoyed, of meeting in worship together in their own congregation. There is reason to believe that the Jewish community in Sardis dated back to the end of the Lydian period, to the days of Croesus. The Sardis synagogue has now been splendidly restored, an outstanding example of Roman architecture without parallel in Asia Minor.

The southern side of the gymnasium was converted into an arcade of vaulted shops early in the Byzantine period. The shops faced a similar arcade on the other side of the avenue, part of the Persian Royal Road, now covered by the modern highway. The twenty-nine structures that have been excavated here date from the fourth century A.D. These were all used for commercial enterprises, many of the establishments identified by inscriptions giving the name of the owner. One of the shopkeepers, a man named Jacob, is also identified as an elder in the synagogue.

The part of the archaeological site south of the highway here is known as the Lydian market area, since it appears to have been the agora of Sardis during the time of the Mermnadae, as evidenced by pottery shards of that period. It continued to be a commercial quarter for a full thousand years afterwards. The major structure in this area is known as the House of the Bronzes, from the large number of bronze objects found here. The most outstanding pieces are now exhibited in the Manisa Museum. The House of Bronzes has been dated to the mid-sixth century A.D. Liturgical objects and an altar found here have led to the suggestion that it was the home of a Christian dignitary, perhaps the Bishop of Sardis. Another recent discovery in this area is a stretch of the ancient Lydian city wall, a massive structure of unbaked brick some 20 meters thick. The wall has been dated to the mid-seventh century B.C., while an older fortification wall beneath it appears to date from the eighth century B.C. or perhaps even earlier.

There are other ancient structures on both sides of the highway about a kilometers or so east of the Pactolus. Just to the north of

The Gymnasium at Sardis

Façade of Gymnasium at Sardis

the highway there are the ruins of a Byzantine church that may have been the cathedral of Sardis, along with the remains of Roman and Byzantine baths. Some 200 meters to the northwest of the church there are the ruins of a late Roman basilica, which seems to have been used as a church in the early Byzantine era. About 200 meters south of the highway at this point we see the ruins of the stadium on the lower slope of the acropolis hill, and just above that the remains of the theater. The theater, which had a capacity of 20,000, was one of the structures rebuilt after the earthquake of A.D. 17. Hamilton examined all four of these structures on his arrival in Sardis, first looking at the two churches and then ascending the lower slope of the acropolis hill to study the stadium and the theater:

> After examining the two massive buildings near the bottom of the hill, which appear to have been erected for churches in the early ages of Christianity, we ascended to the theater and the stadium. The lowest of them [i.e., the churches] consists of several handsome

Roman Synagogue at Sardis

marble piers, supporting brick arches; but the greater part of the brick work is gone, enough only remaining to show the spring of the arches. It is nearly 200 feet long, its greatest length being from east to west, and having a semicircular termination, like the bema of the Greek churches, at both ends, but which does not appear externally. The other, higher up the hill, consisted also of brick arches raised upon six marble piers, made up entirely of architectural fragments plundered from former buildings. Corinthian and Ionic mouldings, shafts of columns, friezes, architraves, and fragments of entablatures, are all worked together with a large quantity of cement: but only four of these piers are now standing.

Some travelers have too hastily concluded that this was the church of Sardis to which allusion is made in the Apocalypse, but besides that the expression can only have referred to the community of Christians then established, the nature of the structure above described shows that its date must have been at least posterior to the overthrow of the Pagan religion and the destruction of the temples, towards the end of the fourth century.

The theater appears to be of Roman construction; it is entirely built of loose rubble, except the wings of the cavea, which are faced with stone; the marble seats, the proscenium and scena, are all gone. Immediately in front, and crossing it at right angles, are the remains of the stadium, the northern side of which have been artificially formed by a wall supported on arches running along the side of the hill.

From hence ascending to the S.E. we soon reached a level platform, on which were the foundation of a small square building, beautifully situated, and from whence we had a splendid view over the plain, bounded by the bold outline of the Phrygian mountains; while to the south the hills of the Acropolis towered up in wild confusion, having, from the soft nature of their sandy beds, been worn by snows and storms into a variety of fantastic shapes, whilst, wherever the roots could hold, the dwarf ilex, arbutus, and other shrubs flourished luxuriantly.

These, then, are the ruins of ancient Sardis, of which the poet

Bacchylides wrote in the first half of the fifth century B.C., lamenting the destruction by fire of the Lydian capital in the Ionian Revolt: "Lo, how it hath ceased, the golden city!"

We now head back eastward along highway E96/300, and some two kilometers along we turn right on highway 45-29, signposted for Birgi and Ödemiş. As we drive southward the view to our east is dominated by the Boz Dağları, whose highest peak rises to an elevation of 2,197 meters. Some 30 kilometers along we pass on our right a turnoff for Gölcük, a drive of six kilometers. Gölcük (Tiny Lake), at an elevation of 970 meters, is a small crater lake in a beautiful setting. It has now been made into a popular resort.

Beyond the Gölcük turnoff the main road winds down through a series of hairpin turns and then, after seven kilometers, brings us to Birgi. This pretty and unspoiled village is the site of Byzantine Pyrgion, whose name it preserves in only slightly different form. Early in the fourteenth century Pyrgion was taken by the Emir of Aydın, after which it came to be called Birgi. Birgi was taken by Beyazit I in 1390, but after his defeat and death at the battle of Ankara in 1402 the town reverted to the Emir of Aydın. Birgi was then captured by Mehmet I in 1425, after which it remained a permanent part of the Ottoman Empire. The oldest part of town is the acropolis hill known as the Kale, where the houses are built on and against the walls of the Byzantine citadel.

The principal monument in Birgi is the Ulu Cami, built on the acropolis hill in 1312 by Mehmet Bey, Emir of Aydın. The building is preceded by a nineteenth-century porch supported by eight wooden pillars. The mosque itself is constructed with marble blocks taken from some ancient building. The minaret is unusual. It rises from the southwest corner of the mosque, its shaft decorated with glazed bricks in red and turquoise arranged in rows of lozenges and zigzags. At the southeast corner of the mosque on its exterior there is a lion carved in high relief, a feature showing Selçuk influence.

The prayer room is the usual forest of columns typical of an Ulu Cami of this period, with sixteen slender marble monoliths arranged in four rows of four each. This divides the room into five north-south aisles, the central aisle being slightly wider than the others. The aisles are divided by arcades, in each of which the columns support a row of six arches of slightly ovoidal shape. The two southernmost columns of the central aisle are connected by a lateral arch, forming a square bay in front of the mihrab that is covered by a dome on straight triangular pendentives. The spandrels of the lateral arch in front of the mihrab are decorated with an inscription from the Koran and geometrical patterns in bi-colored faience mosaic. The mihrab is adorned with Selçuk faience mosaic in turquoise and manganese black; the stalactite niche in the rectangular frame is decorated with varying patterns in the same type of tiles, and below this is a panel with geometric interlacing. The walnut mimber, which is covered with calligraphic inscriptions, is a fine specimen of Selçuk carving, as are the shutters of the eight windows.

The *türbe* of Mehmet Bey, which is dated by an inscription to 1334, is attached to the northwest corner of the mosque. The dome, which is made of red and turquoise bricks, rests on a drum carried by four pendentives decorated with faience mosaics. The graveyard surrounding the mosque has a large number of beautifully carved Turkish tombstones of the fourteenth and fifteenth centuries.

Another important monument in Birgi is the Çakır Ağa Konağı, which in its present form dates from the last quarter of the eighteenth century. This is one of the finest extant examples of an Ottoman *konak,* or mansion, preserving its original carved ceilings and painted panels depicting vases of flowers and panoramas of Istanbul and İzmir. It is one of the most charming dwellings in all of Turkey, now splendidly restored.

We leave Birgi on the road for Ödemiş, a drive of 9 kilometers to the west. We then continue on from Ödemiş on highway 310, which takes us southwest to İlkkurşunköy, after which it heads westward along the north bank of the Küçükmenderes Nehri, or Little Maeander River, the ancient Cayster. Then, after passing

Ulu Cami at Birgi

Derebaşı, we continue along highway 310 as it abruptly turns south, soon crossing the Küçükmenderes. We then turn left on a road signposted for Tire, to which we come after a drive of five kilometers, approaching the town through a vast grove of poplars.

Tire has been identified as the ancient Thyrra, which in the early fourteenth century was captured from the Byzantines by the Emir of Aydın. Beyazit I took Tire in 1390, but after he was defeated by Tamerlane the town reverted to Cüneyt Bey, who was then Emir of Aydın. After the death of Cüneyt Bey the town was restored to the Ottoman Empire in 1425 by Murat II.

The most important monument in Tire is Yahşı Bey Camii, built in 1441 by a general of Murat II. The mosque is preceded by a five-bay portico, now in ruins except for the ornate stalactite entrance porch. The minaret rises from the northeast corner of the building. The plan is an inverted T, with the domed central hall flanked by a pair of side chambers covered by smaller domes. On the south the deep mihrab apse, covered by a semidome with 22 flutes, forms a bold projection on the exterior of the building. This is the earliest example in Ottoman architecture of a structure with a semidome extending from the main dome. The building now houses the Tire Museum, which has antiquities from archaeological sites in the region as well as an extensive ethnographical collection.

The Ulu Cami of Tire was built at the beginning of the fifteenth century by Cüneyt Bey when he was Emir of Aydın. Unfortunately it was gutted in a great fire, it has been largely rebuilt in concrete, and so is now of little architectural interest.

Besides the two edifices above, there are at least 29 other historic mosques of the *beylik* and Ottoman period still standing in Tire. These are, in approximate chronological order: Çanakçı Mescidi (1338); Hafsa Hatun Camii (mid-fourteenth century), founded by a daughter of İsa Bey, the Emir of Aydın; Doğan Bey Camii (fourteenth century); Kazıroğlu Camii (fourteenth century); Mehmet Bey Camii (fourteenth century); Kara Kadı Mecdettin Camii (fourteenth century); Gucur Camii (ca. 1400); Leyse Camii (early fifteenth century); Karahasan Camii (early fifteenth century); Hüsamettin Camii (early fifteenth century); Kara Hayrettin Paşa Camii (early fifteenth century); Süratlı Mehmet Bey Camii (early fifteenth century); Gazazhane Camii (1457); Narin Camii (fifteenth century); Yoğurtçuoğlu Camii (fifteenth century); Kazanoğlu Camii (fifteenth century); Molla Çelebi Camii (fifteenth century); Rum Mehmet Paşa Camii (ca. 1475, founded by a vezier of Mehmet II); Fadıloğlu Camii (late fifteenth century); Molla Arap Camii (late fifteenth century); Tahtakale Camii (1498); Neslihan Camii (ca. 1510); Lütfü Paşa Camii (early sixteenth century); Şeyh Camii (second half of sixteenth century); Yeni Cami (late sixteenth century); Yalınak Camii (end of sixteenth century); Hamza Ağa Camii (second half of seventeenth century); Hacı Mehmet Ali Camii (1799); Alabey Camii (1813); Yunus Emir Camii (late nineteenth century).

The bedesten in the center of town is believed to date from the late fifteenth century. Three massive piers divide the vast hall into eight lofty bays covered by domes on spherical pendentives. The outer periphery of the bedesten is lined with vaulted shops, thirty-two in all, with those at the ends flanking the two entrances.

Other monuments in Tire include: the Süleyman Şah Türbesi (1349); İbn Melek Türbesi (fourteenth century); the Eski Hamam (fifteenth century); the Mir Ali Hanı (fifteenth century); the Neşetoğlu Konağı (nineteenth century); and the delightful library (kütüphane) of Bağdadi Necib Paşa (nineteenth century). The Neşetoğlu Konağı is at No. 12 Kazıroğlu Sokağı in the district known as Yahudiyan, whose name reveals that this is the old Jewish quarter. However, the last Jewish family left Tire in the 1970s.

We leave Tire and head westward on highway 35-36. About 22 kilometers out of Tire we begin to look on the left of the road for two ancient funerary monuments, both of which are to be found some three kilometers to the east of the village of Belevi.

The first monument that we come to, on a low hill beside the road, is known as the Belevi Mausoleum. This has at its core a squared mass of living rock about 25 meters on a side and 15 meters high, formed by cutting away the surrounding hillside. The rock was faced with marble blocks and approached by a flight of marble steps, with a Doric frieze carved at its top. This served as the base of a marble tomb, with a pyramidal roof surmounted by a quadriga, or four-horse chariot. The monument is surrounded by a Corinthian colonnade topped by pairs of winged lions flanking globular urns. Excavation of the Belevi Mausoleum revealed an ornately carved sarcophagus, now in the Ephesus Museum in Selçuk. On the lid of the sarcophagus there is a carving in high relief of the deceased, who is shown reclining on his elbow. The sides are decorated with reliefs representing eleven Sirens, the winged female creatures who conduct the soul of the deceased to the world of the dead. Other parts of the monument are also preserved in the museum, including the statues of the winged lions that once stood on the roof. Archaeological and historical evidence have led to the general agreement that the Belevi monument was created in the mid-third century B.C. It was most probably the tomb of the Seleucid king Antiochus II Theos, who died at Ephesus in 246 B.C. Ancient sources state that

Antiochus was probably killed by his estranged first wife and half sister, Laodice, who had attempted a reconciliation with the king but failed. She then poisoned him.

The second monument is on the hill to the west of the Belevi Mausoleum. This has the shape of a natural tumulus formed from the conical summit of the hill itself, which is surrounded by a well-built wall of ashlar masonry. The entrance is on the south side, where a tunnel nearly 20 meters long burrows into the hill to the core of the tumulus, where there are two burial chambers. The archaeologists who excavated the mound found no sarcophagi in the chambers, which were looted in antiquity. No inscription has been found, but from its size, situation and workmanship the monument has been dated to the fourth or third century B.C. It was probably the tomb of a wealthy dignitary.

We now continue on past Belevi to highway E87/550, where we turn right to head towards İzmir, crossing the Küçükmenderes once again. As we do so we see the ruins of a fortress on a craggy peak just to the west of the highway. This rough structure is called Keçi Kalesi, the Goat's Castle. It was a Byzantine fortress erected to guard the northern approach to Ephesus along the valley of the Cayster.

After a drive of about 18 kilometers we come to Torbalı. Here we make a detour to the site of ancient Metropolis, whose ruins are to be found some five kilometers to the southwest on the north slope of Alaman Dağı. Metropolis takes its name from the Mother Goddess, in Greek, "Mitera," to whom it was dedicated. It is mentioned by Strabo as a town on the road from Smyrna to Ephesus renowned for its excellent wine. Metropolis is also mentioned by Pliny the Younger as one of the free cities that issued coins under Roman rule. Metropolis began to issue coins in the first century B.C., and the supposition is that prior to then the city was subject to Ephesus. The only visible remains of Metropolis were its theater and fragments of its defense walls. Recently the Turkish archaeologist Recep Meriç has unearthed the agora, a gymnasium and a stoa, as well as pottery shards dating back to 725 B.C.

We now return to Torbalı and turn off on to highway 35-26, signposted for Kemalpaşa. After passing turnoffs to Dağkızılca, about two-thirds of the way to Kemalpaşa the road goes through the Karabel Pass. On the right is Mahmut Dağı (1,372 meters), the ancient Mt. Drakon, and on the left Nif Dağı, another one of the peaks that in antiquity was known as Olympus. As we go through the pass we see ahead an ornamental archway over the road, at which point we pull over to look for the famous Karabel relief. This is about 20 meters above the right side of the road, where we see a figure cut in low relief in a panel on the rock facing south. The figure is somewhat larger than life, representing a marching warrior wearing a short tunic or kilt, a short-sleeved vest, a conical headdress, and boots upturned at the toes. He holds a spear in his right hand and a bow in his left. In the upper right-hand corner of the panel there are traces of a hieroglyphic inscription. There was an identical relief on the other side of the road, but this has since disappeared. The surviving relief is very similar to representations of Hittite deities found east of Ankara at Boğazkale, the ancient

Bevlevi Mausoleum

Hittite capital of Hattusha. The Karabel relief may represent the weather god Teshuba, and it is thought to date from the period of the New Hittite Empire, ca. 1500-1200 B.C. This is almost certainly one of the reliefs mentioned by Herodotus in Book II of his *Histories,* where he describes them as figures of the Egyptian king Sesostris. (Sesostris was an almost mythical figure among the Greeks, but it is now known that his name was borne by three pharaohs in the first two centuries of the second millennium B.C.) As Herodotus writes:

> In Ionia also there are two images of Sesostris cut on rock, one on the road from Ephesus to Phocaea, the other between Sardis and Smyrna; in each case the carving is nearly seven feet high and represents a man with a spear in his right hand and a bow in his left, and the rest of his equipment to match—partly Egyptian and partly Ethiopian. Across his breast from shoulder to shoulder runs an inscription in the Egyptian sacred script: "By the strength of my shoulders I won this land." The name and country of the conqueror are not here recorded, and some who have seen the image suppose it to represent Memnon [a mythical king of Ethiopia]; however they are wide of the mark, for Sesostris has made the truth plain enough elsewhere.

Herodotus was unaware of the Hittites, and virtually nothing was known of their empire until the rediscovery of their civilization by modern archaeologists. The first Greeks who saw the reliefs at Karabel seem to have thought that the kilted figures were the women warriors they called the Amazons. This may have given rise to some of the founding legends of the Aeolian cities. The Karabel relief is now known to the Turks as Eti Baba, or Father Hittite.

We now continue along the road to Kemalpaşa, a small town on the Nif Çayı, a stream known to the Greeks as Kryos Potamos, the "Cold River." Kemalpaşa is the ancient Nymphaeum, which would seem to have taken its name from a river shrine sacred to the nymphs. This was shortened to Nymphi and later still to Nif, taking its present name under the Turkish Republic in honor of Mustafa Kemal Paşa, later to be called Atatürk.

Little is known of Nymphaeum in ancient times other than as a stopping place on the road from Smyrna to Sardis. A Roman bath in Nymphaeum was dedicated to the emperor Nero (r. 54-68), who was worshipped there together with Apollo and Artemis.

At the western end of the town we see the ruins of a Byzantine palace built by Andronicus I Comnenus (r. 1183-85). This served as an imperial residence for the emperors of the Lascarid dynasty during the Latin occupation of Constantinople in the years 1204-61, when the Byzantine capital was in Nicaea. The Emperor John III Vatatzes died in the palace at Nymphaeum in 1254. Michael VIII Palaeologus met here with the Genoese ambassadors Guglielmo Vesconte and Guarnerio Giudice to negotiate the historic Treaty of Nymphaeum. This was signed in the palace on 13 March 1261, five months before the Greeks recaptured Constantinople from the Latins. The treaty established an alliance between Byzantium and Genoa that was to endure up until the fall of Constantinople to the Ottoman Turks in 1453. It gave the Genoese lucrative commercial concessions and allowed them to build fortresses to protect the trading colonies they established along the coasts of Asia Minor. Nymphaeum fell to one of the Saruhan emirs in 1313 and was later captured by the Emir of Aydın. In 1415 it was taken by Mehmet I, after which it remained a permanent part of the Ottoman Empire.

After leaving Kemalpaşa we continue in the same direction until we come to highway E96/300. Then we turn westward for İzmir, a drive of 19 kilometers that takes us over the Belkahve Pass at an altitude of 262 meters. Yamanlar Dağı and Mt. Sipylus are to the north and to the south is the Lydian Olympus, Nif Dağı. As we descend into the plain we see off to the west the massed houses of İzmir shining at the head of the Symrnaic Gulf. This completes our tour of the region once known as Lydia.

CHAPTER SIX

IONIA I: WEST AND SOUTH OF İZMİR

Our next three itineraries will take us through the land known in antiquity as Ionia. This comprised the Aegean coast of Asia Minor in the region bounded on the north by the Hermus River and on the south by the Maeander River, known in Turkish as the Büyük (Big) Menderes. The first of these three itineraries will take us along that part of the Ionian coast lying on the great peninsula that extends out into the Aegean west and south of İzmir, forming the southern arm of the Smyrnaic Gulf.

Ionia is one of the most beautiful and historic regions in Asia Minor, and writers since antiquity have sung its praises. The earliest of these encomiums is that of Herodotus, who writes thus of Ionia in Book I of his *Histories:* "These Ionians...had the good fortune to establish their settlements in a region which enjoys a better climate than any other we know of. It does not resemble that which is found farther north where there is an excess of cold and wet, or farther south, where the weather is both too hot and dry." And as Pausanias writes in Book VII of his *Guide to Greece:* "Ionian enjoys the finest of climates and its sanctuaries are unmatched in the world....The wonders of Ionia are numerous, and not much short of the wonders of Greece itself."

The region took its name from the Ionian Greeks, who first settled along this coast and its offshore islands ca. 1000 B.C., shortly after the Aeolians had established themselves along the northern Aegean shore of Asia Minor. Some of the places where the Ionians settled were already inhabited by the peoples whom they called the Pelasgians and Lelegians, as well as by the Phrygians, Maeonians, Lydians and Carians, all of whom eventually became Hellenized. Nor were the Aeolians and Ionians even the first Hellenes to settle in western Anatolia. Legends tell of warriors from Agamemnon's army wandering along this coast after the fall of Troy and founding cities. Archaeological excavations have unearthed evidence of several Mycenaean trading colonies here as well.

The Ionian colonies soon organized themselves into a confederation called the Panionic League, which comprised the Aegean islands of Chios and Samos and ten cities on the mainland opposite them, namely: Phocaea, Clazomenae, Erythrae, Teos, Lebedus, Colophon, Ephesus, Priene, Myus and Miletus. These twelve city-states, also called the Dodecapolis, had their religious center and meeting place at the Panionium, on the mainland opposite Samos. For a long time afterwards they excluded all others from being members. Smyrna, which was originally Aeolian, was, as we have seen, taken over by Ionians from Colophon in the second half of the eighth century B.C.; nevertheless it was not made a member of the Panionic League until 288 B.C., when the confederation was long past the days of its glory.

We leave İzmir and head westward on highway 300, which ten kilometers from the city center comes to a turnoff on the left posted for Agamemnum, a drive of about one kilometer to the south. This brings us to a thermal establishment known as the Baths of Agamemnon, which has been used by local arthritics, asthmatics and hypochondriacs since ancient times, when it was known as the Agamemnonion. According to legend, the baths took their name from the belief that Agamemnon's army was directed here by an oracle after they were defeated by King Telephus of Mysia. The wounded Achaians were healed after bathing in the waters of the spring and, as a token of their gratitude, they hung up on the walls of the baths the helmets of the Mysian warriors that they had taken as trophies after the battle with Telephus. A sanctuary of Asclepius was dedicated here in the Graeco-Roman era. Aelius Aristides often went to the baths here to alleviate his aches and pains, and he writes that the god Asclepius "first began to give oracles at the hot waters" of this shrine. Nothing now remains of the ancient shrine of Asclepius, nor of a temple of

Apollo that Strabo seems to place here. Richard Chandler, who explored the peninsula west of İzmir in January 1765, mentions this temple in his description of the Baths of Agamemnon:

> We now come to a shallow river, over which is a lofty bridge, intended to secure a passage to the traveller, when currents descend from the adjacent mountain formerly called Corax....Nearer the foot are vestiges of an ancient bridge, of which the piers were rebuilt, or repaired, before its final ruin; and in one of them is a maimed Corinthian capital....Some fragments of architecture in the Turkish burying ground not far from hence, it is likely, belonged, with the relic above mentioned, to the temple of Apollo, once seated on the western bank of the stream, by the hot baths. These have been computed forty stadia, or five miles from the city, and were called the Agamemnonion by the people of Smyrna.

We now return to highway 300, which we follow for another ten kilometers until we turn off for Urla İskelesi, a drive of four kilometers.

Urla İskelesi was known to the Greeks as Skala. The Greek poet George Seferiades was born in Skala on 29 February 1900, living there and in İzmir until 1914, when his family moved to Europe. Seferiades returned to his birthplace in 1950, visiting the ruins of ancient Ionian cities west and south of İzmir. This visit made a deep impression on him; he describes it in his memoirs and in several of his poems, most notably in this strophe from "Memory II:"

> Even now I remember:
> he was journeying to Ionian coasts, to empty shells of theaters,
> where only the lizard glides over dry stones,
> and I asked him: "Will they ever be full again?"
> And he answered me: "Perhaps at the hour of death,"
> And he ran across the theater howling,
> "Let me hear my brother!"

Urla İskelesi is the site of ancient Clazomenae, one of the cities of the Panionic League. The original site of the settlement was just to the east of Urla İskelesi, where a causeway leads out to a long and narrow islet. The Clazomenaeans moved out to the islet early in the fifth century B.C. for fear of the Persians, probably after the failure of the Ionian Revolt in 494 B.C., as evidenced by sherds found there. According to Pausanias, the island was connected to the mainland by Alexander the Great, who ordered the building of the first causeway here, the present mole being a modern construction. The islet is now occupied by a quarantine station and a hospital for contagious diseases, and so is off-limits to travelers. In any event, there is virtually nothing left of the ancient city on the islet, though classical architectural fragments can be seen underwater around its periphery, along with the stones of the original causeway. Chandler, the first to identify the site of Clazomenae, made his way out to the islet on this causeway with some difficulty, as he writes:

> The mole was two stadia, or a quarter of a mile in length, but we were ten minutes in passing over it, the waves, which were impelled by a strong inbat [imbat, the daily off-shore wind in the Smyrnaic Gulf], breaking over it in a very formidable manner, as high as the bellies of our horses. The width, as we conjectured, was about thirty feet....We computed the island to be about a mile long, and a quarter broad. The city was small, its port on the NNW side, enclosed by a mole. Traces of the walls are found by the sea; and in a hill are vestiges of a theater. Three or four trees grow on it, and by one is a cave hewn in the rocks, and affording water. The soil was now covered with green corn...

Excavations on the mainland show that the site was inhabited before the Greek migrations, for archaeologists have unearthed pre-Hellenic sherds dating back to ca. 3000 B.C. on Liman Tepe, the low hill on the shore between Urla İskelesi and the foot of the causeway. Excavations have also uncovered the remains of an archaic Greek settlement, presumably the original Ionian city of Clazomenae, with its acropolis on a low eminence some 800 meters south of Urla İskelesi. The most interesting objects found in these excavations are the distinctive Clazomenaean terracotta sarcophagi known as larnaka, many of them with painted decorations. A number of these *larnaka* are exhibited in the archaeological museums in İzmir and Istanbul, as well as in the British Museum and elsewhere in Europe. More than a hundred of these sarcophagi have been found along the shore around Urla İskelesi, most of them dating from the sixth century B.C. It seems that the Clazomenaeans used the original site of their city as a necropolis when they moved out to the islet.

Clazomenae is renowned as the birthplace of the philosopher Anaxagoras, who was born here at the beginning of the fifth century B.C. Aristotle wrote of him:

> Anaxoragoras the Clazomenaean, whom men of that day used to call "Nous" [Mind], either because they admired that comprehension of his, which proved of such surpassing greatness in the study of nature; or because he was the first to enthrone in the universe, not Chance, nor yet Necessity, but Mind pure and simple, which distinguishes and sets apart, in the midst of an otherwise chaotic mass, the substances which have like elements.

We now return to highway 300, where we bypass Urla for the time being and continue driving westward. Twelve kilometers farther along we turn off to the right for Karaburun, which takes us on a long detour out long the eastern shore of the great peninsula that forms the outer arm of the Gulf of İzmir.

Twelve kilometers along the Karaburun road we pass Balıklıova, where a road leads across the narrow waist of the peninsula to its western shore, to which we will return after our detour. About 35 kilometers along we come to the village of Mordoğan, where sherds have been found dating back to the ninth century B.C., along with a Clazomenaean-type sarcophagus that is now exhibited in the

İzmir Museum. After another 19 kilometers we come to Karaburun, a small port on the northeastern promontory of the peninsula, directly across the mouth of the Smyrnaic Gulf from Eski Foça. Near Karaburun, at a place called Pazarlık, Professor John M. Cook has excavated a site that he has identified as ancient Castabus. His excavations unearthed the remains of a hexastyle Ionic temple dating from the fourth century B.C., with an inscription recording that it was dedicated to the deified heroine Hemithea, who is known to have been worshipped at Castabus.

The road continues all the way around the end of the Karaburun peninsula and down its northwestern shore as far as Küçükbahçe, opposite the Greek island of Chios. At the northeastern corner of the peninsula the road passes inland of Karaburun (Black Cape), which retains the meaning of its ancient Greek name, Akri Melaina. The landscape of the northern end of the peninsula is dominated by its central peak, Akdağ (White Mountain), whose summit is 1,212 meters above sea level. This was known to the Greeks as Mt. Mimas, one of the great landmarks on the Aegean coast of Asia Minor, described by Homer in *The Odyssey* as "wind-swept Mimas." The mountain is also mentioned in one of the Homeric Hymns along with other places around this westernmost peninsula of Ionia: "Chios, brightest of the isles, and craggy Mimas, and the heights of Corycus...."

We now retrace our route and go back around the Karaburun peninsula as far as Balıklıova. There we turn right to head across the waist of the peninsula to its western shore, a drive of six kilometers. This brings us to İldir, a seaside village built partly on the site of ancient Erythrae, one of the cities of the Panionic League.

The site is on the headland that forms the north side of a bay almost enclosed on its seaward side by two islands known as Yassıada and Karabağ Adası, part of a group of islands known in antiquity as Hippoi, "the Horses." Farther out to sea there is another group of islets known as Karaada (Black Island). Beyond them is Chios, or Sakız Adası, where another city of the Panionic League was founded at the beginning of the first millennium B.C.

Erythrae's founding was somewhat different from that of the other Ionian cities. Tradition holds that it was first settled by an expedition from Crete, the colonists also including three indigenous peoples from the southwestern regions of Asia Minor—the Lycians, Carians and Pamphylians. A company of Ionians joined them under the leadership of a son of Codrus, one of the legendary kings of Athens. According to one version of the story, the city was named for its founder, Erythrus, "the Red," who was a son of Rhadamanthys, brother of the legendary King Minos of Crete.

Herodotus writes that the Erythraeans and Chians spoke a similar dialect, so they may well have had a common origin. The two cities fought one another in several wars during the archaic period, when Erythrae appears to have been one of the strongest military powers in the Panionic League. One of these disputes concerned the possession of a sacred statue of Heracles, which was found floating on a raft between Chios and Erythrae. As Pausanias tells the tale, the Chians and the Erythraeans both set out in boats to haul in the raft, each group trying to tow it across to their own city. As the tug of war took place, a blind Erythraean fisherman named Phormion had an inspired dream, in which it was revealed to him that the women of Erythrae would have to cut off their hair and braid it into a rope to pull the raft to their side of the strait. The wives of the citizens of Erythrae refused to do this. But the Thracian women who were enslaved there agreed to sacrifice their hair, which was made into a rope and used to pull the raft into the harbor of Erythrae. The statue was then enshrined in a temple called the Herakleion, which Pausanias mentions at the conclusion of his story: "The Thracians are the only women allowed into the Herakleion, and the people there still preserve the rope of hair even in my time; and in fact they say the fisherman's eyes were opened and he could see for the rest of his life." Pausanias, in describing the shrine, writes that "You would gasp at the Herakleion at Erythrae...for its antiquity." He also notes that "the statue [of Heracles] at Erythrae is not like the statues they call Aiginetan or the most ancient Athenian statues, but sheer Egyptian if a statue ever was." The statue of Heracles appears on archaic coins of Erythrae, showing the naked god in his characteristic pose--brandishing a raised club in his right hand and holding a lowered spear in his left.

A shrine of Athena Polias, "of the City," had a colossal cult statue of the goddess done by Endoios, an Attic sculptor of the archaic period who also did a marble group outside the sanctuary. Pausanias describes the shrıne as follows:

> Also at Erythrae is a shrine of Athene of the City, with a wooden statue of great size on a throne with a distaff in one hand and the universe around her head. You can tell the work of Endoios here if only by looking at the workmanship of this statue, and particularly at the white stone Seasons and Graces standing in the open air before you go in.

No trace has been found of the Herakleion, but excavations by Professors Akurgal and Bayburtoğlu have unearthed the remains of the temple of Athena Polias. This is on the acropolis of the ancient city, a hill rising directly from the shore to a summit 85 meters high above the village of İldir, a short stretch of its wall remaining on the western side. The temple was identified by an inscription on a bowl found in one of a number of trenches on the acropolis, along with large quantities of other pottery as well as bronze and ivory offerings. The inscription is now on exhibit in the İzmir Museum.

The theater is on the northern slope of the acropolis, with only its stairways remaining, the rest having been quarried by the villagers for building material. Otherwise all that remains of Erythrae are two stretches of the city wall, one to the north of the acropolis and the other to the southeast. Each of these two surviving sections is over 1,200 meters in length and varies in thickness from 3.7-5.2 meters, constructed of beautiful ashlar masonry, with the remains of towers and gates at intervals. The stream that flows

Ancient City Wall at Erythrae

into the valley between these two stretches of the city wall is the Aleos River, which Chandler mentions in his description of Erythrae:

> The walls of Erythrae were erected on two semi-circular rocky brows, and had square towers at regular distances. They were very thick, the stones massive and rugged, the masonry that called pseudodomum. In the middle is a shallow steam, clear as crystal, which turns a solitary mill in its way through thickets of myrtle and bushes to the sea. This rivulet was anciently named Aleos, and was remarkable for producing hair on the bodies of those who drank it. Near the mouth is a piece of ordinary Mosaic pavement. By a conical hill on the north are vestiges of an ample theater on the mountainside; and farther on, by the sea, three pedestals of white marble. Beyond these is an old square fortress standing on a low spot, a little inland; and by it was a short sepulchral inscription. We searched in vain for a temple of Hercules, which has been mentioned as one of the highest antiquity, and as resembling the temples of Egypt. The god was

represented on a float, on which they related he arrived at Erythrae from Phoenicia.

Erythrae was famous for its Sibyl, a prophetess whose name was Herophile. The Sybils were priestesses who had the power to make known the oracles of Apollo. The most famous were the two Sybils at Cumae and Erythrae, though some said they were the same person since both were named Herophile. Many places claimed to be the birthplace of Herophile, most notably Marpessos in the Troad, but the Erythraeans seem to have the strongest claim. They insist that she was born in their territory in a cave under Mt. Corycus, Greek Korykon, on the southwestern promontory of the great peninsula opposite Chios. The actual seat of the Sibyl was found at the east foot of the acropolis hill at Erythrae in 1891. It was in the form of a fountain house of the second century A.D. bearing a number of inscriptions. One of these inscriptions is in the form of a statement by Herophile proclaiming that she was born in Erythraean territory, but unfortunately this was lost when the fountain house was destroyed. Pausanias gives a lengthy account of the origins and wanderings of Herophile and the claim of Erythrae to be her true home:

> There is a rock sticking out of the earth at which the Delphians say the Sibyl Herophile stood to sing her oracles. I discovered that the earlier Sibyl was among the most ancient in the world. The Greeks say she was the daughter of Zeus and Lamia, daughter of Poseidon; they say she was the first woman to sing oracles and was named Sibyl by the Libyans. But Herophile was younger, though she seems to have been born before the Trojan War even so, and to have foretold Helen in her prophecies; how she would be reared in Sparta for the ruin of Asia and Europe, and how through her Troy would fall to the Greeks. The Delians record her Hymn to Apollo; in the verses she calls herself Artemis as well as Herophile, and then she says she is Apollo's sister and again his daughter. She wrote all this when raving and possessed by the god; elsewhere in the oracles she said

her mother was an immortal one, one of the nymphs on Ida, but her father was a man. This is what the verses say:

> I was born between man and goddess
> slaughterer of sea-monsters and immortal nymph,
> mountain-begotten by a mother from Ida,
> and my country is sacred to my mother,
> red-earthed Marpessos, the river Aidoneus.

> ...At Alexandria they say Herophile was temple keeper to Sminthean Apollo; by the interpretation of a dream she protested to Hecuba that future which we know was to become true. This Sibyl lived most of her life in Samos, but she came to Kolophonian Klaros, and to Delos and Delphi; and whenever she came, she stood by this rock to sing....But the Erythraeans, who dispute possession of Herophile more eagerly than anyone else in Greece, point to Mount Korykon, and a cave in the mountain where they say Herophile was born from a nymph and a shepherd of the district called Theodorus...as for the verse about Marpessos and the river Aidoneus, they expunge it from the oracles.

The Cumaean Sibyl is said to have been brought to Rome during the time of Tarquinius Superbus, whose reign is traditionally dated 534-510 B.C. According to the legend, the Sibyl brought with her to Rome nine collections of prophecies, which she offered to sell to Tarquinius. He found them to be too expensive and refused to buy them, though Herophile repeated the offer several times. After each refusal the Sibyl burnt three of the collections, and so when she offered the last set Tarquinius bought the prophetic offerings and installed them in the temple of Capitoline Jupiter. Her mission accomplished, the Cumaean Sibyl disappeared. Her prophecies, enshrined in the Sibylline Books, have exerted a profound influence over Roman religion for centuries. Virgil, in Book VI of the *Aeneid,* has the Cumaean Sibyl act as a guide for Aeneas in his descent into the Underworld:

> Aeneas the True made his way to the fastness where Apollo rules enthroned on high, and to the vast cavern beyond, which is the Sibyl's own secluded place; here the prophetic Delian God breathes into the spirit's visionary might, revealing things to come.

The inscription in the vanished fountain house indicates that the Sibyl was still issuing her oracles at Erythrae in the second Christian century. But her cult would have been put down during the reign of Theodosius I (r. 379-95), who closed all of the pagan temples and shrines in the Empire, also banning practices such as the consultation of oracles like that of Herophile at Erythrae.

We leave Erythrae and head southwestward on the coast road, which brings us to Ilıca, a resort town whose thermal springs have been noted since antiquity. After passing through the town we rejoin highway 300. Here we turn right and after a short way we come to Çeşme at the western end of the peninsula.

Çeşme is a busy port and resort looking out towards Chios, to which there is a regular ferry service. This was the site of the battle of Çeşme, on 6/7 July 1770, when the Russian navy trapped an Ottoman fleet in the harbor and virtually annihilated it. The only hero to emerge on the Turkish side was Gazi Hasan Paşa, known also as Cezayirli Palabıyık, the "scimitar-mustached Algerian." He escaped on his sinking ship to fight another day, defeating the Russians the following year at Lemnos.

The port at Çeşme is dominated by a Genoese fortress of the late thirteenth century, an impressive structure with a towered citadel surrounded by a double line of defense walls. The fortress now houses the Museum of Ottoman Arms, which in addition to Turkish weapons also includes a small collection of antiquities from the nearby archaeological site of Erythrae. Near the fortress there is an Ottoman caravansaray erected in 1528 by Süleyman the Magnificent. Çeşme also has two seventeenth-century mosques, Hacı Memiş Camii and Hacı Mehmet Camii, as well as the abandoned nineteenth-century Greek Orthodox cathedral.

We now head eastward on highway 300 as far as Urla, a drive

of 35 kilometers. Urla is the oldest and most interesting town on the peninsula west of İzmir, identified as the ancient Hypocremnus. The first foreign traveler to mention it is Richard Chandler, who at first thought it was the site of Clazomenae. He refers to the town as Vourla:

> We continued our journey along the shore. The hills on our left were covered with low shrubs, and villages, some of a clean dry aspect, and several not immediately discernable, though near, the mud-built villages being exactly of the same color with the soil. As we approached Vourla, the little valleys were all green with corn, or filled with native vine-stocks in orderly arrangement, about a foot and a half high....Vourla is distinguished at a distance by its numerous windmills....It is a place of considerable extent, the buildings dispersed on eminences, with a considerable plain towards the sea. The water and air are reputed good. The Turks have seven mosques and the Greeks two churches. At one of these is a small bass-relief, representing a funereal supper, with a short inscription. Another is

The Port and Genoese Fortress at Çeşme, Print from Choiseul-Gouffier

> fixed in a wall over a fountain....A cursory view of this place was sufficient to convince us that it did not stand on the site of Clazomenae.

Three of the mosques of Urla date from the second half of the fifteenth century: Yahşi Bey Camii, Kılıç Ali Camii, and Fatih İbrahim Bey Camii. The first two of these are single-unit mosques, while the third is a multi-unit structure. The central area of its prayer hall is covered by a dome, with each of the side areas having a pair of lower and smaller cupolas.

We leave Urla on the road that heads southeast. After nine kilometers we turn right on highway 36-39, signposted for Seferihisar, a drive of ten kilometers. Chandler stopped in Seferihisar on his way across the peninsula and reported on antiquities that he observed in and around the town. These were probably brought here from the ruins of ancient Teos, on the coast to the south. Chandler wrote of "Sevri-hissar" that it

> is an extensive straggling town, in a valley, two hours from the sea...the country round it is pleasant and well-cultivated....We were lodged in a miserable mud-built khan, and we had here reason to dislike, and to be alarmed at, the carriage of some of our Turkish visitants, but the janizary was our safeguard.
>
> Many scattered remnants of the ancient city occur at Sevri-hissar. One, fixed in the wall of a house, mentions the two societies, the Panathenaists and the Dionysiasts. At the time of the Ionian migration, a colony of Athenians took possession of Teos. These appear to have introduced the Panathenaea, the grand festival of the ancient city. A crown of olive encircles the name of the community which had the care of its celebration; and one of ivy that of the Dionysiasts, who were artificers, or contractors for the Asian theaters, incorporated and settled at Teos under the kings of Pergamum. I copied a long decree made by one of their companies in honor of its magistrates. The slab was placed as a gravestone in the Turkish burying ground of a deserted mosque N.W. of Sevri-hissar....

There are four mosques in and around Seferihisar dating from the second half of the fifteenth century. Two of these—the Ulu Cami and Düzceköy Camii—are multi-unit mosques, both reconstructed in the nineteenth century. The other two—Ulamışköy Camii and Güdük Minare Camii—are single unit mosques, though only the minaret survives of the latter structure.

At Seferihisar we turn right on a road that in 4.5 kilometers brings us to Sığacık, a pretty little seaside town with a Genoese fortress of the late thirteenth century dominating the port. This was the northern port of Teos, one of the cities of the Panionic League. The port was known as Gerae, of whose harbor works there remains part of a mole dating from the Roman era. Chandler stopped here on his way to explore the ruins of Teos, which are scattered across the narrow neck of the peninsula between the northern and southern harbors of the ancient city. He describes the northern harbor, which he calls Segigeck:

> We rode on, and after three hours arrived at Segigeck, which was before us, by the head of a shining bay, land-locked, with an islet near the mouth....Segigeck is a large square ordinary fortress, erected, it is said, by the Genoese, on a flat, with a few brass cannon toward the sea, It was ancient called Gerae, was the port of the city toward the north, and had been peopled with Chalcidensians, who arrived under Geres. It encloses some mean mud-built houses. In the wall next the water are several inscribed marbles, the color a blue-gray, transported from Teos. Another is fixed to a fountain without the south gate. In the hot bath are two large fragments placed upside down, and serving for seats, which I examined, but hastily, fearing some infection, as the plague was known to be near....

The harbor here was the focal point of one of the most important naval battles of the Hellenistic period. The battle was fought late in the year 190 B.C., when the Romans and their Rhodian allies defeated the forces of the Seleucid king Antiochus III, whose commander-in-chief was Hannibal. This and the defeat that

Antiochus suffered early the following year at Magnesia permanently ended Seleucid rule in Asia Minor, with their territory passing to Pergamum and then in 129 B.C. to Rome.

We drive along the waterfront of Sığacık, and then turn inland on a road that leads across the neck of the peninsula to its southern shore. As we approach the shore we see on our left the ruins of ancient Teos, which we approach from the west through the olive grove that has enveloped the site. Except for some evidence of excavation, the site appears much the same as when Chandler came upon it in the spring of 1765. He was looking for the famous temple of Dionysus, whom he calls Bacchus:

> In the morning we crossed the isthmus to Teos, now called Bodrun. We found this city almost as desolate as Erythrae and Clazomenae. The walls, of which traces were extant, were, as we guessed, about five miles in circuit; the masonry handsome. Without them by the way, are vaults of sepulchres stripped of their marble, as it were forerunners of more indistinct ruin. Instead of stately piles, which

Harbor at Sığacık, Teos

once impressed ideas of opulence and grandeur, we saw a marsh, a field of barley in ear, buffaloes ploughing heavily by defaced heaps and prostrate edifices, with illegible inscriptions and time-worn fragments. It was with difficulty we discovered the temple of Bacchus; but a theater on the side of the hill is more conspicuous. The vault only, on which the seats ranged, remains, with two broken pedestals in the area....

The heap of the temple of Bacchus, lay in the middle of a corn field, and is overrun with bushes and olive trees. It was one of the most celebrated structures in Ionia....The town has long been deserted. It has no ruins of churches to prove it existed under the Greek emperors; nor of mosques and baths, to show it was frequented by the Turks....The site is a wilderness; and the low grounds, which are wet, produce the iris, or flag, blue and white. This flower is stamped on the money of Teos. We saw cranes here stalking singly in the corn and the grass, and picking up and disgorging insects and reptiles; or flying heavily with long sticks in their mouths to the tops of trees, and of the remoter houses and chimneys, on which they had agreed to fix their habitation.

Hamilton explored the site early in December 1836, giving a much more detailed description of the ruins than Chandler. He

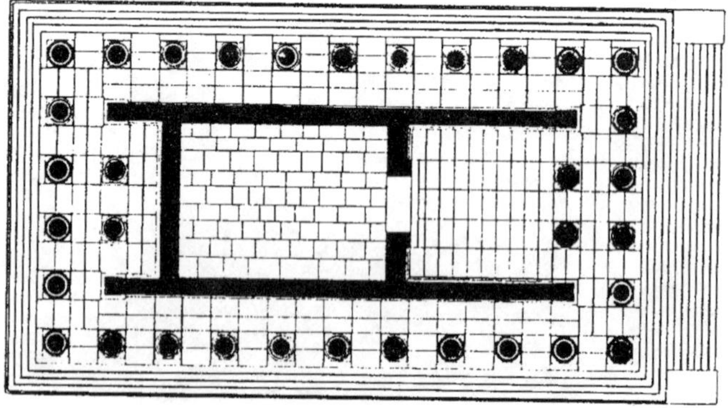

Plan of Temple of Dionysus at Teos

mentions Chandler and also the antiquarian Edmund Chishull, who visited Teos in 1699:

> The ruins of Teos have been partly described by Chishull and by Chandler; but as we spent much time upon the spot, and discovered several ancient buildings, I shall give some account of our proceedings. The principal part of the ancient town appears to have been situated on the eastern and south-eastern slope of the range of hills above mentioned, and to have been bounded on the east by a marshy plain, watered by a small stream flowing into the southern harbor, while toward the north and west the town extended over the hills. The massive walls of the city may be traced along their whole extent, built of a compact semi-crystalline blue limestone found in the neighbourhood...
>
> The building which first attracts the attention of a stranger coming from Sighajik is the theater, on the side of a hill facing S. and bearing N. by W. from the mole of the southern port. It commands a magnificent view, overlooking the site of the ancient city....Half a mile to the S.W. of the theater are the ruins of what is supposed to be the Temple of Bacchus described by Vitruvius. The order is Ionic and the proportions are very grand: the temple itself appears to have occupied but a small area, unless we suppose that the fallen ruins have been heaped together by the subsequent occupiers of the land in clearing the soil....The temple appears to have been surrounded by an oblong Ionic colonnade, the foundations of which are still visible; while the small columns have been used in constructing the neighbouring walls, where we found another inscription.
>
> The whole site of the former city is now covered with olive-trees, and divided into corn-fields by numerous enclosures. These are marked by walls and hedgerows, the former of which consist of ancient fragments, and the latter of luxuriant bay-trees: the fragrance of their bruised branches heightened the pleasure of searching for the written records of the past....

The acropolis of Teos is on the hill that rises halfway between the northern and southern harbors. Most of the surviving structures of the ancient city are between the acropolis and the southern harbor, an area that was enclosed by a defense wall in the third century B.C. The layout of these fortification walls is quite unusual, in that they formed three sides of a rectangle, with the open side facing north towards the acropolis. The only stretch of these walls now visible is at the northwestern end of the circuit, but the foundations of the remainder of the circuit is probably still present under the shrubbery and earth that have buried it. The earliest fortifications that have survived are visible on the southwestern side of the acropolis, where there are some remnants of polygonal wall of the archaic period. At the foot of the acropolis wall to the northeast are the unexcavated remains of a gymnasium, erected in the Hellenistic era and rebuilt in Roman times. On the southwestern slope of the acropolis hill we see the theater, erected in the second century B.C., with its stage building enlarged during the Roman era. Some 300 meters to the southeast of the theater there are the remains of the odeion, a well-preserved structure of the Roman period. Then about 500 meters to the southwest of the odeion, embowered in an olive grove, we see the temple of Dionysus, the most famous edifice of Teos.

The temple was erected in the second quarter of the second century B.C. by the architect Hermogenes of Priene. Hermogenes wrote a book about his work that has survived through a paraphrase in *De architectura,* better known in English as *The Ten Books on Architecture,* a treatise written in the late first century B.C. by the Roman architectural theoretician Vitruvius. Hermogenes was the great theoretician of classical Greek architecture, codifying the rules for the Ionic order that survived through Vitruvius to influence the architecture of Europe from the Renaissance onward. His Ionic temple at Teos was the largest sanctuary of Dionysus ever erected in the ancient world, with a stylobate measuring 18.5 by 30.0 meters. The temple was hexastyle peripteral, surrounded by six columns at its ends and eleven on the sides, with a pair of columns *in antis* in both the pronaos and opisthodomos, the front porch being almost as deep as the cella, while the rear porch was very shallow. Some of the architectural fragments strewn about the site are Hellenistic and others are Roman, the latter coming from a restoration in the time of Hadrian.

As Chandler mentions, Teos was for a time the headquarters of the Asian branch of the Artists of Dionysus, who established themselves here toward the end of the third century B.C. They were a professional guild of actors and musicians who supplied performers for hire at festivals all over the Greek world, with branches in a number of cities beside its main one at Teos. Since Dionysus was the patron deity of drama the members of the guild enjoyed universal privileges, such as freedom from taxation and military service as well as safe conduct wherever they went to perform. The Artists of Dionysus appear to have been a particularly troublesome group; Philostratus refers to them as "a very arrogant class of men and hard to control," and a commentator on Aristotle poses the question, "Why are the Artists of Dionysus in general bad men?" By the middle of the second century B.C. the

Temple of Dionysus at Teos

Artists of Dionysus had worn out their welcome at Teos and were forced to move in turn to Ephesus, Myonnesus, Lebedus, Priene, and then back to Lebedus, where Strabo reports that they were living in his time.

The south harbor has silted up considerably since antiquity, but along the inner side of the narrow peninsula that formed its outer arm one can still see part of the ancient quay, with projecting blocks pierced with holes so that ships could be moored there.

The Teans were great seafarers and established a number of overseas colonies, also joining with a number of other Greek cities ca. 610 B.C. in founding a trading emporium on the Nile delta called Naucratis, Queen of the Sea. Herodotus writes that about that time Thales of Miletus suggested "that the Ionians should set up a common center of government at Teos, as the place occupied a central position; the other cities would continue as going concerns, but subject to the central government, in the relationship of outlying districts to the mother city." But nothing came of this suggestion, and the cities of the Panionic League never had a capital other than their common shrine and gathering place at the Panionium.

After his conquest of Sardis in 546 B.C. King Cyrus of Persia sent his general Harpagus the Mede to subjugate the Greek cities on the Aegean coast, first besieging Phocaea and then Teos. The Teans followed the example of the Phocaeans and fled by sea rather than surrender to the Persians. The Tean exiles then settled in Thrace, where they founded the city of Abdera. This was to be the birthplace of the physicist Democritus, who formulated the first atomic theory, and also of the philosopher Protagoras, who wrote that "Man is the measure of all things."

Many of the Teans later returned to their native city, despite the Persian occupation of Asia Minor. This revived Teos, and in the Ionian Revolt the city contributed 17 ships to the Greek fleet that went down fighting against the Persians at the battle of Lade in 494 B.C., more than any other city in Asia Minor except Miletus.

One of the Teans who fled to Abdera was the poet Anacreon, who was born in Teos ca. 560 B.C. After serving as court poet to the tyrants Polycrates of Samos and Hipparchus of Athens, Anacreon finally returned to Teos in his last years. He died there ca. 483 B.C., when he would have been about eighty-seven, choking on a grape pit while drinking raisin wine. According to Pausanias, Anacreon was honored with a monument on the Athenian acropolis, with "the statue representing him singing in his cups." Pausanias also writes that Anacreon was the "first poet excepting Sappho of Lesbos to make his main theme love." Two of his surviving poems come to mind when one is wandering among the ruins of Teos. The first is entitled "To a Virgin:"

> My Thracian foal, why do you glare with disdain and then shun
> me absolutely, as if I knew nothing of this art?
> I tell you I could bridle you with tight straps, seize the reins and
> gallop you around the posts of the pleasure course,
> But you prefer to graze in the calm meadows, or frisk and gambol
> gaily—having no manly rider to break you in.

The second is a fragment addressed to a servant lad:

> Bring water, lad, bring wine; aye bring them thither,
> for I would try a bout with love.

Critias of Athens wrote of Anacreon in a lyrical passage than can serve as the Tean's epitaph:

> Teos bore thee, thou sweet old weaver of womanish song, rouser of revels, couzener of dames, rival of the flute, the delightful, the anodyne; and never shall love of thee, Anacreon, grow old and die, as long as serving lads bear around bumpers above board, as long as band of maidens does holy night-long service of the dance...

We now retrace our route to Seferihisar, where we head south on the coastal road to Doğanbey, a drive of 16 kilometers. The road continues south beyond Doğanbey around the end of the peninsula, a short distance north of which we see a craggy offshore islet known as Çifit Kalesi, the Jew's Castle. This is the site of ancient Myonnesus, or Mouse Island, an Ionian settlement that was never a member of the Panionic League.

Hecataeus of Miletus, writing ca. 500 B.C., refers to Myonnesus as a city, but the rocky islet cannot have been the site of anything larger than a small town. Nor is there evidence of buildings on the mainland opposite the islet, though the ground there is thinly strewn with ancient shards. The site of Myonnesus is a miniature Gibraltar, a rocky crag some 60 meters high jutting out of the sea just north of Cape Macris, the promontory that forms the southernmost point of the coastline south of Teos. The tiny island was in antiquity connected to the mainland by a causeway whose stones can still be seen underwater. All that remains of the ancient city is part of an archaic defense wall of the type called cyclopean, made of huge irregularly shaped blocks, one of which measures 1.2 by 2.4 meters. The other ruins date from much later times. During the Roman era Myonnesus was little more than a lair of pirates, who found its seagirt offshore rock perfectly suited for their activities. They could tie up their ships hidden away out of sight of the mainland and wait to prey on passing merchantmen.

The only historical incident of any note involving Myonnesus occurred in 190 B.C., just prior to the great naval battle off Teos. The Roman fleet was bound for Teos when they spotted a dozen pirate ships headed for their base at Myonnesus, loaded with loot from a raid they had made on Chios. The pirates escaped safely to Myonnesus, and when the Romans tried to pursue them there they dared not approach too close to the island for fear that rocks would be dropped upon them from above. The Roman historian Livy, in his account of the incident, gives a description of the islet that is still valid today:

> The hill rises like a pyramid from a broad base to a sharp point; it is approached from the mainland by a narrow pathway; on the seaside it is surrounded by cliffs so eaten away by the waves that in some

places the overhanging rocks project farther seaward than the boats sheltering under them.

South of Doğanbey the road turns sharply to the left, after which it heads along the shore eastward of Cape Macris. After passing a turnoff on the left for the village of Ürkmez we come to the site of Lebedus, another city of the Panionic League.

The scanty ruins of Lebedus are to be found mostly between the road and the Kısık peninsula, with the acropolis on a low hill halfway to the shore. The site has never been excavated. Although the ground is thickly strewn with ancient shards, there are no structures to be seen other than the foundations of buildings and walls. The most striking remnant is the defense wall around the seaward periphery of the peninsula. The fortification is some two meters thick and standing to a height of three or four courses; it is made of good ashlar masonry on the inner and outer faces, with a core of rubble. At the southeastern corner of the sea walls there are the foundations of a three-aisled basilica, most probably an early Byzantine church. This may have been the cathedral of Lebedus, which in the early Byzantine period was raised to the status of a bishopric.

Lebedus, along with Myus, was one of the two smallest and least significant cities in the Panionic League, neither of them producing any notable men nor making any mark on history. Lebedus did not contribute a single ship to the Ionian fleet that fought the Persians at the battle of Lade in 494 B.C., and in the Delian confederacy its assessment was only one talent, the lowest in the league. During the second century B.C. Lebedus became the headquarters of the Artists of Dionysus. They were still living there in the time of Strabo, who describes the coast west of Colophon:

After Colophon one comes to the mountain Coracius and to an island sacred to Artemis, whither deer, it has been believed, swam across and gave birth to their young. Then comes Lebedus, which is one

> hundred and twenty stadia distant from Colophon. This is the meeting place and settlement of all the Dionysiac artists in Ionia as far as the Hellespont; and this is the place where both games and a general festal procession are held every year in honor of Dionysus. They formerly lived in Teos, the city of the Ionians that comes next after Colophon, but when the sedition broke out they fled to Ephesus. And when Attalus settled them in Myonnesus between Teos and Lebedus the Teians sent an embassy to beg of the Romans not to permit Myonnesus to be fortified against them; and they migrated to Lebedus, whose inhabitants gladly received them because of the dearth of population by which they were then afflicted.

A short distance beyond Lebedus our route crosses the Dereboğaz Deresi and comes to Gümüldür, after which the road heads southeastward along the coast, passing under the seaward slopes of Karacadağ (770 meters). After crossing a small river we come to the site of ancient Notium, its acropolis approached by a steep path from the road.

Notium was originally an Aeolian city, established far to the south of the other members of the Aeolian League. (In fact, its name means "South," or "Southern."). But early in its history Notium became the port of Colophon, an Ionian city some ten miles inland to the north, and thenceforth the two cities formed parts of one civic unit. Later, with the growth of the local seaborne commerce, much of the population moved down to the port, which was known as New Colophon. The inland city came to be called Old Colophon.

The ruins of Notium are poorly preserved but extensive, spreading across the slopes of two hills and the saddle between. Its defense walls, built early in the Hellenistic period, had a periphery of some four kilometers, enclosing an area measuring about 1,000 meters from east to west and 300-500 meters from north to south. From there it extended out onto two steep promontories flanking the double-cusped bay that served as Notium's harbor. The wall was built with large square blocks and fortified with square towers, a number of which survive, particularly in the northeast angle of the circuit. Two of the city gates are still visible, one on the west side and the other one on the north. A flight of stone-hewn steps in the southeast corner of the circuit indicates that there was another portal there. Excavations by French archaeologists in 1921 unearthed the foundations of a Corinthian *templum-in-antis* on the western hill; this dates from the time of Hadrian, and an inscription records that it was dedicated to Athena Polias. The stylobate of the temple measures 7.5 by 16.0 meters, and immediately to its east there are the foundations of an altar measuring 5.3 by 17.7 meters. The temple and the altar were together surrounded on all four sides by Doric stoas, the temenos measuring 17.1 by 38.2 meters, with shops arrayed around the outer periphery of the arcades on the east, west and north sides. The remains of a small temple of unknown dedication were uncovered about 100 meters to the northeast of Athena's sanctuary. An agora was discovered in the center of the city, with the bouleuterion just to its east. Another agora was unearthed near the northeastern angle of the defense walls, with the theater to its northwest. The theater dates from the Hellenistic era, with renovations in Roman times. The extensive necropolis is on the western slopes of the hill to the north of the city.

We now head inland on highway 35-51, signposted for Değirmendere. After about two kilometers we turn off to the right on a secondary road, signposted for ancient Claros, which is a short way from the highway.

The site of Claros is in the valley of a small stream known in antiquity as the Ales, which Pausanias claimed was the coldest in Ionia. By the beginning of the twentieth century the river and its silt had completely covered the ruins of Claros and its famous oracular temple of Apollo. The site was first excavated in 1907 for the Istanbul Archaeological Museum by Theodore Macridy, who unearthed two columns from the propylon at the entrance to the sanctuary. A more thorough excavation was made in the years 1950-60 by a group of French archaeologists under the direction of Louis Robert, who found and cleared the sanctuary of Apollo and a number of other structures. The site is below the local water table, and so the ruins are kept visible only by constant pumping.

Claros was never a city, but rather a sanctuary under the aegis of Colophon, in whose territory it was located. The Colophonians claimed that the oracular sanctuary of Clarian Apollo was very ancient, and that it was one of the places where the Sibyl Herophile gave her prophecies. There is a reference to the sanctuary in the Homeric Hymn to Delian Apollo, dating perhaps to the seventh century B.C., where the poet sings of "gleaming Claros." The reference to "vine-clad Claros" in the Homeric Hymn to Aphrodite is probably of somewhat later date. But there is an even earlier reference to the shrine in the first of nine surviving fragments of Hesiod's *Melampodia,* dated ca. 700 B.C. This was a series of stories about the famous seers of antiquity, most notably Mopsus, Calchas, Amphilochus, Teiresias and Melampus, for whom the *Melampodia* was named:

> It is said that Calchas the seer returned from Troy with Amphilochus the son of Amphiarus and came on foot to this place [Colophon]. But happening to find near Claros a seer greater than himself, Mopsus, the son of Manto, Teiresias' daughter, he died of vexation...

Although the sanctuary at Claros certainly existed in classical times, there is virtually no mention of the oracle in that period. The first record of one of its responses is the prophecy that led to the founding of the new city of Smyrna under Mt. Pagus at the beginning of the Hellenistic era, which is when the present temple was built. Later in the Hellenistic period the oracle at Claros seems to have declined in popularity, but then it had a great revival in the imperial Roman age. The temple was rededicated by Hadrian toward the end of his reign, and delegations came from all over the Graeco-Roman world to consult the oracle, as evidenced by inscriptions, including one recording a visit by pilgrims from Britain. One of the notables who came to Claros was Germanicus, the adopted son of Tiberius, who in A.D. 18 was told by the oracle that his death was imminent. Within the year he died in Antioch of poison. The Roman historian Tacitus, in his account of this incident, describes the procedure followed by the oracle of Clarian Apollo:

> There is no woman there as at Delphi, rather a priest, after hearing merely the number and names of the clients, goes down into a cave; there he drinks from a secret fountain, and though generally illiterate, issues responses in various matters in the consultants' minds.

The oracle at Claros was one of the last to survive in Christian times, closed in 392 by an edict of Theodosius I banning all pagan practices in the Empire. The temple was destroyed in an earthquake and its ruins covered with mud by the river, burying the shrine until it was rediscovered and unearthed by archaeologists.

The sanctuary stood in Apollo's sacred grove of ash trees, which pilgrims arriving by sea approached from the south, passing through the propylon that formed the ceremonial entrance to the shrine.

Sanctuary of Apollo at Claros

Propylon of Sanctuary of Apollo at Claros

This was a monumental entryway in the Doric order erected in the second century B.C., with four columns on the south side and two each on the east and west. The inner surfaces of the surviving columns are carved with numerous inscriptions of the second century B.C., including lists of the various groups of pilgrims and their place of origin as well as the names of the young people who sang in the choirs at festivals of Apollo. On the left side of the propylon was a stoa used for commercial purposes, and on its right side a semicircular exedra, measuring some eight meters in diameter. It has survived completely intact.

The propylon marks the beginning of the Sacred Way, which was flanked by statues and stelae erected in the first century B.C. in honor of various notables, principally governors of the province of Asia. The Sacred Way led northwestward to the east front of the temple of Apollo. This was a Doric temple standing on a five-stepped crepidoma, with its stylobate measuring 26 by 46 meters, its peripteral colonnade having six columns on the ends and eleven on the sides. Some 150 of the column drums, 1.60 meters in diameter, lie arrayed on the ground along with seven Doric capitals. The style of the temple suggests that it was built in the late fourth or early third century B.C., while an inscription on the architrave records that the peripteral colonnade was not erected until the time of Hadrian. Excavations within the cella indicate there was an earlier sanctuary of Apollo here before the erection of the present temple.

At the rear of the temple there was a colossal cult statue of Apollo. The god was represented in a sitting position, with a laurel wreath in his right hand and his left hand resting on a cithara. He is flanked by the standing figures of his mother Leto, on his left, and his twin sister Artemis—her quiver on her shoulder, on his right. Large fragments of these statues were discovered within the cella, with the remains indicating that the figure of Apollo was 7-8 meters high. The figures of Apollo and Artemis were exactly as they were represented in the coins of Colophon, which were used as models in reconstructing the statues from their fragments.

The adyton, or inner sanctuary, was beneath the west end of

Oracular Chamber of Sanctuary of Apollo at Claros

the cella, directly under the statues of Apollo, Leto and Artemis. This consisted of two vaulted chambers separated by a massive wall 2.7 meters in thickness. The western room served as a waiting room for the pilgrims, while the eastern one was reserved for the oracle. The pilgrims approached the waiting room via two stairways at the eastern front of the temple, from where they were led along a labyrinthian passageway under the cella. Since the oracles were always delivered at night, this subterranean approach further added to the mystery of the whole experience. The inner chamber had at its rear a rectangular well from which the oracle drank before making his prophecy. This well is mentioned by Pliny the Elder, who writes of "a pool in the cave of Clarian Apollo, a draft of which inspires wonderful oracles, but shortens the life of the drinker." The oracle, a priest of Apollo, was assisted by one or two scribes and a thespode, or professional bard, whose duty it was to render the prophet's pronouncements into verses which were chanted to the pilgrims in the waiting room. The pilgrims would have been unaware of who was chanting the verses, which is why Tacitus thought it was the "generally illiterate" oracle himself. The waiting room had benches for the pilgrims, and there was also a votive stone of bluish marble in the shape of half an outsize ostrich egg, some 0.7 meters high, discovered intact by the French archaeologists. This represented the legendary omphalos, or navel stone, which was originally in Apollo's shrine at Delphi. According to the legend, Zeus, desiring to find the center of the earth's surface, started two eagles of equal speed from opposite ends of the world, and they met at Delphi. Afterwards the spot was marked by the omphalos stone, which was flanked by statues of two golden eagles. As time passed the omphalos came to be regarded as the symbol of Apollo himself, and similar stones were set up in other places where he was worshipped.

Some 27 meters east of the temple there is a great marble altar measuring 9.0 by 18.5 meters. On it there are two separate tables for votive offerings, one for Apollo and the other for Dionysus. This is one of numerous examples of the two gods sharing a shrine as they did at Delphi. During the three winter months Apollo went off to enjoy the sunshine with the Hyperboreans beyond the north wind, while Dionysus was worshipped at Delphi in his place. North of the altar there is a well-preserved stone sundial, with an inscription recording that it was dedicated during the Hellenistic period by the agoranomos, the director of the market. South of the altar there is a stone with an inscription recording that it was set up by Quintus Tullius Cicero, younger brother of Marcus Tullius Cicero, the famous orator and writer. The younger Cicero was governor of the Roman province of Asia during the years 61-59 B.C. Farther south there are a well-preserved exedra and a stone chair, whose arm rests are shaped like winged serpents.

South of Apollo's sanctuary and aligned parallel to it is a smaller temple of the Ionic order, with an altar in front of it. The temple was identified by an archaic statue of a young woman found by the altar, with an inscription of the sixth century B.C. recording that it was dedicated to the Clarian Artemis. The worship of the divine huntress here at her brother's shrine is mentioned in one of the Homeric Hymns to Artemis, quoted in part earlier in reference to her shrine on the river Meles in Smyrna:

> Muse, sing of Artemis, sister of the Far-shooter, the virgin who delights in arrows, who was fostered with Apollo. She waters her horses in Meles deep in reeds, and swiftly drives her all-golden chariot through Smyrna to vine-clad Claros, where Apollo, god of the silver bow, sits waiting for the far-shooting goddess who delights in arrows.
>
> And so hail to you Artemis, in my song, and to all goddesses as well. Of you first I sing and with you I begin; now that I have begun with you I will turn to another song.

We now return to the road and continue driving northward. Then after about 13 kilometers we come to Değirmendere, a large village near the site of ancient Colophon, one of the cities of the Panionic League. The site is approached via a pathway leading off from the southern end of the village, a walk of about 1.5 kilometers.

The poorly-preserved ruins of Colophon are spread along the lower slopes of three interconnected hills and their enclosed valley, the periphery of the ancient city defined by a three-sided defense wall. The city wall, studded with a dozen defense towers, is dated to the end of the fourth century B.C., probably erected by Lysimachus. Excavations by American archaeologists indicate that the original settlement was founded on a hill overlooking the plain to the southwest, at an elevation of about 200 meters. The most notable remains within the Hellenistic walls are those of a temple dedicated to Demeter, a commercial stoa, and a complex of houses separated by a labyrinth of streets. All of the structures of this complex date from the fourth century B.C., with the dwellings erected on the foundations of buildings from the archaic period. At the west end of the complex a stepped street leads to a large Roman baths.

Colophon was the largest and most powerful city in the Panionic League during the early history of the confederation. During the second half of the eighth century B.C. exiles from Colophon seized control of Aeolian Smyrna, which thereafter was an Ionian city. The Colophonians also took control of Aeolian Notium, which thenceforth became the port of Colophon. This enabled Colophon to become a naval power, and ca. 700 B.C. the Colophonians established colonies at Myrleia on the Propontis and at Siris in southern Italy. The Colophonians were famous for their cavalry, which ranged over the broad plain they controlled south of Smyrna, using fierce dogs as auxiliaries. Strabo writes of the renowned Colophonian cavalry in his account of the city's early history:

> The Colophonians once possessed notable naval and cavalry forces, in which latter they were so far superior to the others that whenever in wars that were hard to end, the cavalry of the Colophonians served as ally, the war came to an end; whence arose the proverb, "he put Colophon to it," which is quoted when a sure end is put to any affair.

> Native Colophonians, among those of whom we have record, were: Mimnermus, who was both a flute-player and an elegaic poet; Xenophanes, the natural philosopher, who composed the "Silloi" [Satires]; and Pindar speaks also of a certain Polymnastus as one of the famous musicians: "Thou knowest the voice, common to all, of Polymnastus the Colophonian." And some say that Homer was from there.

Mimnermus is believed to have been born in Colophon in the mid-seventh century B.C. and to have lived on into the first quarter of the following century. In one of his surviving fragments the narrator tells of the founding of Colophon and of the subsequent capture of Smyrna by the Colophonians: "After leaving Pylos, the lofty city of Neleus, we came in our voyage to the long-wished for Asia, and settled at Colophon, and hastening then from the river Asteeis, by the will of god we took Aeolian Smyrna." In another of his poems, "The Warrior of the Past," he writes of the military prowess of a Colophonian warrior in the days of his ancestors:

> None could match the strength of him and the pride of his courage.
> Thus the tale told of my fathers who saw him there
> breaking the massed battalions of armored Lydian horsemen,
> swinging the ashwood spear on the range of the Hermos plane.
> Pallas Athene, goddess of war, would have found no fault with
> this stark heart in its strength, when at the first-line rush
> swift in the blood and staggered collision of armies in battle
> all through the raining shafts he fought out a bitter path.
> No man ever in the strong encounters of battle was braver
> than he, when he went still in the gleaming light of the sun.

By the time that Mimnermus wrote these lines Colophon was under Lydian control, having been taken by King Gyges in the second quarter of the seventh century B.C. Soon after the fall of Sardis in 546 B.C., Colophon was conquered by a Persian army under Harpagus the Mede, after which a number of Colophonians fled from Asia Minor. One of those who left was the philosopher Xenophanes, then about twenty-five years old, who spent the rest of his long life at Elea in southern Italy, where he died ca. 480 B.C., when he was at least ninety two. In one of his works he tells of how the wealth of the Colophonians led them into a decadent way of life, which eventually brought about the downfall of their city:

> They had acquired useless luxuries in Lydia while still free of her odious tyranny, paraded to the marketplace in sea-purple robes, often in bright swarms of a thousand. They were proud and pleased with their elaborate coiffures, and hid their body-odors with rare perfumes.

Although Xenophanes is renowned as a philosopher, founder of the Eleatic philosophical school, he is also numbered among the great elegaic poets of ancient Greece. One of his surviving poems, "The Well-Tempered Symposium," evokes the spirit of the good life in Ionia in the archaic age, which ended with the year of his death:

> Now the floor is swept clean, and the hands of all who are present
> are washed, and the cups are clean. One puts the garlands on,
> another passes the fragrant myrrh on a dish. The mixing
> bowl is set up and stands by, full of the spirit of cheer,
> and more wine still stands ready and promises no disappointment;
> sweet wine in earthen jars, preserving its own bouquet.
> In the middle of all frankincense gives out its holy fragrance,
> and we have water there too, cold and crystal and sweet.
> Golden-brown leaves are set nearby, and the lordly table
> is weighed down under its load of honey and cheese.
> The altar, in the center, is completely hidden in flowers.
> Merriment and singing fill all the corners of the house.
> First of all, enlightened men should hymn the God, using
> words of propriety, and stories that have no fault.

> Then, when they have made libation and prayed to be able
> to conduct themselves like gentlemen as occasion demands,
> it will not be drunk-and-disorderly to drink as much as one can
> and still get home without help—except for a very old man.
> Best approve that man who in drinking discloses notable
> ideas as they come to his mind and his good disposition directs.
> Its no use to tell the tale of the battles of Titans and Giants,
> or Centaurs either, these fictions of our fathers' imaginations,
> nor wars of the Gods; there's no good to be got from such subjects.
> One should be thoughtful always and right-minded toward the Gods.

In another work, apparently written not long before he died, Xenophanes reminisces about the Colophon of his youth and the lost world of archaic Ionia:

> Three score and seven years have crossed my careworn soul up and down the land of Hellas, and there were then more than five and twenty years from my birth, at least if my addition is right....Such things may be said beside the fire in wintertime when a man reclines full-fed on a soft couch drinking sweet wine and munching chick peas, such things as who and whence art thou? And how old are thou good sir? And of what age was thou when the Mede appeared?

We now retrace our route on highway 35-51, driving southward to the coast. There we turn left on to highway 35-39, which curves around the bay beyond Notium and soon brings us to the seaside village of Pamucak. We turn left there on the road to Selçuk, where our first itinerary through Ionia comes to an end.

CHAPTER SEVEN

IONIA II: EPHESUS

The second of our three itineraries in Ionia will take us to Ephesus, using the town of Selçuk as our base. Travelers approaching Ephesus from İzmir head south along highway E87/550 to Selçuk, a drive of about 75 kilometers, the last stretch taking one across the valley of the Küçükmenderes, the Greek Cayster.

As we enter Selçuk we see above and to the right the acropolis hill of medieval Ephesus, known in Turkish as Ayasuluk. Passing through Selçuk, we approach the site of Ephesus on the Kuşadası road, which leads out of town to the west. Just outside of town we come on our right to the isolated site of the Artemisium, the most renowned monument of ancient Ephesus. The main entrance to the archaeological site, where the ruins of the Graeco-Roman city of Ephesus are located, is about 1,200 meters farther along on the left.

We can see from these scattered ruins that the site of Ephesus changed several times in its long history. The local topography has changed as well. In antiquity the sea came in as far as the Ayasuluk hill, whereas now the coast is some twelve kilometers away, the intervening countryside created by silt carried down to the coastal plain by the Cayster river. The original Ionian settlement, founded ca. 1000 B.C., was on the northern slope of Mt. Pion, now known as Panayır Dağı, and the ancient harbor was on the shore below this. Mythology has it that the leader of the expedition which founded the city was Prince Androclus, grandson of the legendary King Codrus of Athens. According to Pausanias, when the Ionians first arrived they found that the people who lived here included Amazons from Thermodon in the Pontus, who worshipped at an ancient shrine of Ephesian Artemis:

The sanctuary at Apollo at Didymoi and the oracle there are more

> ancient than the Ionian settlement, and Ephesian Artemis is much older still. It seems to me that, when Pindar said the Amazons founded this sanctuary on their expedition against Theseus of Athens, there are things he did not know about the goddess. The women of Thermodon sacrificed to the Ephesian goddess because they knew the sanctuary from old days. When they fled from Herakles, and some of them from Dionysos in an even earlier age, they threw themselves on its mercy....The countryside was occupied by Lydians and Carian Leleges; and, among others, women of the Amazon race lived around the sanctuary for the refuge it offered. Androklos, son of Kodros's son Androklos, was accepted as king of the Ionians who sailed against Ephesos, but those who lived around the sanctuary had nothing to fear; they swore a treaty with the Ionians and kept out of the war....

The city of Ephesus was originally ruled by kings, who may have exercised a quasi-feudal sovereignty over the other cities of the Panionic League. It was apparently under their rule that the Ephesians erected the Artemisium, the first sanctuary of Artemis, replacing an earlier shrine of Cybele, the fertility goddess worshipped by the earlier inhabitants. This stood at the same site as the Artemisium we see today, at the southern foot of the Ayasuluk hill. The monarchy at Ephesus was eventually supplanted by an aristocratic regime. The Ephesian aristocracy were dominated by a clan of royal descent known as the Basilidae, who held power until ca. 600 B.C. Then one of the aristocrats, Pythagoras, seized control and ruled as a tyrant, redistributing the wealth of the rich among the poorer people to gain their support. The Basilidae were thereafter relegated to the rule of hereditary chief priests in the Artemisium, which was rebuilt on a larger scale by Pythagoras. This temple turned out to be the salvation of the city when King Croesus of Lydia invaded Ionia in 560 B.C., at the beginning of his reign. Herodotus reports in Book I of his *Histories:*

> The first Greek city that Croesus attacked was Ephesus. The

EPHESUS and SELÇUK
Map VII
Ayasuluk Hill
Byzantine Fortress
Gate of
Persecution
Church of
St. John
SELÇUK
Museum
N
İsa Bey
Mosque
Artemisium
Hellenistic walls
Main entrance
Magnesia Gate
EPHESUS
ARCHAEOLOGICAL SITE
(see large-scale plan)

View of Ephesus, Allom Print

Ephesians, when he laid siege to them, ran a rope from their walls to the temple of Artemis, putting the town by means of this link, under the protection of the goddess. The distance between the temple and the old town which was then under siege is just under a mile. Having started with the Ephesians, Croesus subsequently attacked all the Ionian and Aeolian cities in turn on various pretexts, substantial or trivial, according to what ground of complaint he could find against them. He forced all the Asiatic Greeks to pay him tribute, and then turned his attention to shipbuilding in order to attack the islanders. However, when everything was ready to begin building, something happened which persuaded him to desist.

Herodotus goes on to explain how one of the eastern Greeks, either Bias of Priene or Pittacus of Mytilene, persuaded Croesus to change his mind so "that he abandoned the idea of building a fleet, and formed a treaty of friendship" with the Ionians. The treaty that Croesus made with the Panionic League forced the Ephesians to abandon their strongly fortified city on the northern slope of Mt. Pion and move inland to a new unwalled site on level ground south of the Artemisium. Soon afterwards the Ephesians replaced the earlier Artemisium with a temple on a truly colossal scale, to which Croesus contributed munificently. The size and grandeur of the new temple reflected the great wealth of Ephesus under the Lydians, a prosperity that continued under the Persians after Croesus was defeated and killed by Cyrus in 546 B.C. The Persian king Darius I (r. 521-486 B.C.) built a great highway, the Royal Road, which linked his capital at Susa with Ephesus, . Ephesus thenceforth became the greatest port on the Aegean coast of Asia Minor.

Ephesus was at the time controlled by two tyrants, Athenagoras and Comas, who ruled as clients of Darius. One of the opponents of this dictatorship who was banished from the city was the poet Hipponax. He is noted as the inventor of the choliambic, sometimes called the "scazon," or "limping verse," which reverses the stress at the end of each line so as to bring the reader down on the wrong foot, as it were. The three unconnected verses that follow are typical of Hipponax, all of them characterized by rough colloquialisms and sarcastic humor:

Hermes, dear Hermes, Maia's son from Kyllene,
I pray to you, I'm suffering from extreme shivers,
so give an overcoat to Hipponax, give him
a cape, and sandals, and felt overshoes, sixty
pieces of gold to bury in his strong chamber.

Keep travelling you swine, the whole way toward Smyrna.
Go through the Lydian land, past the tomb of Alyattes,
the grave of Gyges and the pillar of Megastyrs,
the monument of Atys, son of Alyattes,
big chief, and point your paunch against the sun's setting.

Hold my jacket, somebody, while I hit Boupalos in the eye.
I can hit with both hands, and I never miss punches.

Ephesus produced one of the great philosophers of nature during the reign of Darius. This was Heraclitus, a member of the Heraclidae clan who, according to tradition, renounced his hereditary priesthood in favor of his younger brother, preferring to devote all of his time to his intellectual pursuits. Heraclitus envisaged the transformations that take place in the physical world as an endless series of interchanges between opposites. His fundamental principle was *panta rhei*, that is, "all things are in a state of flux;" he expressed this in sayings such as: "You can never step into the same river twice." He believed that the underlying unity in nature was the Logos, or Word, by which he meant the harmonious principles through which the cosmos came into being and which govern all phenomena. Another of his sayings was: "All human laws are fed by one divine law," which in his view was the Logos. He went on to emphasize that "the people must fight for this law as for a city rampart." Heraclitus expressed himself in an oracular style that caused him to be known as Skoteinos, or the Obscure, saying that his purpose was "neither to say nor conceal but rather to indicate" the truth.

The archaic Artemisium was destroyed by fire in the mid-fourth century B.C. The Ephesians immediately set out to build a new and more splendid temple, which was completed in the third quarter of the third century B.C. By that time the site of the city had changed once again, for in the late fourth century B.C. Lysimachus moved it to what is now the main archaeological zone. It lies in the valley between Mt. Pion and the eminence to its west, the Greek Mt. Coressus, known to the Turks as Bülbül Dagı, the Mountain of Nightingales. Lysimachus then built a defense wall nearly six miles in circumference around the city, its circuit extending along the ridges and peaks of Mt. Pion and Mt. Coressus. An inner line of fortifications enclosed the commercial quarter of the city. Its western side opened out on to a new harbor, created by dredging a channel through the silt that had been deposited by the Cayster. But after all of this work the Ephesians were reluctant to move to the new city until Lysimachus resorted to drastic measures. Strabo mentions Lysimachus' diabolical solution after describing of the successive sites of Ephesus up to that time:

> The city of Ephesus was inhabitated both by Carians and Leleges, but Androclus drove them both out and settled the most of those who had come with him round the Athenaeum and the Hypelaeus, though he also included a part of the country situated on the slopes of Mt. Coressus. Now Ephesus was thus inhabited until the time of Croesus, but later the people came down from the mountainside and abode round the present temple [the Artemisium] until the time of Alexander. Lysimachus built a wall round the present city, but the people were not agreeably disposed to change their abodes to it; and therefore he waited for a downpour of rain and himself took advantage of it and blocked the sewers to inundate the city; and the inhabitants were then glad to make the change....

The prosperity of Ephesus, which had declined in the classical period, revived as soon as it had been reestablished on its new site, with a harbor that once again gave it access to the sea. During the third century B.C. Ephesus was a pawn in the struggle between the Ptolemies of Egypt and the Seleucid kingdom for control of Asia Minor. The city was occupied in 196 B.C. by Antiochus III, but after his defeat at Magnesia in 189 B.C. it became part of the Pergamene kingdom. Then after the Attalid dynasty came to an end in 133 B.C. Ephesus passed under the control of Rome, becoming capital of the province of Asia four years later. The city surrendered to Mithridates VI of Pontus at the beginning of his first war against Rome in 88 B.C. Mithridates established his headquarters at Ephesus, where soon afterwards he issued secret orders to have all Romans in Asia Minor put to death on an appointed day one month later. His order was carried out at the scheduled time and on a single day some 80,000 Romans and other Italians, women and children included, were slaughtered. The toll was highest in Ephesus, the principal city in the province of Asia. Ephesus remained under the control of Mithridates until 84 B.C., when a Roman army under Sulla recaptured the city.

After the end of the First Mithridatic War Ephesus began a long period of peace and prosperity under the mantle of the *pax Romana.* The city reached its prime during the imperial Roman era, when its citizens proudly proclaimed that Ephesus was the "First and Foremost Metropolis in Asia." Strabo, whose career spanned the first half-century of that era, wrote of Ephesus that "the city by the advantages which it affords, daily improves and is the largest mart in Asia within the Taurus." Ephesus had by then surpassed Smyrna as the busiest port on the Aegean coast of Anatolia, and it was also the most important commercial and financial center in the Asian dominions of Rome. Its population reached 400,000 at its peak in the second century A.D. Ephesus also attracted pilgrims from all over the Empire, including a number of emperors beginning with Augustus. All of them, commoners and royalty alike, came to pay homage to Artemis Ephesia, as the goddess was called—"she whom all Asia and the world adore."

During the latter half of the first century A.D. Ephesus became a center for the new Christian faith that would replace the old pagan religion of the Graeco-Roman world. Paul made numerous conversions among both the Jews and Greeks during his two visits to Ephesus, the first in the year A.D. 54 and the second beginning two years after that. It was during Paul's second stay in Ephesus that the famous riot of the silversmiths took place, an incident reported in *Acts* 19:23-31:

> It was during this time that a rather serious disturbance broke out in connection with the Way. A silver smith named Demetrius, who employed a large number of craftsmen making silver statues of Diana [the Roman Artemis], called a general meeting of his own men with others in the same trade. "As you men know," he said, "it is on this industry that we depend for our prosperity. Now you must have seen and heard how, not just in Ephesus but nearly everywhere in Asia, this man Paul has persuaded and converted a great number of people with his argument that gods made by hands are not gods at all. This

> threatens not only to discredit our trade, but also to reduce the great goddess Diana to unimportance. It could end up by taking away the prestige of a goddess venerated all over Asia, yes and everywhere else in the world." This speech aroused them to fury, and they began to shout, "Great is Diana of the Ephesians!" The whole town was in an uproar and the mob rushed to the theater dragging along two of Paul's Macedonian travelling companions, Gaius and Aristarchus. Paul wanted to make an appeal to the people, but the disciples refused to let him; in fact some of the Asiarchs [state officials], who were friends of his, sent messages imploring him not to take the risk of going into the theater.

The crowd was eventually calmed and dispersed, and Paul decided that it would be wise to leave Ephesus, whereupon he said good-bye to his disciples there and headed off to Macedonia. There is a tradition that Paul was imprisoned for a time during his second stay in Ephesus, though there is no evidence of this in any of the sources. Nevertheless, the tradition lingers on, and there is a ruined building on Mt. Coressus that is still pointed out as "St. Paul's Prison."

There is also a tradition that St. John the Apostle lived out his last years in Ephesus along with the Blessed Virgin. There has been much discussion as to whether John the Apostle is here being confused with St. John the Theologian. The latter, according to tradition, is buried on the Ayasuluk hill, where a small church was dedicated to him in the second century. The church was demolished in 535 by the Emperor Justinian, who built in its place the huge cathedral whose impressive ruins on the southern side of the Ayasuluk hill are now being restored. Another tradition has it that the Virgin died near Ephesus in a place called Panaya Kapulu, known in Turkish as Meryemana. This place is some eight kilometers south of Selçuk by road and has now become an internationally famous shrine.

Ephesus was one of the Seven Churches of Revelation. As we read in *Revelation* 2:1-7:

> Write to the angel of the church in Ephesus and say, "Here is the message of the one who holds the seven stars in his right hand and who lives surrounded by the seven golden lamp stands: I know all about you, how hard you work and how much you put up with. I know you cannot stand wicked men, and how you tested the imposters who called themselves apostles and proved they were liars. I know, too, that you have patience, and have suffered for my name, without growing tired. Nevertheless, I have this complaint to make; you have less love now than you used to. Think where you were before you fell; repent, and do as you used to at first, or else, if you will not repent, I shall come to you and take your lamp stand from its place. It is in your favor, nevertheless, that you loathe as I do what the Nicolaitans are doing. If anyone has ears to hear, let him listen to what the Spirit is saying to the churches: those who prove victorious I will feed from the tree of life set in God's paradise."

Ephesus continued to flourish under the mantle of the *pax Romana* until the year 262, when it was sacked by the Ostrogoths. The Artemisium was partly restored on a smaller scale during the reign of Diocletian. It remained in use until 392, when it was closed by the edict of Theodosius I banning paganism throughout the Empire. The temple was then wrecked in 401 by a mob inflamed by the sermons of John Chrysostom, Patriarch of Constantinople, who saw the destruction of the Artemisium as the final triumph of Christianity over paganism. By that time a Roman basilica in Ephesus had been converted into a church dedicated to the Virgin Mary. Gradually, the belief in Christ and the veneration of his Blessed Mother replaced the worship of Artemis and all of the other older deities of the Graeco-Roman world. Nevertheless, some pagans continued to sacrifice to the older gods for at least a century afterwards.

During the medieval Byzantine era Ephesus shared the fate of the other cities of Asia Minor, enduring successive invasions by the Persians, Arabs and Selçuk Turks, the latter holding the city during the years 1190-96. These centuries of almost continual warfare took their toll on Ephesus, transforming the magnificent Roman city of late antiquity into a smaller and more humble Byzantine provincial town. Byzantine Ephesus originally had two centers, one in the harbor quarter and the other on the Ayasuluk hill, where a citadel and defense walls had been built by Justinian. But by the end of the Byzantine period the harbor had been so completely silted up that ships could no longer use it. The harbor quarter was then abandoned and thereafter the townspeople lived only on the citadel hill. The hill was known to the Greeks as Haghios Theologos, after the cathedral of St. John the Theologian erected by Justinian. The Venetians and Genoese who traded there changed Theologos in their tongue into Altoluogo. The Turks later changed it to Ayasuluk, the name by which Ephesus was known in Ottoman timcs.

Ephesus was taken by the Aydınıd Türkmen tribe in 1304 and became the capital of their *beylik*, which included the whole of the Cayser and Maeander valleys. In 1374-75, the Emir of Aydın, İsa Bey, erected the large mosque that stands at the foot of the Ayasuluk hill below the church of St. John. Beyazit I captured the town in 1390, but the Aydınıd regained it after Tamerlane's defeat of the Ottomans at Ankara in 1402. Murat II recaptured Ephesus in 1402. It then became a kaza and the seat of a kadı, or judge, who upheld the sultan's laws and dispensed his justice.

The population of the town in the mid-fifteenth century appears to have been about 2,000. A census at that time records that there were 481 houses divided into 24 quarters, three of them inhabited by Greeks and the others by Turks, all dwelling within the walls of the citadel on the Ayasuluk hill. The Ottoman town, though small, appears to have prospered at first, for a government mint was built there, as well as a small mosque, a medrese and an imaret. But towards the end of the sixteenth century Ephesus began an irrevocable decline, for its harbor had been silted up and it had been bypassed by the main trade routes. Smyrna supplanted it as the principal port on the Aegean coast. The Turkish chronicler Evliya Çelebi, writing in the mid-seventeenth century, describes Ephesus as having only about a hundred houses, all with earthen roofs, along with a mosque, a public bath, and a caravansaray for travelers. The whole region around Ephesus was in deep decline by that time, for the silted-up delta of the Cayster had become a malarial swamp. Murderous bandits lay in wait there to prey on passersby, as the English traveler Covel reported in 1670. Like Sardis, Ephesus eventually degenerated into a broken-down village, with its most famous monument, the Artemisium, having apparently vanished without a trace. Richard Chandler, who visited the site twice in the years 1764-65, writes that he and his companions had searched for the Artemisium, but "to as little purpose as the travellers who had preceded us....We now seek in vain for the temple; the city is prostrate and the goddess gone." Chandler paints a dismal picture of Ephesus, although the Greek peasants he encountered there were cheerful enough, as we gather from his account of his attempt to excavate the ruins:

> The Ephesians are now a few Greek peasants, living in extreme wretchedness, dependence and insensibility; the representatives of an illustrious people, and inhabiting the wreck of their former greatness; some, the substrutures of the glorious edifices which they raised; some, beneath the vaults of the stadium, once the crowded scene of their diversions; and some, by the abrupt precipice, in the sepulchres, which received their ashes. We employed a couple of them to pile stones, to serve instead of a ladder, at the arch of the stadium and, to clear a pedestal of the portico by the theater from rubbish. We had occasion for another dig at the Corinthian temple; and sending to the stadium, the whole tribe, ten or twelve, followed; one playing all the way before them on a rude lyre, and at times striking the sounding board with the fingers of his left hand in concert with the strings. One of them had on a pair of sandals of goatskin, laced with thongs, and not uncommon. After gratifying their curiosity, they returned back as they came, with their musician in front.
>
> Such are the present citizens of Ephesus, and such is the condition to which that renowned city has been gradually reduced. It was a ruinous place when the emperor Justinian filled Constantinople with

> its statues, and raised his church of St. Sophia on its columns. Since then it has been almost quite exhausted. Its streets are obscured and overgrown. A herd of goats was driven to it for shelter from the sun at noon; and a noisy flight of crows from the quarries seemed to insult its silence. We heard the partridge call in the area of the theater and of the stadium. The glorious pomp of its heathen worship is no longer remembered; and Christianity, which was there nursed by apostles, and fostered by general councils, until it increased to fulness of stature, barely lingers on in an existence hardly visible.

The Artemisium eluded discovery for more than a century after Chandler's visit. The first archaeological excavations of ancient Ephesus were begun in 1863 by the engineer John Turtle Wood in a project sponsored by the British Museum. After searching for more than six years, Wood finally unearthed part of the marble pavement of the temple on the last day of 1869, after having dug down some six meters. Wood continued excavating the site until 1874, but even then he had not cleared the temple to its lowest levels. This task was accomplished by D. G. Hogarth in a two-year campaign for the British Museum beginning in 1904. In the course of time, he excavated the temple to its foundations, determined the several periods of its construction, and recovered important architectural members and works of art, including precious dedicatory offerings. A team of Austrian archaeologists had been excavating elsewhere in Ephesus since 1895, and their successors continue to work here to the present day. These excavations have been accompanied by the restoration of several important structures in both the ancient and medieval sites of the city, so that today we can see some of the great edifices of Ephesus in something of their former splendor.

We begin our exploration of Ephesus below the southern foot of the Ayasuluk hill, on the site of the Artemisium. The earliest shrine of Artemis discovered on this site is a protogeometric (ninth-eighth century B.C.) temple measuring 8.4 by 13.5 meters, surrounded by a peripteral colonnade with four columns on the ends and eight on the sides, of which only the foundations remain. Archaeologists also unearthed an altar dated ca. 700 B.C., which was presumably erected on the site of the ancient sanctuary of Cybele, where the earlier inhabitants of Ephesus had worshipped the Anatolian fertility goddess before the arrival of the Ionian Greeks. The altar would have enshrined the sacred cult objects of Cybele-Artemis, including her ancient xoanon, or wooden idol, which seems to have included a meteoritic stone. During the following century the Ephesians enclosed this altar in a baldachin inside the unroofed cella of the temple, which was rebuilt on a larger scale ca. 600 B.C., probably by the tyrant Pythagoras.

The archaic Artemisium was begun ca. 560 B.C. The chief architect was the Cretan Chersiphron, assisted by his son Metagenes and also by Theodorus of Samos, who a few years before had designed and built the famous temple of Hera on his native island. Theodorus brought to the project the vast experience he must have gained in the construction of the Samiam Heraeum, which, like the Artemisium, was built on an immense platform that had to be filled in on marshy ground. These two Ionic edifices were the largest temples ever built in the Greek world, monuments to the extraordinary flowering of Hellenic culture in the Ionian cities of the Aegean coast of Asia Minor and its offshore islands in the archaic period.

The archaic Artemisium stood on a two-stepped crepidoma, with its stylobate estimated to have measured 50.16 by 103.26 meters, more than three times the area of the platform of the Parthenon in Athens. A highly unusual feature of the Artemisium, which it shared with the temple of Artemis at Sardis, was that it faced west rather than east. Some 40 meters beyond the west front of the temple and aligned with it there was an altar dedicated to Artemis, a rectangular structure some 40 meters wide by 20 meters deep. The temple was dipteral, that is, one surrounded by a double row of columns, with eight at the front, nine at the rear, and twenty on the sides, along with eight more on its pronaos between the antae, making 106 columns in all, according to the reconstruction just described. At the east end there was an adyton which could be entered only from the cella. The lower diameters of the external columns varied from 1.51 meters at the corners to 1.725 meters at the center of the west front, while their height is estimated by some scholars to have been ca. 19 meters. The lowest drum of each of 36 columns at the west front of the temple was carved with larger-than-life reliefs, 1.82 meters high, the famous columnae caelatea shown on coins of Ephesus. Some of these columnae caelatea are now preserved in the British Museum, including one with an inscription recording that it was "presented by Croesus." This inscription verifies a statement by Herodotus in Book I of his *Histories,* where he writes that the Lydian king dedicated "the golden cows and most of the columns at Ephesus."

The archaic cult statue of Artemis stood at the rear of the unroofed cella under a baldachin. The statue of Artemis is believed to have been done by Endoios, who did the statue of Athena at Erythrae, but nothing remains of this work. According to Pausanias, Endoios was an apprentice of Daedalus, the legendary artist, inventor and craftsman of ancient Greece, who is credited with building the famous Labyrinth at Knossos in Crete for King Minos. Another famous sculpture of the archaic Artemisium that has now vanished is the bronze statue of an Amazon by Polyclitus, a renowned sculptor who flourished in the second half of the fifth century B.C. .

The archaic Artemisium stood undamaged for two centuries, but then in 356 B.C. it was burned down by a madman named Herotratus, who thus sought to gain immortal fame. Later tradition held that this catastrophe occurred on the night that Alexander the Great was born. The Ephesians immediately set out to rebuild the temple, a project that seems to have taken more than a century to complete. The original architects of his edifice were Paeonius and Demetrius, both of Ephesus, the latter identified as a "slave of Artemis." The new Artemisium was still being built in 334 B.C., when Alexander the Great stopped briefly in Ephesus after taking Sardis. When he saw the partially rebuilt temple Alexander of-

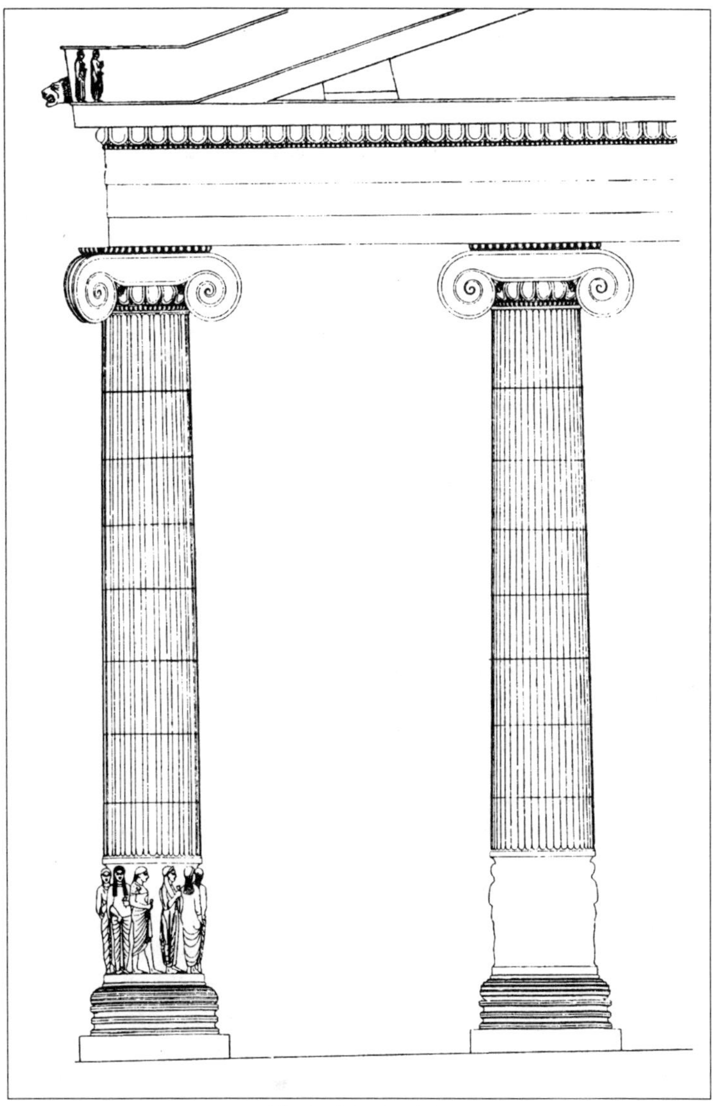

The Archaic Artmisium

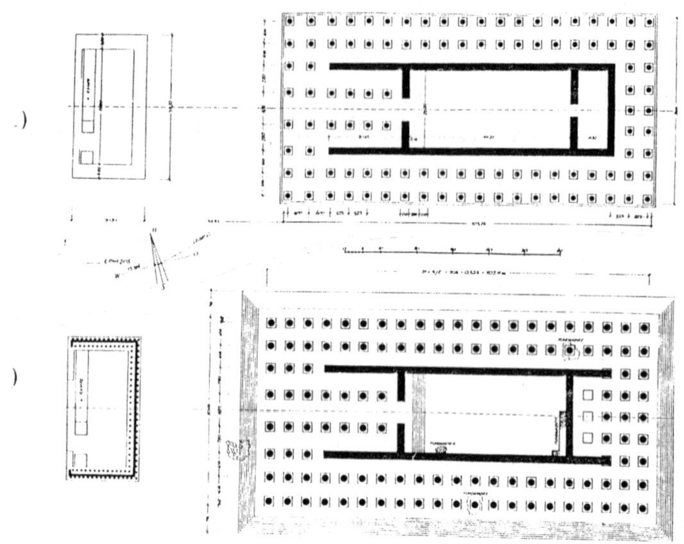

Plans of the Archaic (top) and Hellenistic (bottom) Artemisium

fered to pay all the expenses for its reconstruction. The Ephesians politely refused, saying that it was not fitting for one god to make a dedication to another deity. Alexander in any event ordered that the tribute formerly paid by Ephesus to Persia be transferred instead to the Artemisium, which allowed the Ephesians to go on with the restoration of the Artemisium. They appointed as head architect a Macedonian whose name is given variously as Deinocrates or Cheirocrates, the latter being the one given by Strabo. The Hellenistic Artemisium was built on the same colossal scale as its archaic predecessor. Its size and magnificence earned it a place among the Seven Wonders of the ancient world, along with the pyramids of Egypt, the Colossus of Rhodes, the statue of Zeus at Olympia, the hanging gardens of Babylon, the lighthouse at Alexandria, and the Mausoleum at Halicarnassus.

The Hellenistic Artemisium stood on a thirteen-stepped crepidoma, 2.68 meters in height, with its stylobate measuring

55.10 by 115.14 meters. It was slightly larger than its predecessor, on whose foundations it rested. The plan and dimensions of the new temple were virtually the same as the archaic edifice, except that a third row of columns was added at the west front of the temple and an opisthodomos was created at the rear, with six columns between the antae. This reconstruction gives a total of 120 columns, which are estimated to have been 17.65 meters tall. The lowest drum on each of 36 columns in the front row was carved with reliefs, a feature inherited from the archaic temple. (Some authorities think that the uppermost drum on each of these columns also was decorated with reliefs.) On one of these columnae caelatea, now preserved in the British Museum, the reliefs represent five larger than life-size figures, three of which have been identified as Hermes, Thanatos (Death), and a woman thought to be either Alcestis or Iphigeneia, who is being led away to the Underworld. Pliny the Younger attributes this relief to the great Scopas, but modern scholars are doubtful.

Beyond the west front of the temple there was an altar dedi-

The Hellenistic Artemisium

cated to Artemis. This was on the same site as the altar of the archaic temple and had the same dimensions, the only difference being that the Hellenistic structure had a double colonnade of tall and slender Ionic columns around all sides except its west, with representations of the four-horse chariots known as quadrigas at the two rear corners. According to Pausanias, this altar was decorated by Praxitiles, one of the most renowned sculptors of the fourth century B.C.

After its final destruction the Artemisium was used as a quarry for other buildings, particularly the church of St. John on the Ayasuluk hill. Today all that remains to be seen of the temple is a single column, its fallen drum reerected by archaeologists, the former sanctuary filled with water that has seeped into the excavation pit. In order to evoke its vanished glory wc might refer to a description of the Artemisium by Pausanias, who writes of why this was one of the most famous shrines in the Graeco-Roman world:

> [E]very city recognizes Ephesian Artemis, and people individually honor her above all the gods. I think the reason is the glory of the Amazons who have the reputation of having established the statue, and also the fact that the sanctuary was built so very long ago. Three other things have contributed to make it famous: the size of the temple which overtops every other human construction, the flourishing strength of the city of Ephesus, and the glittering position of the goddess in the city.

We now continue along the Kuşadası road for a little over a kilometer, after which we turn left to approach the main entrance to the archaeological zone. The road enters the zone at the site of the Coressus Gate, the northern gateway to the Graeco-Roman city of Ephesus. Excavations have been made in an attempt to unearth the gateway, but as yet no traces of it have been found.

As we walk south on the road from the site of the gateway we come on our left to a large structure identified as the Gymnasium

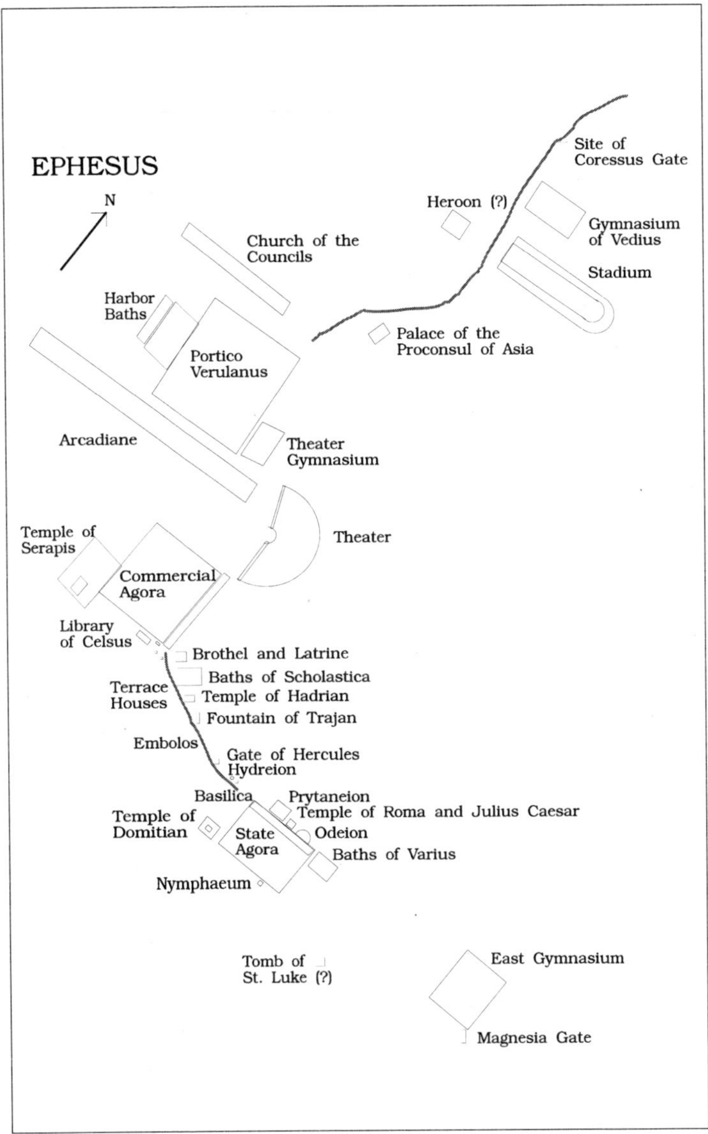
EPHESUS
N
Site of
Coressus Gate
Heroon (?)
Gymnasium
of Vedius
Church of the
Councils
Stadium
Harbor
Baths
Palace of the
Proconsul of Asia
Portico
Verulanus
Arcadiane
Theater
Gymnasium
Theater
Temple of
Serapis
Commercial
Agora
Library
of Celsus
Brothel and Latrine
Baths of Scholastica
Terrace
Houses
Temple of Hadrian
Fountain of Trajan
Embolos
Gate of Hercules
Hydreion
Basilica
Prytaneion
Temple of Roma and Julius Caesar
Temple of
Domitian
State
Agora
Odeion
Baths of Varius
Nymphaeum
Tomb of
St. Luke (?)
East Gymnasium
Magnesia Gate

of Vedius. An inscription records that this was erected in A.D. 150 by Publius Vedius and his wife Flavia Papiana, who dedicated it to Artemis and to the Emperor Antoninus Pius, their close friend and patron. This was a combined gymnasium and public baths, the best-preserved of the eight gymnasium-bath complexes that have been unearthed in Ephesus. One entered through the propylon near the eastern end of the north side of the complex, where the entrance was flanked by statues. The long chamber to the left of the entrance was a latrine, which had entrances on its west and south sides. The propylon leads to the palaestra, a colonnaded courtyard of some 40 by 50 meters that takes up the entire eastern side of the complex, surrounded by a portico with 18 columns to east and west and 14 to north and south, all of them some five meters in height. Opening off the left side of the courtyard there was a large hall, measuring about 10 by 20 meters, surrounded by a colonnade; this was used for ceremonial functions and was reserved for the Emperor when he visited Ephesus. West of this was a large room that extended across the entire width of the building, an area devoted to sports and gymnastics. Beyond this was the natatio, or swimming pool, which at the center of its west side opened on to the frigidarium, or cold baths, on either side of which there was an apodyterium, or dressing room. Beyond the frigidarium was the tepidarium, or warm baths, and to the west of these were the calidarium, or cold baths.

Just beyond the gymnasium is the stadium, a huge horseshoe-shaped structure 28 meters wide and 229 meters long, its great round-arched entrance still intact at the east end. The stadium dates to the Hellenistic era, but it was rebuilt during the reign of Nero, as recorded in an inscription, and altered further in the third or fourth century A.D. The tiers of seats on the south side were hollowed out of the slope of Mt. Pion, while those on the north were supported on a vaulted substructure. Most of the seats were removed in the medieval Byzantine era, when the stadium served as a quarry during construction of the citadel on the Ayasuluk hill.

Entrance to the Stadium

The small hill just to the west of the stadium is believed to have been the acropolis of the original Ionian settlement. Recent excavations have revealed the fortification wall that surrounded the hill, as well as the foundations of an unidentified building of the seventh or sixth century B.C. on the summit of the acropolis. On the south side of the hill there are the remains of a Byzantine fountain of the seventh century A.D., with three niches for statues and the remains of a trough used for watering animals. Nearby there are the remains of a structure that some authorities have identified as a heroon and others as a macellum, or meat market.

We now continue along the road, passing on our right an excavation site where archaeologists are looking for the Olympium, a colossal temple erected ca. A.D. 125 in honor of Hadrian, who was worshipped here as Zeus Olympius. According to ancient sources, the Olympium was the eighth largest temple in the Graeco-Roman world, but during the medieval Byzantine period its ruins served as a quarry until it virtually disappeared. The excavations have so far unearthed only a single Corinthian capital some two meters in height; this is twice as high as the Ionic capitals of the Artemisium, evidence of the colossal size of the Olympium.

Some 250 meters beyond the stadium we see on the right a complex known in times past as the Byzantine Baths. This has now been identified as the palace of the proconsul of Asia, the provincial governor, and probably dates from the reign of Diocletian.

Just beyond the pronconsul's palace a side path to the right leads westward towards the ancient harbor, now a swampland. This brings us to the extensive ruins of a structure of the early second century A.D. known as the Church of the Councils. This is an extremely long and narrow basilica, measuring some 30 by 260 meters, divided by two rows of columns into a nave and side aisles, with an apse-shaped exedra at either end. Opinion is divided as to the original function of this building, with some holding that it was a corn exchange and financial center, while others are of the opinion that it was a museion, or shrine of the Muses, an institution of higher learning concentrating on medicine and other sciences. The building was abandoned for a time in the latter half of the third century B.C., after Ephesus was sacked by the Ostrogoths. At the beginning of the fourth century somewhat more than the western half of the basilica was converted into a church dedicated to the Virgin Mary. An apse and flanking side chapels were constructed 116 meters from the eastern end of the basilica to create the new church, whose was 75 meters long. The narthex, or vestibule, was 12 meters to its west, and beyond that was an atrium 48 meters long ending in an apse at the western end of the building. The atrium was paved with slabs of ancient marble taken from other buildings in Ephesus, while the narthex had a floor mosaic in geometric designs. A baptistery was erected on the north side of the atrium, a domed structure with six exedrae surrounding a circular pool that served as the baptismal font. The church was dedicated to the Blessed Virgin Mary after a decree of Constantine the Great in 313 (eleven years before he became sole emperor), allowing Christians to worship together in public places.

During the reign of Justinian two churches were created where there had been one before. The central area of the western church was covered by a small dome and had an exonarthex, or outer vestibule, between it and the original narthex. The large marble basin in the center of the western church was brought from the Harbor Baths, a huge Roman edifice to the south of the basilica. The eastern church, which was somewhat smaller then the western one, used the apse of the original church, flanked by side chapels. In addition, a tiny chapel was built up against its southern side.

The remainder of the basilica to the east of the eastern church was used as a meeting hall by the Third Ecumenical Council, which was convened here by Theodosius II (r. 408-50). The assembled patriarches and bishops eventually condemned the Nestorian heresy, which held that Jesus had both human and divine natures, and that Mary was the mother only of Christ the man. The council decreed that Christ had a single nature, which was both human and divine, and that Mary was the Theotokos, the Mother of God. The basilica was also the site of the infamous "Robber Council" of 449, which the Greek Orthodox Church condemned as heretical. When Pope Paul VI came to Ephesus, on 26 July 1967, he led a large congregation in prayer here, commemorating the fact that this was apparently the first church ever dedicated to the Virgin, and that it was here that her role as the Theotokos was confirmed. A large crucifix and an inscription in the apse commemorates the pope's historic visit.

The area to the south of the church is a vast field of ruins that was originally, but erroneously, known as the Baths of Constantius (r. 337-61), son and successor of Constantine the Great. Now it has been identified as a gymnasium-baths complex dating from the reign of Domitian, revetted in marble during Hadrian's reign by Claudius Verulanus, chief priest of the province of Asia. The Harbor Baths, as they are now called, were part of the most enormous complex of public buildings in Ephesus, all erected during the reign of Domitian. This vast complex covered an area of some 360 by 500 meters and comprised, besides the baths themselves, the Harbor Gymnasium, which had a palaestra 90 meters on a side, as well as another exercise ground called the Portico Verulanus, which measured 200 by 240 meters and was surrounded by a triple colonnade.

South of the gymnasium-baths complex we come to the Arcadiane, an impressive and remarkably well-preserved colonnaded avenue that led from the ancient harbor to the theater, a distance of some 600 meters. The avenue dates back to the first century B.C., but it did not take its final form until the reign of the Emperor Arcadius (r. 395-408), for whom it is named. It was eleven meters wide and was flanked with covered walkways five meters in width, the latter paved in mosaics and lined with shops. According to an inscription, fifty street lamps illuminated the promenade in the evening. There were propylae at either end of the avenue, of which only the foundations remain. About halfway along the Arcadiane we see two pairs of monolithic marble columns flanking the avenue, a monument dated to the reign of Justinian. Each of the monuments is capped with a Corinthian capital and stands on a four-stepped platform above a high circular base ringed with columnar niches that once contained statues. There were also statues on each of the four capitals, and it is thought that these represented the Four Evangelists.

At the eastern or inner end of the Arcadiane, we see on the right a pretty fountain set into the terrace wall of the theater. The pool of the fountain was fed by water spouts in the form of marble lion heads. In front of the pool there were two pairs of columns, the inner ones fluted and capped with Ionic capitals, the outer pair unfluted and without capitals. The elegance of the monument and the fine carving of the Ionic capitals date the fountain to the third or second century B.C., with the plain columns in front added in the fourth century A.D.

Excavations just to the north of the inner end of the Arcadiane have unearthed the palaestra of what is known as the Theater Gymnasium. The palaestra measured 70 meters along the Arcadiane and 30 meters in depth. It was surrounded by a portico on all but

The Theater

its inner side, where there was a flight of steps that served as viewing stands during athletic competitions on the exercise grounds. Above the steps was the entrance to the main building of the gymnasium, which included baths, lecture halls, conference rooms, a library, and a ceremonial chamber reserved for the Emperor on his visits to Ephesus. The Theater Gymnasium is dated to the second century A.D., probably from the Hadrianic era.

The focal point of Ephesus is the great theater, the largest in Asia Minor, with a seating capacity of 24,000. It dates from the early Hellenistic period, with extensive additions and reconstructions in the imperial Roman era. The auditorium extends through an angle of 220 degrees and has a diameter of 154 meters, with a vertical rise of 38 meters from its orchestra to the uppermost tier of seats, whose middle section is still surmounted by an arcade. Two diazomata divide the auditorium into three sections, the first of which have twelve radial stairways and the third twenty four. The diameter of the orchestra, which is slightly larger than a semicircle, is about 34 meters. The actors in ancient Greek drama originally performed alongside the chorus in the orchestra; later, in the Hellenistic period, they acted on a raised stage, the proscenium, which was erected in front of the skene, the stage building. The core of the Hellenistic skene in the Ephesus theater remains within the monumental stage building erected in the imperial Roman era. This grandiose structure originally had three stories, with colonnaded frontals alternating with statues and reliefs set in niches; in front of it was the broad stage, raised high above the level of the orchestra on three rows of Doric columns, whose stumps remain in place.

Aside from the usual theatrical performances, the theater at Ephesus was also the focal point of the annual mid-winter festival celebrating the birth of Artemis. Early in the morning of that day the xoanon of Artemis was taken from the Artemisium and carried in procession by the eunuch priests known as the Megabyzi. The first stage of the procession took it around the eastern slopes of Mt. Pion to the Magnesia Gate, the southeastern entryway to the city. There the procession was met by the ephebes, the young men in military training, who formed a guard of honor for the xoanon as it was carried through the city to the theater. There the principal festivities were held, and at their conclusion the ephebes led the way as the Megabyzi carried the xoanon back to the Artemisium, leaving the city through the Coressus Gate. The route of the procession is recorded in an inscription of A.D. 104 found in the theater by John Turtle Wood, who was thus able to determine the location of the Artemisium after six years of fruitless digging.

By the time the above inscription was recorded Christianity had already taken root in Ephesus, and the cult of Artemis was being supplanted by Christianity. Graphic evidence of this is recorded in a Syriac chronicle dating from the early Byzantine period, which describes how St. John the Theologian converted a great assemblage of Ephesians who had been summoned to the theater by the procurator, the Roman governor of the city. The Syriac account is paraphrased by Clive Foss in his *Ephesus After Antiquity:*

The procurator called an assembly of the people to confirm the conversion and discuss the fate of the idol worshippers: as was the custom, the meeting took place in the Theater, where the ruler sat on his throne. Meanwhile the priests of Artemis blew horns and opened the gates of the Temple, where a multitude assembled. St. John, standing on the highest, or easternmost, row of seats, blessed the Ephesians and baptized some 40,000 of them.

One of the main streets of ancient Ephesus—the Marble Way—begins below the theater perpendicular to the Arcadiane, running southward from there into the center of the city. The street takes its name from the fact that it is paved in marble, which was laid down in the fifth century A.D. at the expense of a wealthy Ephesian named Eutropius. The Marble Way was designed as a thoroughfare for wheeled vehicles, whose tracks can still be seen in the pavement, with the pedestrians using a raised walkway on the west side under a Doric portico. The relief panels depicting gladiators that we see along the walkway were brought here from other places in Ephesus. Notice also the crude carving on the pavement, showing a woman's head, a pubic triangle and a foot, the latter indicating the direction to a brothel at the southern end of the Marble Way.

A short walk along the Marble Way brings us to the eastern side of the main commercial agora, a vast square area measuring 110 meters along each side. This agora was originally built in the Ionic order in the third century B.C., but then it was reconstructed in the Corinthian order during the imperial Roman era, achieving its final form early in the third century A.D. during the reign of Caracalla. The double colonnade in two stories that forms the eastern side of the agora was erected in the reign of Nero. In the middle of the agora archaeologists unearthed numerous honorific statues, as well as the foundations of a horologion, or clock tower, which included a sundial and a clypsedra, or water clock. There were also numerous inscriptions that have shed considerable light on the social, economic and political life of ancient Ephesus, for the commercial agora was the center of its day-to-day activities.

More recent excavations have unearthed the market square of the archaic city five meters below the level of the Roman agora. These excavations have also unearthed pottery dating back in an almost continuous spectrum from the archaic period to the Mycenaean era, indicating that this site was inhabited for centuries before the founding of the Ionian settlement.

Near the southeast corner of the agora is a marble gateway in the form of a triple triumphal arch. Inscriptions in Greek and Latin on the attic of the gateway record that it was erected in 4/3 B.C. by Mithridates and Mazeus, two rich freedmen, who dedicated it to their former owners: the Emperor Augustus, his daughter, Livia, and his son-in-law, Agrippa. The panels with the Latin inscription have now been assembled beside the gateway. An inscription of the third century A.D. on the wall between the gate and the courtyard to its west praises a certain market inspector for keeping down the price of bread. A roughly-scrawled graffito on the opposite side of the gate gives a warning to passersby: "Whosoever shall relieve himself here shall suffer the wrath of Hecate."

Just beyond the southeast corner of the agora, perpendicular to the Gate of Mithridates and Mazeus, we see the splendidly restored Library of Celsus. Inscriptions in both Greek and Latin record that the library was founded in A.D. 110 by the consul Gaius Julius Aquila as a funerary monument to his father Gaius Celsus Polemaenus, who had been a Roman senator and proconsul of the province of Asia. The library stands over vaulted substructures on a podium 21 meters in width at the western end of a marble courtyard, approached by a flight of nine steps that were once flanked by statues of Celsus. The façade is in two stories, at the front of each of which there are eight Corinthian columns arrayed in pairs. On the ground floor there are doors between pairs of columns, with the central door higher and wider than the other two. The architrave above the columns in each pair on the lower story support the pair of columns above. Between the lower pair of columns there are niches containing statues of female figures personifying the virtues of Celsus, identified by inscriptions as Sophia

The Library of Celsus

(Wisdom), Arete (Valor), Ennoia (Thought), and Episteme (Knowledge). The statues are copies of the originals, which are in the Ephesus Museum in Vienna. The columns in the upper story are slightly smaller than the lower ones. Each of the column pairs frames a high plinth that once supported a statue, now vanished. Between the columns in adjacent pairs an architrave supports a frontal, the central one triangular and the other two round; beneath them are two windows, the central one higher and wider than those on the sides.

The interior of the library consisted of a single lofty hall, its floor area measuring 10.92 by 16.72 meters. The three-tiered, horseshoe-shaped gallery is lined with niches in which some 12,000 books and scrolls were stored in cupboards and shelves. In the central niche is a semicircular arch rising to the height of the uppermost tier of the gallery; this almost certainly framed a statue of Athena, represented as the goddess of wisdom. The locked tomb of Celsus is located directly below this niche, his skeleton still intact inside his lead coffin.

At the southwest corner of the agora a flight of steps leads up to the ruins of a large building that has been identified as a temple of Serapis. This was erected in the latter half of the second century A.D. by Egyptian merchants living in Ephesus; an inscription records that in the second decade of the following century it was also dedicated to the deified Caracalla. The temenos of this temple extended northward to a long and narrow stoa that stretched for 160 m, from the west gate of the agora. The temenos was bordered on three sides by colonnades, and on the southern side a wide staircase led up to the temple of Serapis, whose pronaos was fronted by eight Corinthian monoliths some 14 meters in height and with a lower diameter of 1.5 meters. The cella of the temple was a square 29 meters on a side covered with a stone vault. Early in the Byzantine era it was converted into a church, whose baptistery is at the east end of the building.

The Marble Way ends at a junction just past the agora and the library, and from there another street leads off half-left to extend up the valley between Mt. Pion and Mt. Coressus. This thoroughfare was generally known as the Embolos, or Colonnaded Way, but it was also called the Street of the Curetes, after an order of Ephesian priests.

At the outer angle of the two streets, on our right as we start up the Embolos, we see the ruins of a monumental gateway of the second century A.D., probably from the Hadrianic era. This opened on to a square and street that have not yet been excavated. Probably the latter led to an important sanctuary, given the original grandeur of the gateway, which would have resembled Hadrian's Gate in Athens. It was a triple gateway, with a round arch over the central entrance. Those on the sides were framed by Ionic columns, with an upper arcade of six Ionic columns and a pediment over the central pair.

At the lower end of the Embolos on its left side, just opposite the gateway, are the remains of a building complex that contained the public latrines. An inscription in the latrines indicates that the complex also included a brothel, which comprised a reception hall,

Street of the Curetes

bedrooms, a dining room, a bath, and a pool. Several of the chambers still retain their original mosaic decoration, though their frescoes have all but disappeared. The phallic statue of Priapus, now in the museum in Selçuk, was found in a well within the brothel. The complex was originally built in the late first century A.D. or early in the following century. Around the year 400 the structure was extensively renovated and converted into a large baths by a wealthy Christian lady named Scholastica, who presumably would have eliminated the brothel. The Baths of Scholastica included a large colonnaded hall used as a public meeting place. Some of the columns in this hall were taken from the temple of Hestia Boulea; inscribed on them are lists of the Curetes who served in this sanctuary. Near the entrance to the baths there is a headless statue, believed to be a representation of the lady Scholastica.

On the right side of the Embolos, just beyond the gateway, we see the remains of a Byzantine fountain with crosses on the panels of its basin. This was originally built in the Augustan age as an heroon, converted into a fountain in the early Byzantine era.

Just beyond the fountain there are eight inscriptions recording decrees by Valentinian I (r. 364-75), Valens (r. 364-78) and Gratian (r. 367-83), all of them concerning the restoration of Ephesus after the city had been devastated after an earthquake in the mid-fourth century.

The next monument on the right side of the street is a Roman mausoleum known as the Octagon. The octagonal tomb has a pyramidal roof and stands on a rectangular base surrounded by columns with Corinthian capitals. The tomb was built during the years 40-20 B.C.; when excavated it proved to contain the skeleton of a young woman aged eighteen to twenty, but there was no inscription to identify her.

Continuing up the Embolos, we now come on our left to the temple of Hadrian, one of the most attractive structures in Ephesus. This little Corinthian temple consists of a pronaos and a cella, which was originally covered by a stone vault. The façade of the porch consists of two pillars at the corners and between them a pair of columns. The architrave and frieze over the openings on either side curve in a semicircular arch over the two columns, with the keystone carved in relief with the bust of Tyche, the goddess of good fortune. This is one of the earliest examples of an arch supported on columns rather than piers, an amalgamation of Greek and Roman forms that led directly into Romanesque architecture. The arch was originally framed in a triangular pediment, of which only the two corners remain. The inscription above the architrave records that the temple was built by an Ephesian named Publius Quintilius and dedicated by him to the deified Hadrian, ca. A.D. 128. The temple was restored in the late fourth century, when figurative reliefs were added in the lunette over the doorway and in the upper zone of the front wall of the cella, extending along the antae. The reliefs that we see today are plaster copies of the originals, which are preserved in the Selçuk museum. The relief in the lunette shows the nude figure of a young woman emerging from a cluster of acanthus leaves. Most of the other reliefs were taken from a building of the third century A.D., including: a scene from

Temple of Hadrian

the founding legend of Ephesus, in which Prince Androclus is shown killing a wild boar; the fight between Heracles and Theseus;" and a scene showing Amazons among a group of deities. The only relief done during the fourth century reconstruction is one showing Theodosius I, a great foe of paganism, surrounded by his family and a group of Graeco-Roman deities including Athena and Ephesian Artemis. A podium against the end wall of the cella once supported the cult statue of Hadrian, now vanished.

Outside Hadrian's temple we see four pedestals standing in front of the piers and columns of the porch. Inscriptions show that these supported statues of the Tetrarchs, the Emperors of East and West and their Caesars. The Tetrarchy was instituted by Diocletian in 293 as an attempt to share the responsibilities of ruling the vast Roman Empire, but after he abdicated and retired in 305 the system broke down in a series of civil wars, which ended only when Constantine the Great became sole emperor in 324.

Across the street from Hadrian's temple we see a row of ten small shops opening off from a colonnaded sidewalk paved in charming mosaics, in which the figures of birds are interspersed in a geometrical design. The colonnade was built in the first century A.D., with the mosaic decoration added in the fifth century. This is part of one of the latest excavations at Ephesus, which has unearthed an entire residential quarter of the late Roman period on the lower slopes of Mt. Coressus, along with the row of shops in front of them along the Embolos. The inhabitants of this quarter were the wealthiest in Ephesus, as evidenced by their luxurious dwellings, usually comprising a congeries of rooms around a peristyle court. Some of the villas retain their marble and mosaic pavements, along with large areas of their original frescoes. They are called the Terrace Houses, because they are built on a series of tiers rising up the slope of Mt. Coressus from the Embolos, so that often the roof of a lower house serves as the terrace of the one above. The Terrace Houses were built in the first century A.D. and remained inhabited until 616, when they were destroyed by the Sassanids under Chosroes II along with the rest of Ephesus.

A short way beyond the temple of Hadrian a side street to the left leads from the Embolos to the upper level of the theater. Just beyond the intersection is a partially-restored nymphaeum, or monumental fountain. An inscription records that the fountain was built in A.D. 102-04 by Tiberius Claudius Aristion, who dedicated it to the Emperor Trajan. The fountain was dominated by a colossal statue of Trajan, twelve meters high, of which only the feet and the base remain. Some of the other sculptures that decorated the fountain are now in the Selçuk museum, including representations of Trajan's family and a beautiful statue of Dionysus. The pool of the fountain was surrounded on three sides by a two-storied colonnade, the columns in the lower tier in the so-called composite order, the upper ones Corinthian. The colonnade has now been partially reassembled, although in truncated form, so as to give one an idea of its general appearance.

The Embolos continues uphill as far as the so-called Gate of Heracles, which marked the end of the avenue for vehicles, the rest of the way being for pedestrians only. The gateway is a two-story structure dating from the early fourth century A.D., with a

Nymphaeum of Trajan

passageway under a wide circular arch. The upper level has a colonnade with six columns, with reliefs of Nikes, or winged victories, at the upper corners of the archway. The gate takes its name from the two reliefs of Heracles on the lower sides of its central pillars; in both of them the god is shown wearing the skin of the Nemean Lion, which he killed in one of his twelve labors. These pillars and their reliefs date from the second century A.D.; they originally stood elsewhere in the city and were erected here only in the fourth or fifth century.

At the upper end of the Embolos on its left side there are the remains of two monuments. The first of these is a fountain called the Hydreion, whose long and narrow pool has a central area with a semicircular section at the rear, with four Corinthian columns standing on its walls. When the fountain was rebuilt at the end of the third century A.D., statues of the four Tetrarchs were erected in front of it, with only their bases now remaining.

Just beyond the Hydreion is the Monument of Caius Memnius, which was originally in the form of a four-sided triumphal arch resting on a four-stepped base. This was erected in the second half of the first century B.C. On each facade there were semicircular niches linked by arches springing from pillars. The monument was decorated with reliefs, some of which have survived and have been reerected in their original places. The pillars were decorated with the figures of dancing females, and above the arches there were reliefs representing Caius Memnius, his father Caicus, and his grandfather Sulla, who ruled in Rome as Dictator during the years 84-80 B.C. Sulla sacked Ephesus in 84 B.C. to punish the Ephesians for their support of Mithridates and for having massacred the Roman colonists living in the city.

Just beyond these two monuments we come to a square at the upper end of the Embolos, beyond which the two streets diverge half-left and half-right at the northwest corner of the State Agora. At the center of the intersection there is a round Roman altar decorated with a garland strung on bulls' heads, brought here from another part of Ephesus in the fourth century A.D. Next to it is a

The Hydreion

relief of a Nike that was originally part of the Gate of Heracles.

The State Agora was so called because it was used for political and religious functions rather than for commercial functions, as in the case of the lower agora. This upper agora measured 56 meters from north to south and 160 meters from east to west, with stoas along its north and south sides. Its construction began in the first century A.D., but it did not take its final form until the third quarter of the fourth century. Within the agora, about a third of the way along its major axis from west to east, we see the foundations of a temple of Augustus, erected in the last quarter of the first century B.C. The temple was subsequently destroyed, after which it was served as a quarry for stones used in buildings erected in later times.

We now turn right into the ancient street that leads along the west side of the agora. After passing on the left a monument known as the Socle Monument, we see a conspicuous structure which has on its right side a large semicircular archway. This is the Pollio Fountain, erected ca. A.D. 8 by Caius Offilus Proclus in honor of Caius

Sextilius Pollio, a philanthropist who commissioned an aqueduct to bring water into Ephesus during the reign of Augustus. An inscription records that the monument was embellished in A.D. 93 by the addition of a fountain with a group of statues in the large apsidal niche behind the archway. The statues consisted of pedimental figures from the temple of Augustus in the State Agora. This group, now in the Selçuk museum, dates from the last quarter of the first century B.C., and represents the slaying of the Cyclops Polyphemus, a story told by Homer in Book IX of *The Odyssey*.

On the right side of the street we come to the northeast corner of a large temenos that surrounded the temple of Domitian, of which only fragments remain. The temple was erected early in the reign of the Emperor Domitian, who granted Ephesus the right to be called Neocorus, or Temple-Warden, the first of four times—more than any other city in Asia Minor—that it was awarded this title. The temenos of the sanctuary measured 50 by 100 meters. The stylobate of the temple, which stood on an eight-stepped crepidoma, was 254 by 34 meters, with an altar ten meters to its east. The peripheral colonnade had eight columns at its ends and twelve along the sides. The temple was preceded by a porch with four columns in front of the antae, with the cella measuring 9 by 17 meters. The colossal cult statue of Emperor Domitian stood at the rear of the cella. It was toppled by a mob in A.D. 96, when word reached Ephesus that Domitian had been assassinated. As we have seen, the head of this famous statue and an arm are preserved in the İzmir museum, while other fragments are in the Selçuk museum.

The terrace that supported the statue had a very elaborate façade, of which two piers and their entablature have been reerected. These are surmounted by a pair of columns decorated with reliefs representing robed figures. At the eastern end of the temple precincts is a vaulted passageway called the Inscription Gallery. This is used to display some of the more than two thousand inscriptions that have been discovered at Ephesus, the oldest dating back to the seventh century B.C.

At the southwest corner of the agora there are the remains of another monumental Roman fountain. This comprised a rectangular courtyard surrounded on all sides except the rear by a two-tiered colonnade, with two pools at the front. There were 14 columns on each side and 20 on the front façade, which was surmounted by a pediment nine meters high. The columns on each tier were arrayed in pairs, with frontals over the statues in niches between them. The statues unearthed here during recent excavations include figures of two Nymphs and Triton, a son of Poseidon, all of which are now exhibited in the Selçuk museum. An inscription records that the fountain was built during the years A.D. 75-80 by Gaius Laecanius Bassus, governor of the province of Asia.

There was another nymphaeum opposite the southern side of the agora, about two-thirds of the way from the southwest corner of the square. This fountain was originally constructed in the years A.D. 4-14; it was subsequently modified a number of times and took on its final form only in the fourth century. The nymphaeum contained the statues of a number of emperors and prominent Ephesians, some of which are exhibited in the Selçuk museum.

We now retrace our steps to the intersection at the end of the Embolos, where we now turn right on the ancient street that borders the north side of the State Agora. On either side of the street near its beginning there is a statue base with two reliefs on its sides, all dating from the third century A.D. One of the reliefs on either side shows the nude figure of Hermes, who on the left is shown holding a ram by its horns and in the other leading a goat. These bases formed part of a gateway that served as one of the entrances to the State Agora.

The street along the north side of the agora was known as Clivus Sacer, the Sacred Way, taking its name from the fact that it led to one of the holiest places in Ephesus. This was the shrine of Hestia Boulea, which was within the Prytaneion, or Town Hall. We see the ruins of the Prytaneion on our left after passing the colonnade that lines the street for its first 70 meters.

The Prytaneion was originally constructed in the third century B.C. and reached its final form during the reign of Augustus. It comprised a large hall preceded by a courtyard surrounded on three sides by Doric colonnades. After it was destroyed, probably when the Ostrogoths sacked Ephesus, its columns and other architectural members were used in the construction of the Baths of Scholastica. Some of these have now been restored to their original site. Two of the reerected columns are covered with inscriptions of the first century A.D., some of them recording lists of the priests known as Curetes. The Curetes originally served as priests only in the Artemisium, but from the time of Augustus onwards they were also assigned to the Prytaneion. There they served in the shrine of Hestia Boulea, which was in a small room behind the main chamber of the Prytaneion. The focal point of this shrine was the sacred hearth and its undying fire, a fire originally lit in Athens at the shrine of Hestia, goddess of the hearth. The flame was carried by the colonists who founded Ephesus, where it was kept burning as long as her cult endured in the city. Several statues of Artemis were found in the shrine of Hestia Boulea within the Prytaneion. They were apparently buried there in 392, when the worship of the ancient pagan deities was banned by Theodosius I.

Just beyond the Prytaneion the ruins of some early Byzantine houses cover the site of the double temple of Dea Roma and Divus Julius Caesar. This was erected on the order of Octavian in 29 B.C., two years before he became Augustus, deifying the city of Rome and his adoptive father Julius Caesar.

We now come to the most prominent monument around the agora—the odeion, a small theater whose cavea was carved out of the south slope of Mt. Pion. The odeion had a capacity of about 1,400, with a single diazoma separating the semicircular auditorium into two zones, the lower one divided by six radial stairways and the upper by seven. The stage building was in two stories, and a wooden roof probably extended from its top to the upper gallery of the auditorium. An inscription records that the odeion was built ca. A.D. 150 to serve as the bouleuterion, the founders being Publius Vedius Antonius and his wife Flavia Papiana. It also served as a concert hall, as did many of the council chambers in Graeco-Roman cities.

Directly in front of the odeion we see the best-preserved stretch of a double colonnade that originally extended along the entire north side of the agora. This stretch of the colonnade is referred to in an inscription as a basilica. The basilica was erected late in the Augustan age, with its central nave separated from the side aisles by two rows of columns that carried a flat wooden roof. The basilica was originally in the Ionic order, with each of the capitals decorated on two sides with a prominent bull head relief. Late in the Roman imperial era, when the basilica was renovated, columns with Corinthian capitals were placed between the original Ionic columns so as to strengthen the structure. The basilica was probably used for meetings of the law courts and for other municipal affairs. Excavations have revealed the foundations of a stoa of the Hellenistic era 1.3 meters beneath the basilica.

Beyond the northeastern corner of the agora we see the remains of the so-called Baths of Varius. This structure originally com-

Colonnade in front of the Odeion

prised a baths complex and a palaestra, to which other sections were added in the late Roman and early Byzantine eras. An inscription records that a hall in the baths was donated toward the end of the second century A.D. by Flavius Damianus, a prominent Ephesian sophist.

We now walk over to the parking lot at the southeast entrance to the main archaeological zone. Here we come to the road that leads from Selçuk to Meryemana, the supposed House of the Virgin, which we will visit at the end of our itinerary. At the moment we head in the direction of Selçuk, pausing after a short distance to look at a minor monument to the right of the road.

This is a circular building some 16 meters in diameter, dated to the first century B.C. Crosses inscribed on the building led to the belief in times past that this was the Tomb of St. Luke, but there is no evidence to support this tradition.

We continue along the road and soon come to the Magnesia Gate, so called because it was the starting point for the road from Ephesus to Magnesia ad Maeandrum. The gateway, along with the city walls, were originally built late in the fourth century B.C.; during the reign of Vespasian (r. 69-79) it was remodelled and converted into a triple triumphal archway. This is the only surviving gateway of ancient Ephesus, and although it is now in ruins there are plans to restore it.

The large structure just to the north of the Magnesia Gate is known as the East Gymnasium. This is a gymnasium-baths complex built at the end of the second century A.D. by the sophist Flavius Damianus and his wife Vedia Phaedrina.

Just beyond the East Gymnasium a road leads back to Selçuk, following the course of the ancient processional way between the Magnesia Gate and the Artemisium. About two-thirds of the way along this road a path leads off to the left around a shoulder of Mt. Pion, on whose northern slope there is a large necropolis and the remains of an early Christian basilica at the mouth of a cave.

The cave is the legendary Grotto of the Seven Sleepers of Ephesus. The legend originates in the persecution of Christians during the reign of Decius (r. 249-51). At that time seven Christian youths took refuge in this grotto when pursued by Roman soldiers, who sealed up the mouth of the cave and left the young men for dead. But the youths survived in a deep sleep, which ended nearly two centuries later when they awoke toward the end of the reign of Theodosius II. They were very hungry and so one of them went into Ephesus to buy bread, which he paid for using coins from the reign of Decius. The baker was astonished by this and followed the youth back to the cave, where he learned the story of the Seven Sleepers of Ephesus. When news of this miracle reached Constantinople the Emperor Theodosius immediately came to Ephesus to meet the youths, accompanied by multitudes of the curious. The seven eventually died in the normal span of years (not counting their nearly two centuries of suspended animation), and they were buried in the grotto on Mt. Pion. The Grotto of the Seven Sleepers became an extremely popular shrine, whose fame endured throughout the Byzantine period and on into the Ottoman era. Accounts of medieval pilgrims indicate that the graves of St. Timothy and St. Mary Magdalene were also believed to be in or close by the grotto. The tradition that Mary Magdalene spent her last years in Ephesus can be traced back to Gregory of Tours in the sixth century. In 1952 it was lent some credence by the French archaeologist Louis Massignon, who claimed that he identified her tomb at the entrance to the grotto.

We now go on to visit the Islamic and Christian monuments on the Ayasuluk hill, taking the path that leads upwards past the Artemisium. A short distance above the site of the temple this brings us to İsa Bey Camii, the most important Islamic monument in Ephesus.

İsa Bey, who dedicated this mosque on 5 January 1375, was a grandson of the Emir Aydın, founder of the Aydınıd *beylik*. Prior to that the Aydınıd Türkmen had converted the church of St. John into a mosque and worshipped there. İsa Bey Camii is built on a platform that compensates for the slope of the Ayasuluk hill, creating a level area measuring 51 by 57 meters, one third of which is taken up by the mosque and the rest by its courtyard, which was originally surrounded by a portico. This is the earliest known example of a Turkish mosque preceded by a courtyard. One of the two entrances to the mosque is on the southern side of the courtyard, where one enters the central area of the prayer room through an arcade of three pointed arches carried on a pair of columns. Two domes along the longitudinal axis of the mosque cover the central area of the prayer room, which is flanked by long transepts with double shed roofs supported by colonnades along the transverse axis. The second entrance to the mosque is through an ornate portal in the Selçuk style at the end of the western transept. The mosque is a fine example of the Islamic architecture of the *beylik* period, which flourished in Anatolia in the last century before the Ottoman conquest of Constantinople.

After leaving İsa Bey Camii we climb up the steep path that leads to the medieval ghost town of Ayasuluk, entering its lower enclosure through what was once the main gateway in the lower defense walls. The gate and the walls of which it is a part were constructed during the medieval Byzantine period, making considerable use of material from more ancient structures. Fragmentary reliefs above its arched entrance have been identified as scenes from *The Iliad,* including the deaths of Patroclus and Achilles. These scenes of violent death led an early European traveler to call this the Gate of Persecution, a curious name that is still in use today.

After passing through the gate we make our way to the church of St. John the Theologian. This is now being superbly restored by Turkish and American archaeologists, whose work has progressed to the point where one can make out the plan of Justinian's cathedral. The plan is based on that of Justinian's long-vanished church of the Holy Apostles in Constantinople, which was also the archetype for the basilica of San Marco in Venice.

The church of St. John is 110 meters in length and 60 meters in width along its major axes. It was preceded on its western side by an atrium measuring 47 by 35 meters, which because of the downward slope of the hill had to be supported on a great vaulted substructure. The atrium was surrounded on three sides by a portico carried on a double colonnade. At the east side were the entrances to the exonarthex, and from there the congregation passed on through the narthex into the nave. The church itself was a cruciform basilica with four domes along its longitudinal axis, the third from the rear covering its central area, which was flanked by a pair of domes over the transepts. The central area of the nave was separated from the side aisles by a pair of two-tiered colonnades that extended around the periphery of the transepts and on into the chancel, which ended in a semicircular apse. The colonnade consisted of a series of brick arches carried by blue-veined marble columns between massive stone piers, with the lower tier carrying a gallery that extended all the way around the sides of the church. Some of the capitals on the columns that have been reerected in the nave bear the imperial monogram of Justinian and his empress Theodora. The floor of the nave was paved in marble and mosaic, of which large sections have been restored, while the

The Church of St. John

domes and the upper zones of the walls were undoubtedly decorated with mosaics.

The large baptistery of the church adjoined the left aisle of the nave. At its northwest corner was the skeuphylakion, or treasury, whose main entrance was from the south side of the north transept. At the northeast corner of the treasury a door opened into a small apsidal chamber that in the tenth century was converted into a chapel. One can still see frescoes depicting Christ, St. John the Theologian, and another saint, who is unidentified.

The altar table under the central dome was raised on a two-stepped platform, which was approached by an inclined ramp ten meters in length along the central axis of the nave. Behind the altar there was a synthronon, a semicircular tier of seats for the clergy.

Beneath the altar is the crypt, approached by a flight of six steps. This contained the tomb of St. John the Theologian, the goal of the multitudes of pilgrims who flocked to Ephesus during the medieval Byzantine era. After descending into the crypt one entered a small chapel containing the grave of St. John and three very precious relics: a fragment of the True Cross, a seamless garment woven by the Blessed Virgin which she wore during her last years in Ephesus, and the original manuscript of the *Book of Revelation* written by the Theologian himself. According to the popular belief, St. John was not dead, but only sleeping deeply in his tomb here in Ephesus, where he would awaken at the Second Coming of Christ. This belief seems to have been perpetuated by the monks serving at the shrine, as attested by Jordanus Catalanus, who made a pilgrimage to Ephesus ca. 1330: "As I heard it from a certain monk, who was there and heard it with his own ears, from hour to hour, a very loud sound is heard there, as of a man snoring." Pilgrims were also led to believe that the grave of St. John exuded a fine dust, which they called manna, and to which they attributed magical and curative powers.

The higher and steeper northern end of the Ayasuluk hill is ringed with the walls of the Byzantine citadel, built by Justinian.

During the medieval Byzantine period Ephesus declined to the status of a small town on the Ayasuluk hill, its people huddling for protection within the citadel as invading armies repeatedly swept across the plain below. Villagers were still living within the citadel up until fairly recent times, but they were moved down to the town of Selçuk when archaeological excavations and restorations began on the Ayasuluk hill. The only structures remaining within the citadel now are a small mosque and a Byzantine church, the latter with a cistern built into its structure.

We now return to Selçuk to visit the very attractive and interesting museum. In the garden of the museum we see the sarcophagus from the Belevi Mausoleum, dating from the fourth or third century B.C., surmounted by a carving in high relief of the deceased reclining on his funerary bier. Also in the garden is a reconstruction of the pediment of the temple of Augustus in the State Agora, representing the slaying of the Cyclops Polyphemus. The exhibits in the museum are grouped in a seies of six galleries. The Hall of the Residential Relics contains principally objects found in the excavation of the Terrace Houses, including mosaics and frescoes as well as sculptures—the most notable being a marble head of Socrates, a bronze miniature of Eros on a dolphin, and a bronze statuette of Priapus. The Hall of the Fountain Relics comprises statuary from the Roman nymphaea in Ephesus, the most striking being a marble statue known as the Resting Warrior. The most beautiful items in the Hall of the Recent Finds are an ivory frieze of the first century A.D. and a fourth-century head of the Emperor Marcus Aurelius, as well as marble theatrical masks and Byzantine crosses. The Hall of the Funerary Relics contains mostly antiquities unearthed in an archaic necropolis in the State Agora and in the early Christian cemetery around the Grotto of the Seven Sleepers, the oldest being a Mycenaean vase found in a grave under the church of St. John and dating to the thirteenth century B.C. The Hall of the Imperial Cults and Portraits has mostly Roman statuary and portrait busts, the most interesting exhibits being the original reliefs from the temple of Hadrian. Finally, we come

Statue of Resting Warrior, Selçuk Museum

to the Hall of Artemis, which contains two large statues of the goddess as well as dedicatory offerings found in the Artemisium dating back to the eighth century B.C. The two statues of the goddess, both discovered in the Prytaneion, are known as the Great Artemis and the Beautiful Artemis. The first of them is 2.92 meters in height and dates from the first century A.D.; the second is 1.75 meters tall and dates back to the second century A.D. Both of these extraordinary statues represent the goddess as Artemis Polymastros (Artemis with Many Breasts), referring to the cluster of large pendant nodules each wears above her waist. These are now thought to be bull testicles, symbolic of her role as a fertility deity.

We now go on to visit the shrine of the Blessed Virgin at Panaya Kapulu, Turkish Meryemana. It is eight kilometers to the south of Selçuk and is approached via the road near the Magnesia Gate.

The shrine at Panaya Kapulu is an ancient house where the Blessed Virgin is supposed to have spent the last years of her life,

Statue of Artemis, Selçuk Museum

when, according to tradition, she dwelt in Ephesus in the company of St. John the Apostle. The site of the house was revealed in a dream to Catharina Emmerich (1775-1824), a German nun who never visited Ephesus. Nevertheless, her dream was so vivid and detailed in its topographical description of the countryside south of Ephesus that it led to a search for the supposed house of the Virgin. The Lazarist fathers in İzmir explored the region south of Ephesus and found the ruins of this ancient house at Panaya Kapulu, whose setting seemed to fit the description in Catharina Emmerich's dream. Their report was so convincing that in 1896 the Roman Catholic Church officially declared the house at Panaya Kapulu to be the last home of the Blessed Virgin, whereupon the building was restored and converted into a shrine. The house soon became an extremely popular place of pilgrimage, attracting not only Roman Catholics but also people of other faiths from around the world. Many cures and other miracles have been attributed to the Virgin by those who came here to pray for her help. On 26 July 1967 Pope Paul VI made a pilgrimage to Panaya Kapulu, and afterwards he granted a plenary indulgence to all pilgrims who visited the Virgin's shrine.

Four kilometers to the southeast of Panaya Kapulu we see the peak known as Ala Dağ, the Greek Mt. Solmissus. Strabo mentions this peak as a landmark in identifying Ortygia, the place where, in his version of the myth, Leto gave birth to both Artemis and Apollo. Most other sources place the birth of Apollo on the isle of Delos. Ortygia has been identified as ancient Arvalia, whose site is four kilometers due west of Panaya Kapulu. The birth of the divine twins is mentioned in the Homeric Hymn to Delian Apollo, where the poet sings to the goddess: "Rejoice, blessed Leto, for you bear glorious children, the lord Apollo and Artemis who delights in arrows, her in Ortygia and he in rocky Delos..." Strabo's account of the birth of Artemis here mentions the Curetes, the Cretan demigods who gave their name to the order of Ephesian priests who served at the Artemisium. He goes on to describe the surrounding coast:

Then comes the harbor called Panormus, with a temple of the Ephesian Artemis; and then the city Ephesus. On the same coast, slightly above the sea, is also Ortygia, which is a magnificent grove of all kinds of trees, of the cypress most of all. It is traversed by the Cenchrius River, where Leto is said to have bathed herself in her travail. For here is the mystical scene of her birth and of the nurse Ortygia, and of the holy place where the birth took place, and of the olive tree nearby, where the goddess is said first to have taken a rest after she was released from her travail. Above the grove lies Solmissus, where, it is said, the Curetes stationed themselves, and with the din of their arms frightened Hera out of her wits when she was jealously spying on Leto, and when they helped Leto to conceal from Hera the birth of her children. There are several temples in the place, some ancient, and the others built in later times; and in the ancient temples are many ancient wooden images, but in those of later times there are works of Scopas; for example Leto holding a sceptre and Ortygia standing beside her with a child in each arm. A general festival is held here annually; and by a certain custom the

House of the Virgin at Panaya Kapulu

youths vie for honor, particularly in the splendor of their banquets there. At that time, also, a special college of the Curetes holds symposiums and performs mystic sacrifices.

The ancient festival of celebrating the birth of Artemis was replaced in the Christian era by the feastday of the Assumption of the Blessed Virgin on 15 August. This was was celebrated here by the Greeks of the nearby village of Kerkince up until the exchange of populations in 1923. On the old calendar the feastday of Artemis, the virgin huntress, would have been celebrated at about the same time as that of the Virgin Mary. The fact that the birthplace of Artemis is in the same Ephesian countryside as the last abode of the Virgin is no coincidence. It would seem that the worship of the pagan goddess continued in popular belief in the veneration of Mary, who in the council of Ephesus was declared to be the Mother of God. Such is the continuity of culture in this ancient land.

CHAPTER EIGHT

IONIA III: SOUTH OF EPHESUS

Our last itinerary will take us to the sites of the ancient Ionian cities south of Ephesus, starting from Selçuk.

We leave Selçuk on highway 515 leading to Kuşadası, a drive of 17 kilometers, the first stretch taking us past Ephesus westward along the valley of the Cayster. The highway then turns south into the valley of the Cenchrius, a tributary of the Cayster. This is the river in which, according to Strabo, Leto washed herself after giving birth to Artemis (and perhaps Apollo too). The point where the road turns south is believed to be the site of Panormus, an ancient town whose silted-up harbor is now five kilometers from the sea. Another ancient town named Phygela was located a short distance to the south of Panormus, and to the south of that and some way inland was Ortygia, the legendary birthplace of Artemis. At the southern end of the Cenchrius valley the highway turns westward again for about two kilometers before turning south, and then after another six kilometers it brings us to Kuşadası, the ancient Neapolis. The ancient sites we have just passed are all mentioned by Strabo in his description of the Ionian coast, proceeding northward from Mycale, the mountainous cape opposite the Greek island of Samos:

> After the Samian strait, near Mt. Mycale, as one sails to Ephesus, one comes on the right to the seaboard of the Ephesians; and a part of the seaboard is held by the Samians. First on the seaboard is the Panionium, lying three stadia above the sea where the Pan-Ionia, a common festival of the Ionians, are held, and where sacrifices are performed in honor of Heliconian Poseidon, and Prienians serve as priests at this sacrifice...Then comes Neapolis, which in earlier times belonged to the Ephesians, but now belongs to the Samians....Then

> comes Phygela, a small town, with a temple of Artemis Munychia, founded by Agamemnon....Then comes the harbor called Panormus, with a temple of the Ephesian Artemis; and then the city Ephesus. On the same coast, slightly above the sea is also Ortygia...traversed by the Cenchrius River....

The countryside around Kuşadası was in antiquity known as Anaea, a fertile plain long disputed among the Ionians of Samos, Priene and Ephesus. During the Roman period the port of Anaea came to be called Neapolis, which in the mid-second century A.D. was raised to the status of an independent city by the emperor Antoninus Pius. Then in the late Byzantine era, after the signing of the Treaty of Nymphaeum in 1261, Neapolis became the property of the Genoese, who called it Scala Nova, the New Landing Place. After the Ottomans conquered the region in the second quarter of the thirteenth century the port become known in Turkish as Kuşadası, the Isle of Birds. This name stemmed from the sea birds who nest at the southern side of the harbor on an offshore islet, now connected to the mainland by a causeway.

Kuşadası today is completely devoted to tourism, with a large yacht marina and a pier where cruise ships stop to disembark sightseers bound for Ephesus. There is also a regular ferry service to Samos.

Kuşadası has two prominent historical monuments. One of these is the Genoese fortress on the islet from which the town takes its name, a well-preserved structure dating from the late thirteenth century. The other is the caravanserai of Öküz (the Ox) Mehmet Pasha, dated 1619, which has now been converted into a luxury hotel. Both of these monuments are mentioned by Chandler, who in April 1765 made his second visit to Scala Nova. He travelled here from Ephesus, by the same route we have followed, in a fruitless attempt to find the shrine of Artemis at her birthplace in Ortygia:

> As the site of Ortygia is marked by a mountain and a river, we

expected to find it without much difficulty; and with that view preferred, in our second journey from Ephesus, the lower way to Scala Nova, going from the gymnasium where we had pitched our tent, to the extremity of the plain and then along the sea. We came in sight of the town sooner than before, and turned into the road near Phygela, a little beyond the broken wall, without meeting any thing remarkable.

The improved face of a country is perishable, like human beauty. Not only the birthplace of Diana and its sanctity are forgotten, but the grove and sacred buildings which adorned it appear no more; and, perhaps, as I have since suspected, the land has encroached on the sea, and the valley, in which Arvisis is, was once Ortygia...

Scala Nova is situated on a bay, on the slope of a hill, the houses rising one above the other, intermixed with minarees and tall slender cypresses. A street through which we rode was hung with goatskins explosed to dry, dyed of almost lively red. At one of the fountains was an ancient coffin, used as a cistern. The port was filled with small craft. Before it is an old fortress on a rock or islet, frequented by gulls and seamews. By the waterside is a large and good khan [the caravansarai of Oküz Mehmet Pasha], at which we passed the night on our return....

Chandler then headed south along the coast in an attempt to find the site of the Panionium. The previous year he had found an ancient inscription referring to the Panionium in a church at the village of Güzelçamlı. Then, and in his second expedition, he failed to find the sanctuary and the church has since been destroyed. However, excavations by German archaeologists in 1958 unearthed some fragmentary remains of the Panionium near Güzelçamlı.

The site of the Panionium can now be reached by road from Kuşadası. We start out on the highway for Söke, turning off to the right on a secondary road signposted for Davutlar and Güzelçamlı. The site of the Panionium is about a kilometer southwest of the village center of Güzelçamlı, on a hilltop overlooking the sea. The German excavations unearthed the precinct wall of the sanctuary;

at its center they found traces of an ancient stone altar, with all of the remains dating to the sixth century B.C. A small theater with eleven rows of seats was also excavated on the southwest slope of the hill, below a cave about ten meters in diameter and ten meters deep. The theater was subsequently identified as the bouleuterion, the council chamber where the delegates of the Panionic League held their meetings.

The shrine at the Panionium was dedicated to Heliconian Poseidon, so named from the city of Helice in the Peloponnesus where that particular cult of the sea god originated, and from where it was brought to Asia Minor by the Ionian colonists. Strabo writes about the sacrifices in his description of Helice, which was engulfed by a tidal wave in 373 B.C. and submerged in the Gulf of Corinth:

> For the sea was raised by an earthquake and it submerged Helice, and also the temple of Heliconian Poseidon, whom the Ionians worship even to this day, offering there [at the Panionium] the Pan-Ionian sacrifices. And, as some suppose, Homer recalls this sacrifice when he says [in Book III of *The Iliad*]: "but he breathed out his spirit and bellowed, as when a dragged bull bellows round the altar of the Helicionian lord." And they infer that the poet [Homer] lived after the Ionian colonisation, since he mentions the Pan-Ionian sacrifice, which the Ionians perform in honor of the Heliconian Poseidon in the country of the Prienians; for the Prienians themselves are also said to be from Helice; and indeed as king for this sacrifice they appoint a Prienian young man to superintend the sacred rites....

Herodotus mentions the Panionium several times, most notably in his account of the Ionian migration in Book I of his *Histories:*

> The twelve cities [of the Panionic League] marked their pride by building a temple for their own use which they called the Panionium, and by excluding from it all the other Ionians—although in fact only Smyrna ever applied for admission....The Panionium is a consecrated

spot on the north side of Mycale, chosen by common consent of the Ionians and dedicated to Poseidon, who was previously worshipped at Helice. Mycale itself is a promontory of the mainland running out in a westerly direction towards Samos, and it was here that the Ionians gathered from their various cities to keep the festival called the Panionia....

Herodotus then goes on to tell of what happened to the Panionic League after the fall of Sardis to the Persians in 546 B.C., when Cyrus sent Harpagus the Mede to subdue the Greek cities on the Aegean coast:

When the news reached the various cities, the Ionians began to erect defenses and hold meetings at the Panionium. The meetings were attended by all except the Milesians, who were the only ones who obtained the same terms from Cyrus as from Croesus...

The men of Phocaea and Teos were the only Ionians who preferred voluntary exile to the prospect of slavery; the others remained where they were. All of them, except the Milesians, fought Harpagus as the Phocaeans and Teians had done, but in spite of individual acts of great courage in defense of their homes they were defeated; their towns were taken, and they were forced to submit to their new masters...

In spite of their defeat the Ionians continued the practice of meeting at the Panionium, and I was told that it was at one of these meetings that a man of Priene, called Bias, made a most admirable suggestion which, had they taken it, might have made them the most prosperous people in the Greek world. The proposal was that all the Ionians should unite and sail for Sardinia and settle together in a single community; there, living in the biggest island in the world, they would escape subjection, rule over their neighbors and be rich and happy. If, on the other hand, they stayed in Ionia, there was little chance, as far as he could see, of ever regaining their freedom. This proposal was made by Bias after the Ionian defeat, but there was another, hardly less excellent, which had been made before it by

> Thales of Miletus, a Phoenician by remote descent; this was that the Ionians should set up a common government at Teos, as that place occupied a central position; the other cities would continue as growing concerns, but subject to the central government, in the relation of outlying districts to the mother city. Such were the two proposals.

The Ionian cities revolted against Persian rule in 499 B.C., but they were ultimately defeated at the battle of Lade five years later. The activities of the Panionic League were then suspended until western Asia Minor was liberated from Persian rule by Alexander in 334 B.C., after which the cities of the confederacy once again began meeting at the Panionium. They continued to meet there on into the Roman era, though by that time they had lost their independence and had long passed the period of their greatest brilliance.

The Ionians also met once every four years on the Aegean isle of Delos, where they celebrated the feastday of Apollo, one of their patron deities. This festival is described in the Homeric Hymn to Delian Apollo, evoking a vision of the golden age of the Ionians:

> Yet in Delos do you most delight your heart, for the long-robed Ionians gather in your honor with their children and shy wives. Mindful, they delight you with boxing and dancing and song, so often as they hold their gathering. A man would say they are deathless and unageing if he should come upon the Ionians so met together. For he would see the graces of them all, and would be pleased in heart gazing at the well-girded women and the men with their swift ships and great renown.

We now retrace our route to Davutlar, where we continue eastward to rejoin the main road, turning right for Söke. Then after a short drive we come to Söke, a lively market town on the Maeander plain. Söke is a good base for visiting the ancient Ionian cities south of Ephesus, and it is also a strategic starting point for exploring the archaeological sites along the Maeander valley to the east.

We leave Söke and drive south on highway 525 for about five kilometers, after which we turn right on a secondary road signposted for Priene. A drive of about eight kilometers brings us to the pretty village of Güllübahçe, from which a path leads to the site of ancient Priene, one of the cities of the Panionic League.

Priene is the most splendidly situated of the ancient Ionian cities, standing on a tiered terrace of Mt. Mycale well above the Maeander plain. An enormous crag of the mountain juts up behind it to a height of more than 400 meters. The ruined city is quite different from Ephesus in its appearance, for it is Greek rather than Roman in its architecture. This is because the city reached its full development on this site in the third quarter of the fourth century B.C. It was not rebuilt nor did it expand in later periods, preserving its Hellenic character as if time had stopped for it at the end of the classical age.

According to Strabo, Priene "was founded by Aepytus, the son of Neleus, and then later by Philotas, who brought a colony from Thebes." The original settlement, which would have been founded in the great Ionian migration ca. 1000 B.C., was probably on the seacoast under Mt. Mycale. But subsequent silting by the Maeander isolated the original settlement, and in the mid-fourth century B.C. the Prieneans founded a new city on the present site. The original site of Priene has never been found, probably buried deep beneath the soil near the ancient mouth of the Maeander. The entire topography of this coastal site has changed enormously since Priene was first built on its present site, for the whole of the lower Maeander is an alluvial delta. The Aegean in antiquity penetrated well past Mt. Mycale, which at the time of the Ionic migration was a seagirt promontory, with Miletus founded on the next cape to the south. Now the ruins of these two cities are stranded far inland.

Priene is the finest extant example of an ancient city built on the Hippodamian model. That is to say, it was laid out in the manner set forth by Hippodamus of Miletus, who in the mid-fifth century B.C. became the first city planner in the Greek world. Hippodamos planned Greek cities on a rectangular grid pattern, with straight streets intersecting at right angles, as contrasted with the labyrinthine confusion of more ancient settlements and of medieval towns. This plan has been preserved to a greater extent at Priene than at Miletus or any of the other cities planned by Hippodamus.

The city faces south for the most part, with a jagged cliff of Mt. Mycale at its back. The main avenues run east-west on the level along terraces built on the southern slope of Mt. Mycale, while the stepped side streets rise from south to north between the successive tiers of this inclined shelf above the Maeander plain. The city's lower defense wall extended around the periphery of this shelf on all sides except the north, where the cliff provided a natural fortification. This lower wall was penetrated by three gates, one to the northeast, a second to the southeast, and a third to the west, the latter opening on to the main avenue of the city and its principal public buildings. The acropolis of the city was on the summit above the cliff, a site known in antiquity as the Telonoia. The acropolis was guarded by two stretches of walls, one facing

The Acropolis at Priene, with the Temple of Athena below

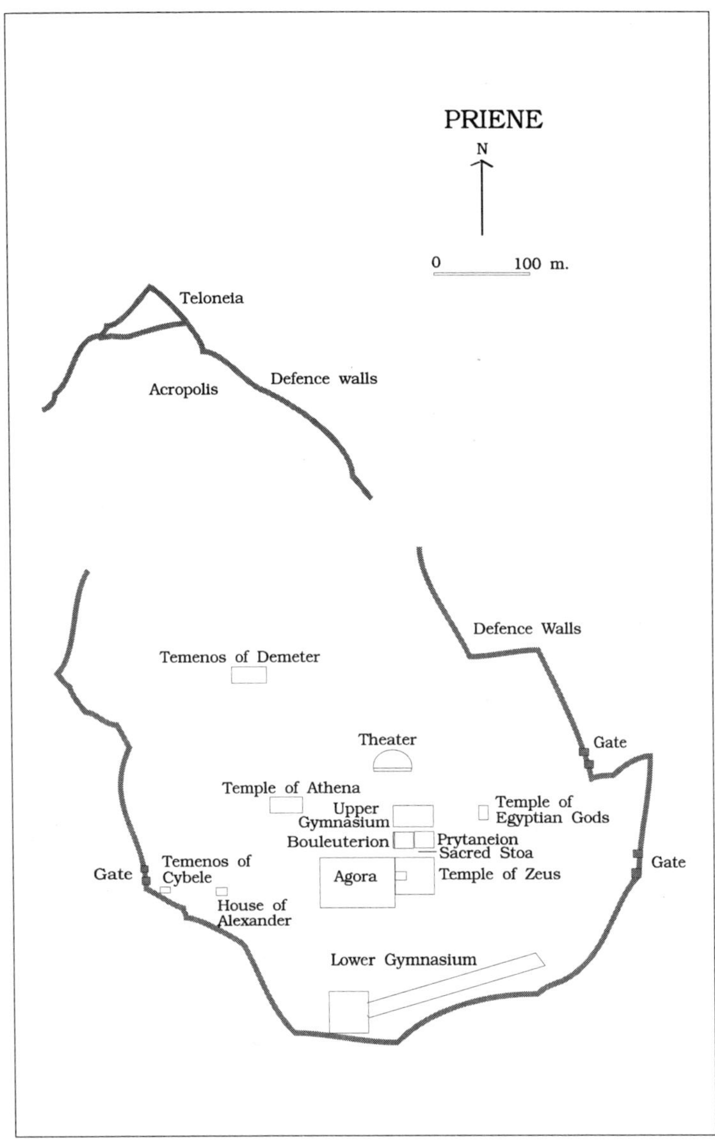
PRIENE
N
0 100 m.
Teloneia
Acropolis
Defence walls
Defence Walls
Temenos of Demeter
Theater
Gate
Temple of Athena
Upper Gymnasium
Temple of Egyptian Gods
Bouleuterion
Prytaneion
Sacred Stoa
Gate
Temenos of Cybele
Agora
Temple of Zeus
Gate
House of Alexander
Lower Gymnasium

northwest and the other northeast, with a cross wall forming a citadel at the angle formed by the two lines.

An aqueduct brought water into the city through the northeastern stretch of the defense walls. This led to three pools just inside the walls, from where the water flowed through earthenware pipes to numerous fountains throughout the city.

We enter the ancient city through the northeast gate, from where a path leads to one of the main east-west avenues of Priene. About 100 meters along this avenue on the left we come to the so-called sanctuary of the Egyptian Gods, a small temenos measuring 14.60 by 7.31 meters. An inscription on an altar stone records that it was dedicated to Isis, Serapis and Anubis, whose sanctuary here was founded by Egyptian merchants during the Hellenistic period.

Continuing along in the same direction, after another 100 meters we come to the theater, whose cavea is hollowed out of the hillside above the street. This is one of the finest theaters that has survived from the Hellenistic world, and though it was modified in the Roman era it remains as quintessentially Greek as the rest of Priene. Here we see the best extant example of the horseshoe-shaped orchestra which in Hellenistic times replaced the full circular form of the classical period. The horseshoe shape developed as a result of the broadening of the stage, which began to encroach upon the orchestra during this period, as the actors performed there rather than with the chorus on the dancing floor. The theater, which seated 5,000—the entire population of late classical Priene, was used not only for performances of drama and other cultural activities, but also for meetings of the ecclesia, the popular assembly of the city.

The civic center of Priene was just to the south of the theater. Its principal edifices faced one another across the main east-west avenue, with the agora and the temple of Zeus Olympius to the south and the Sacred Stoa to the north, with the northeast side of the latter opening up to the bouleuterion and the prytaneion.

The agora, which dates from the third century B.C., was founded on three sides by Doric stoas, with its north side open to the main avenue. There were shops on its west side and along the ends of its south side, the latter flanking a chamber divided longitudinally by a row of eight columns. At the center of the market square there is an altar dedicated to Hermes, and immediately to the east of this there are two stone platforms where dignitaries took their places during ceremonial occasions in the agora. Around the square there were a large number of honorific statues, whose pedestals were usually in the form of benches or exedrae. Adjoining the agora on its northwest side there was a smaller market square where food-stuffs and clothing were sold.

The temenos of Zeus Olympius was built adjacent to the east side of the agora in the third century B.C., with only the foundations surviving. This was a small prostyle temple of the Ionic order, its stylobate measuring 8.50 by 13.50 meters, with four columns in its pronaos. The ruins in the northeast corner of the temenos are the remains of a small Byzantine fort.

The Sacred Stoa was erected in 130 B.C. directly across the avenue from the agora and the temenos of Zeus. The founder is identified by an inscription as King Ariarthes VI of Cappadocia. This grand stoa was 160 meters long and 12 meters wide under the portico, outside which there was an open promenade almost 6.5 meters in width along the avenue, approached by a flight of six steps. The stoa had 49 Doric columns along its façade on the avenue, with a colonnade of 24 Ionic columns supporting the wooden roof, dividing the inner hall into two aisles.

The east end of the Sacred Stoa opened into the bouleuterion, on the left, and the prytaneion, on the right, both dating from ca. 150 B.C. The bouleuterion is one of the best-preserved and most distinctive council chambers in Asia Minor, with rectangular tiers of seats rising from three sides of the almost square room, in whose center there are the remains of an altar. The adjoining prytaneion was the meeting place and dining hall of the executive committee of the city council, who were responsible for the day-to-day operation of the polis, or city-state. As at Ephesus, the prytaneion had an inner sanctum dedicated to Hestia Boulea, which

The Theater at Priene

The Bouleuterion at Priene

is why the portico leading to the council chamber was called the Sacred Stoa.

Across the street just to the north of the bouleuterion and the prytaneion are the remains of the upper gymnasium. When this was originally built in the fourth century B.C., it consisted of a peristyle surrounding a palaestra; then in Roman times baths were added to the north side of the gymnasium.

The lower gymnasium, a larger structure than the upper one, is just inside the southernmost of the city walls, with the stadium abutting its inner side. Both of these structures seem to have been erected ca. 130 B.C. The palaestra of this lower gymnasium was surrounded by four stoas of the Doric order; its propylon, which was also Doric, was on the west side, where it opened on to a stepped street that led up into the center of town. The stadium was 190 meters long; parallel to its northern side there was promenade six meters wide bordered by a Doric stoa.

Another stoa extended westward from the Sacred Stoa past the south side of the temple of Athena Polias, the most famous edifice in Priene. Five columns of the temple's peripteral colonnade have been reerected, their mottled columns and exquisite Ionic capitals standing out vividly against the background of the rugged cliff behind them.

The temple was designed and built by Pythius, one of the architects of the famous Mausoleum in Halicarnassus. The temple was begun by Pythius in 340 B.C., but it may not have been completed for some two centuries. An inscription, now in the British Museum, records that "King Alexander presented this temple to Athena Polias." This dedication may have been made by Alexander the Great on his way from Ephesus to Miletus in 334 B.C., but his biographers do not record that he actually visited Priene. Other inscriptions indicate that at the beginning of the Roman imperial era the deified Augustus was worshipped in the temple along with Athena. According to Vitruvius, the temple was described in detail by Pythius in a lost work that made it an archetype of Ionic architecture. The temple had a peripteral colonnade with six columns at the ends and eleven on the sides, with a pair of columns *in antis* in both its front and rear porches. This was the first Ionic temple to have an opisthodomos, a feature that Pythius adopted from the Doric order. Thenceforth, through his influence, it became customary to have a rear porch in all large Ionic temples. Here, as elsewhere, the opisthodomos was screened off so that it could be used as a treasury. The stylobate of the temple, made of marble from Mt. Mycale, measured 37.20 meters by 19.55 meters. The cella was 14.75 meters in length, the pronaos 8.85 meters and the opisthodomos 3.53 meters. The sides of the temple were 14.75 meters high, the same as the length of the cella, with the columns rising to a height of 12.69 meters and the entablature an additional 2.06 meters. At the rear of the cella there was a large cult statue of Athena Polias, which Pausanias thought to be one of the most remarkable works in Asia Minor. It is a half-size copy of the famous statue of the goddess done by Pheidias in the Athenian Parthenon.

At the eastern end of the stylobate there was a large altar, of

Temple of Athena at Priene

which only the foundations remain. The base of the altar was decorated with a Gigantomachia in high relief, some sculptures of which are now in the Istanbul Archaeological Museum. The style of these reliefs, which are dated to the late second century B.C., suggest that they were modelled on those that decorated the Altar of Zeus in Pergamum. The stoa south of the temenos dates from the same period as the altar, and also seems to have been based on a Pergamene model. The stoa, which was 78.40 meters long and faced south, had a single row of 22 Doric columns standing on a terrace seven meters in height.

About 100 meters north of the temple of Athena we see on the hillside a sanctuary of Demeter, whose daughter Persephone was also worshipped there. Demeter's symbol, a sheaf of corn, appears on the coins of Priene. The temple, whose temenos measures 45.05 by 17.75 meters, dates from the fourth century B.C. Just inside the sanctuary, on the right side, there are the remains of a Roman altar. Outside the temple to the southeast there is a small sunken chamber with a saddle roof. This was used as a sacrificial pit, where the blood of slaughtered animals was poured as an offering to Demeter and Persephone, and to other deities of the Underworld.

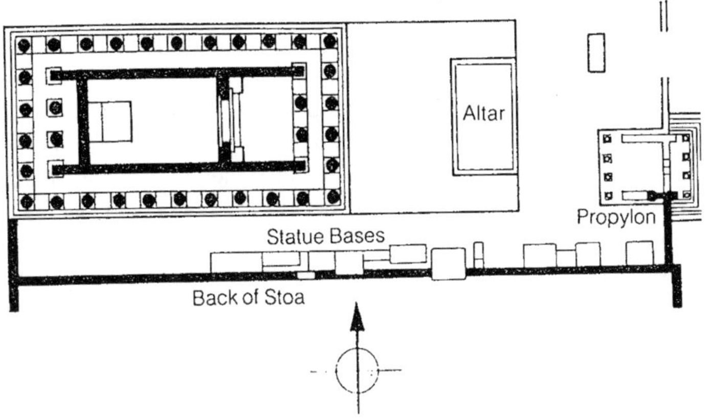

Plan of Temple of Athena at Priene

There is another sanctuary just inside the west gate of the city, this one dedicated to Cybele. Here too there is a sacrificial pit, where blood offerings were made to Cybele as the Earth Mother, the great fertility goddess of ancient Anatolia. A headless statue of Cybele discovered in this pit is now in the Istanbul Archaeological Museum.

One block in from the west gate there are the remains of a house that has been identified as a shrine of Alexander the Great. The identification was based on a statuette of Alexander found there during excavations that began in 1896 under the direction of the German archaeologists Wiegand and Schrader. An inscription discovered on the left doorpost recorded the holding of a priesthood, adding this injunction: "No admission to this sanctuary except to the pure, and in white rainment."

Several blocks of ancient houses stand along the rectangular grid of streets between the town center and the west gate, the shrine of Alexander being one of them. These all date from the Hellenistic period, and are among the finest and best-preserved dwellings that have survived from that era in Asia Minor.

A path at the rear of the theater leads up to the acropolis, passing through the walls at the point where the aqueduct enters the city. The climb to the summit is steep and takes about ninety minutes, with the winding pathway indicated by paint marks on the rocks along the way. At the summit we come to the Teloneia, the three-sided citadel on the acropolis, which dates from the mid-fourth century B.C. The most prominent remnant of the citadel is a ruined tower, whose surviving fragment stands to a height of fifteen courses of squared stones. The Teloneia was manned by a permanent garrison, whose commander was elected for a four-month period and forbidden to leave the acropolis during that time. The view from the summit is superb, looking down on the ancient city far below, with the Maeander river shining here and there in its sinuous course across the great alluvial plain that it has created across the centuries. Richard Chandler visited the site in April 1765 and described the scene:

> We then arrived on the summit of Mycale, large, distinct and rough, with stunted trees and deserted cottages, encircled, except toward the plain, by an ancient wall of masonry called pseudoisodomum. This had been repaired, and made tenable in a later age by additional earthworks. A steep high naked rock rises behind; and the area terminates before in a most abrupt and formidable precipice, from which we looked down in wonder on the diminutive objects beneath us. The massive heap of a temple below appeared to the naked eye but as chippings of marble.

After returning to Güllübahçe, we continue driving westward on the same road until we come to a turnoff on the left signposted for Miletus. There we head southward across the Maeander plain, this part of which was in antiquity a great indentation of the sea known as the Latmian Gulf. After crossing a branch of the Maeander we come to the ruins of Miletus, the most renowned of all the cities of the Panionic League.

As contrasted with Priene, the present situation of Miletus is anything but superb. The remains of this once great maritime city are marooned more than eight kilometers from the sea, surrounded by a swampy morass that makes the site almost unapproachable in any season other than summer, when it becomes a burnt-out wasteland covered with scrub. Nevertheless, the ruins themselves are very interesting and impressive, particularly when one bears in mind the illustrious history of this incomparable city, which the Milesians proudly called "the first settled in Ionia, and the mother of many and great cities in Pontus and Egypt, and in various other parts of the world."

Miletus is probably the oldest of all of the original cities of the Panionic League, archaeological excavations having revealed evidence of human habitation going back to at least the sixteenth century B.C. The first settlers appear to have been from Crete, part of the thalassocracy, or maritime empire, that the Minoans developed throughout the Aegean in the first half of the second millennium B.C. Thucydides credited the establishment of this thalassocracy to King Minos, the eponymous founder of the Minoan dynasty on Crete. According to legend, Minos gained supremacy by defeating his brother Sarpedon, who left Crete with his followers and settled along the southwestern coast of Anatolia. One tradition has it that it was these Cretan settlers who gave rise to the Lycian race in Asia Minor. According to Strabo, one of the places founded by Sarpedon and his followers was Miletus, originally known as Milatos, which they named after their native city on Crete. Another tradition has it that the Ionians settled here later under the leadership of Prince Neleus, a son of King Codrus of Athens.

These traditions have been confirmed to some extent by archaeological excavations at Miletus, which reveal evidence of a Minoan settlement much predating the Ionian migration. This settlement appears to have been taken over by the Mycenaeans in the late Bronze Age, ca. 1400 B.C. This would have been about the same time that the Mycenaeans became the dominant power on Crete itself, ending the Minoan era. Scholars have in recent years deciphered correspondence between the Hittites and the Achaians inscribed on clay tablets found at Boğazkale, the ancient Hittite capital of Hattusha. There reference is made to a city on the southwest coast of Anatolia known as Millawata or Millawanda, which has been identified as Miletus, known to the Mycenaeans as Milwatos.

The Minoan-Mycenaean settlement of Milwatos was probably a trading station rather than a permanent colony, similar to others established by the Cretans around the Aegean in the late Bronze Age. There is no evidence of any interaction between them and the indigenous people of southwestern Anatolia, the Carians. When the Ionians established their colony at Miletus, at the beginning of the first millennium B.C., they came to stay, killing all the native males and taking the younger Carian women as their wives. Herodotus mentions this when he writes of the Ionian settlers at Miletus in Book I of his *Histories:*

Even those who started from the Government House in Athens and believe themselves to be of the purest Ionian blood, took no women with them but married Carian girls, whose parents they had killed. The fact that these women were forced into marriage after the murder of their fathers, husbands and sons was the origin of the law, established by oath and and passed down to their female descendants, forbidding them to sit at table with their husbands or to address them by name. It was at Miletus that this took place.

Miletus was one of the original cities of the Panionic League, of which it was the most powerful member throughout the history of the confederacy. During its early years Miletus greatly surpassed all of the other Ionian cities in its maritime ventures and commerce, founding its first colonies in the eighth century B.C. on the shores of the Pontus Euxinos, the Black Sea. During the following two centuries Miletus founded a far greater number of colonies than any other city-state in the Greek world, including more than thirty in the Black Sea and its approaches in the Dardanelles and the Sea of Marmara. Miletus also had a privileged position at Naucratis, the great emporium on the Nile delta founded by the Greeks ca. 610 B.C., with the Milesians establishing there a fortified trading station known as Milesionteichos.

The same dynamism also manifested itself in the intellectual activities of the Milesians, who surpassed all of the other eastern Greeks in the great flowering of culture that began among the Ionians in the archaic period. Miletus gave birth to the first physicists: Thales, Anaximander and Anaximines, as well as the geographer Hecataeus, the city planner Hippodamus, the poets Timotheus and Phocylides, and the orator Aeschines. The city also produced another figure of renown in late antiquity; this was Isidorus of Miletus, a distinguished mathematician and physicist who was one of the architects of the great church of Haghia Sophia in Constantinople.

Miletus played a leading role in the Ionian Revolt against the Persians that began in 499 B.C. The last battle in this revolt was fought in 499 B.C. off Lade, then an islet off the harbor of Miletus, which had been besieged by the Persians throughout the war. There an armada of 600 Phoenician ships decisively defeated an Ionian fleet of 353 triremes, after which the Persians captured Miletus and burned it to the ground, enslaving those of its surviving inhabitants who had not escaped. This catastrophe deeply shocked the Athenians, who had strongly supported the Ionians in their revolt. Herodotus writes about this in a moving passage in Book VI of his *Histories:*

> The Athenians...showed their profound distress at the capture of Miletus in a number of ways, and, in particular, when Phrynicus produced his play, the *Capture of Miletus,* the audience in the theater burst into tears. The author was fined a thousand drachmas for reminding them of a catastrophe which touched them so closely, and they forbad anyone ever to put the play on stage again.

Miletus was resettled and rebuilt after the Ionian Revolt. But then it was destroyed again in 479 B.C. by Xerxes, who thus took his revenge for the defeats that the Greeks had inflicted on the Persians at Salamis and Plataea. Nevertheless Miletus endured, and the survivors who escaped captivity returned to the city and soon began to rebuild it. By the mid-fifth century B.C. Miletus was once again a flourishing port and commercial center, as evidenced by the fact that in the Delian Confederacy the Milesians contributed only slightly less than the Ephesians. The city was rebuilt according to the plans of Hippodamus, who laid it out in the rectangular grid pattern that became the archetype for city planning in both ancient and modern times. But by then the golden age of Miletus was over, and during the remainder of antiquity its history and record of accomplishment are generally undistinguished, except for giving birth to one of the architects of Haghia Sophia. Miletus went into an inexorable decline in late antiquity, for by then the Maeander had almost completely silted up the Latmian Gulf and carried the shoreline westward far beyond the city. By the early Byzantine period the Milesians had to keep a long river channel dredged clear in order to give their shipping access to the sea. Then in the medieval Byzantine era Miletus was engulfed by the waves of invasions that eventually destroyed it and all the other Greek cities of Asia Minor, leaving them either abandoned or lingering on as desolate villages huddled among the ruined monuments of their illustrious past.

The Turkish village that grew up around the ruins of Miletus was known as Balat, a variation of the Greek "palatia," or "palace," from the popular belief that its monuments had been the palaces of some great king in ancient times. This was a common legend in Anatolia. During the late fourteenth and early fifteenth century Balat was part of the Menteşeoğlu *beylik*, one of the Türkmen principalities into which Anatolia was divided after the collapse of the Selçuk Sultanate of Rum. The most important extant monument of this period is İlyas Bey Camii, the handsome old mosque that stands near the entrance to the archaeological zone. The mosque was erected in 1404 by the Menteşeoğlu emir, İlyas Bey, who had been reinstated in his *beylik* two years before following Tamerlane's victory over Beyazit I at the battle of Ankara. İlyas Bey Camii is one of the most impressive mosques of the *beylik* period still standing in Anatolia, with a dome nearly 15 meters in diameter. The complex also includes a medrese and a *hamam*. Unfortunately the mosque is no longer in use and is beginning to deteriorate. Balat was abandoned after it was severely damaged by an earthquake in 1955, whereupon the villagers were resettled some five kilometers to the south in the village of Akköy, where they reside today. The original village and the mosque of İlyas Bey are mentioned by Chandler in his description of Miletus, which he visited in the autumn of 1764.

> Miletus is a very mean place, but still called Palat or Palatia, the Palaces. The principal relic of its former magnificence is a ruined theater, which is visible afar off, and was a most capacious edifice, measuring in front four hundred and fifty-seven feet....The whole site of the town, to a great extent, is spread with rubbish and overrun

with thickets. The vestiges of the heathen city are pieces of wall, broken arches, and a few scattered pedestals, and inscriptions, a square marble urn, and many wells....Some fragments of ordinary churches are interspersed among the ruins, and traces remain of an old fortress erected upon the theater...From the number of forsaken mosques, it is evident, that Mohametanism has flourished in its turn at Miletus. All these have been mean buildings; but one, a noble and beautiful structure of marble, is in use, and the dome, with a palm tree or two, towers amid the ruins and some flat-roofed cottages, inhabited by a very few Turkish families, the present citizens of Miletus.

The ruins of Miletus are far more impressive than they were in Chandler's time, for since 1899 the site has been under excavation by the German Archaeological Institute in Istanbul, which has superbly restored a number of the surviving monuments. The ruins that one sees today at Miletus all date from after the reconstruction of the city following its destruction by Xerxes in 479 B.C., with

İlyas Bey Camii, Miletus

many of the monuments being much later than that. The reconstructed city has been laid out according to a rectangular grid plan on a long and tapering peninsula which was at the time washed by the sea on all sides except its south, where it was connected to the mainland by an isthmus. There were two indentations of the sea on the western side of the peninsula, and these served as the city's harbors. The one to the south is now known as the Theater Port and the other is called the Lion Port—once the principal harbor of Miletus, so called because of the statues of the two lions that guarded its entrance.

The impressive and well-preserved theater faces southward across the southernmost of the two ports. The theater was originally erected in the first half of the fourth century B.C., with a seating capacity of 5,300. It was enlarged in both the Hellenistic and imperial Roman periods, finally reaching its present capacity of 15,000 in the latter era. The Roman restoration involved building a barrier to separate the auditorium from the orchestra, where gladiatorial bouts and wild animal fights were staged. The seats in the lower zone of the auditorium are well preserved, and one can still see the lower part of the stage building and some of the reliefs with which it was decorated, along with the *paradoi,* or vaulted passages, on either side. Four columns in the front row of the auditorium, of which two remain standing, once carried a baldachin that supported the imperial loge.

On the hill above the theater we see the substantial ruins of a castle and defense walls from the Byzantine period, along with the remains of an Hellenistic heroon and a late Roman synagogue. The existence of a substantial Jewish community in Miletus has long been known; an inscription in the theater records that it marks the "place of the Jews, also called the God-fearing."

The large structure of rectangular plan on the level ground in front of the theater is a Turkish caravanserai, the İlyas Bey Hanı. This was built by İlyas Bey at the same time that he erected his mosque. The caravanserai measures 32 by 25 meters, with 14 chambers arrayed around a central courtyard of 17 by 11 meters,

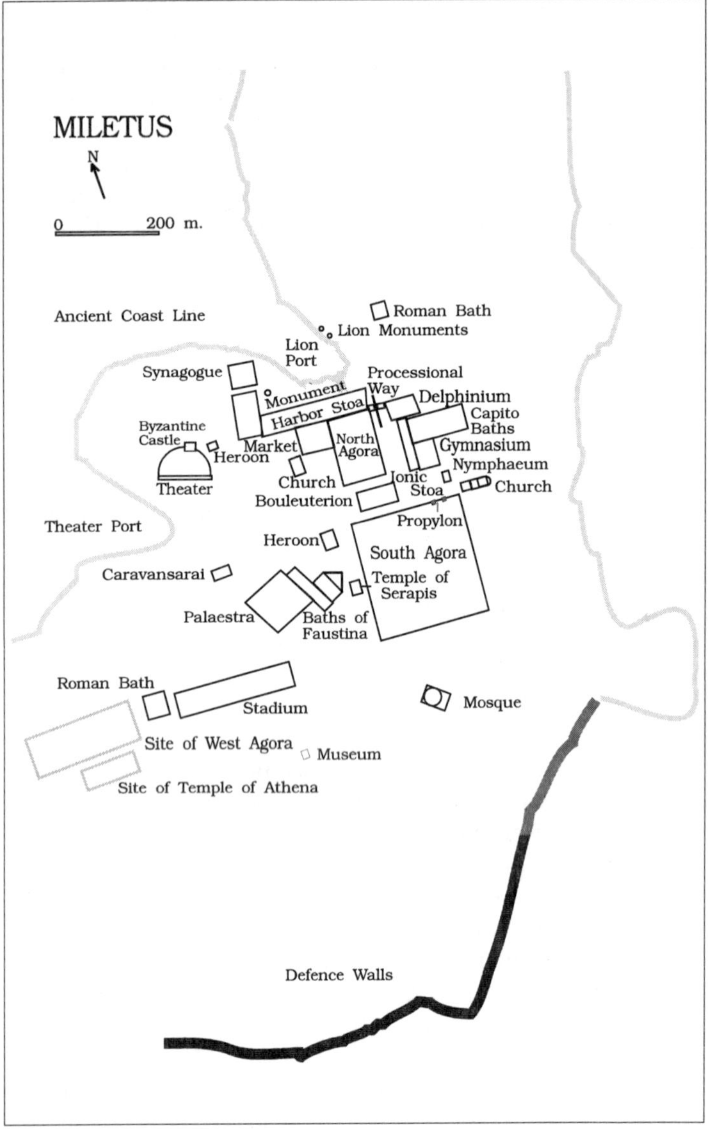
MILETUS
N
0 200 m.
Ancient Coast Line
Roman Bath
Lion Monuments
Lion Port
Synagogue
Processional Way
Monument
Harbor Stoa
Delphinium
Capito Baths
Byzantine Castle
Heroon
Market
North Agora
Gymnasium
Theater
Church
Ionic Stoa
Nymphaeum
Church
Bouleuterion
Propylon
Theater Port
Heroon
South Agora
Caravansarai
Temple of Serapis
Palaestra
Baths of Faustina
Roman Bath
Stadium
Mosque
Site of West Agora
Museum
Site of Temple of Athena
Defence Walls

its arched entrance on the north side. There was originally a second story, but only the stairway that led to this level has survived in the southeast corner of the court. The chambers on the ground floor were used as stables and storage areas, while those on the upper level housed travelling merchants.

About 150 meters south of the caravansaray we see the partially restored stadium, 29.5 meters wide and 191 meters in length. This was originally built ca. 150 B.C. and then enlarged in the third century A.D.; in its final form it had a capacity of 15,000, with tiers of seats on the long sides supported on vaulted substructures. The original Hellenistic entryway was at the west end of the stadium. Then in the late Roman era a more elaborate entryway was erected at the east end; this was a seven-arched propylaea, in which each archway was framed by two pairs of columns with Corinthian capitals supporting entablatures.

A short distance to the west of the stadium there are traces of a Roman bath, of which only the north and east walls remain. A short way beyond the bath to the west we see an Ottoman grave-

The Theater of Miletus

yard, which covers the site of the west agora. Soundings indicate that this market square measured ca. 190 by 80 meters. Just to the south of this a stone podium marks the site of the temple of Athena, erected in the second quarter of the fifth century B.C. This was an Ionic temple measuring 18 by 30 meters, with a peristyle formed by six columns at the ends and ten on the sides.

Excavations in the area of the temple of Athena have unearthed the foundations of houses interspersed with Minoan and Mycenaean shards from the epoch 1500-1100 B.C. Protogeometric and geometric pottery dating from the period 900-700 B.C., indicate that this was the site of both the late Bronze Age settlement and the first Ionian city.

The civic center of Hellenistic and Roman Miletus was towards the eastern side of the peninsula, extending from a line south of the Theater Port up to one north of the inner end of the Lion Port. The southeastern corner of this area is taken up with the remains of the largest monument that has survived from ancient Miletus. This is the south agora, an enormous colonnaded courtyard measuring 196 by 164 meters, with its propylon at the east end of the north stoa and another near the middle of the west stoa. The Doric stoas that bordered the courtyard were erected in the second century B.C.; those on the east and south sides contained shops that alternately opened on to the agora square and the surrounding market streets.

Just outside the west side of the agora there was a long and narrow stoa that extended northward for 168 meters from the west entrance of the market square. This was also erected in the second century B.C., serving as a storage area for the shops in and around the agora. Just beyond the south end of this stoa we see the remains of a small Corinthian temple of Serapis, dating from the third century A.D. The temple is basilical in plan, preceded by a four-column porch. The central area of the cella is separated from the side aisles by two rows of four columns each.

A short way to the west of this temple we come to the enormous and well-preserved Baths of Faustina. These are named for the Empress Faustina, wife of Marcus Aurelius, and are dated to the period of his reign, 161-80. This is the only major building in the civic center that does not conform to the Hippodomean plan, its axes making an angle of approximately 45 degrees with the coordinates of the rectangular grid on which the rest of the city is laid out. The almost square palaestra on the west side of the complex measures approximately 78 meters on each side, surrounded by remains of Corinthian colonnades. Statues of a lion and the river god Meandros, both of which adorned fountains, can still be seen in their original places within the baths, while other sculptures are now in the Istanbul Archaeological Museum. About 50 meters north of the baths there is a heroon dating from the Roman imperial era.

The other buildings of the civic center are all to the north of the south agora. These were approached from the south through the propylon of the agora, a monumental gateway on the north side of the market square dating from the second century A.D. The remains of the gateway were unearthed in 1908 by German archaeologists and are now incorporated in the rebuilt propylon in the State Museum in Berlin. The propylon opened on to a square that formed the southern terminus of a grand processional way that was the main promenade of Ephesus in the Hellenistic and Roman periods, flanked by some of the most important public buildings in the city.

The building at the southwest side of the square is the bouleuterion. This was entered through a Corinthian propylon, through which one passed into a courtyard with Doric stoas on three sides. Then from there one went on into the bouleuterion proper, a roofed auditorium with a seating capacity of 1,500. An inscription on the architrave of the bouleuterion records that it was founded by the Seleucid king Antiochus IV Epiphanes (175-164 B.C.).

Outside the propylon at the southeast corner of the square are the remains of a basilical church of the sixth century, its atrium preceded by a four-columned Roman propylon of the third century A.D. The circular structure adjoining the apse of the basilica to the south is a martyrium, the shrine of a Christian martyr, while the square building to the north of the atrium is believed to be the baptistery of the church.

Just to the west of the baptistery there are the remains of a monumental Roman nymphaeum dating from the second century A.D. Two reservoirs at the rear of the fountain stored water brought into Miletus from a source six kilometers to the southeast. The water that was not used in the nymphaeum flowed through a network of earthenware pipes to fountains elsewhere in the city. The fountain was 20 meters wide and was originally in three stories, the lower two with side wings projecting to flank the huge basin, into which water poured from the mouths of marble fish around the sides and from amphorae carried by marble nymphs. The statues of the nymphs and of various deities, 27 figures in all, were framed in columnar niches with architraves on three stories. The lower three niches survive, though without their marble revetment; otherwise all that remains are some architectural fragments. Some of these statues are now in the Istanbul Archaeological Museum, while others are in the Berlin State Museum.

We now start walking up the processional way, whose roadway was 100 meters long and 28 meters in width, with pedestrian walkways six meters wide on either side. Along the entire east side of the avenue there is an Ionic stoa, now being restored in all of its magnificence, with a row of arcaded shops at its rear. Behind the south half of the stoa are the remains of a gymnasium of the second century B.C., with a palaestra on its south side and on the north five rooms where the young athletes engaged in their studies. The splendid four-columned propylon of the gymnasium has recently been reerected and restored to its original condition. North of the gymnasium are the enormous Capito Baths, whose palaestra is behind the northern half of the Ionic stoa of the processional way. An inscription records that the baths, currently being restored, were built by Cornelius Vergilius Capito, who was procurator of the province of Asia in the mid-first century A.D.

The west side of the processional way bordered the east side of the north agora, which was originally built late in the classical

View Northward from South Agora, Miletus

period and enlarged in both the Hellenistic and Roman eras. When this agora reached the final stage of its development, in the imperial Roman era, it was surrounded on all four sides by Corinthian stoas, with two other Corinthian porticoes opening off its western side, the larger one on the north being a marketplace surrounded by shops. A short distance to the west of these porticoes we see the remains of a sixth-century basilical church dedicated to St. Michael. Adjacent to this is a structure identified as the Episcopal Palace, with part of its mosaic pavement still intact. It has been suggested that St. Michael's served as the cathedral of Byzantine Miletus. Excavations have revealed that the basilica was erected over a temple of Dionysus.

Close by are the remains of the so-called Mosque of Forty Steps. This was built in the late fourteenth century by the Menteşeoğlu Türkmen, taking its name from the flight of stairs that led to its minaret. Only 17 of the original 40 steps remain to this day.

At the northern end of the processional way one veered left to

North End of the Processional Way, Miletus

Ionic Stoa of Capito Baths

pass through the harbor gate, a sixteen-columned portal that formed the entryway to the avenue from the Lion Port. Adjoining the gateway on the east at the end of the avenue are the ruins of the oldest and most important sanctuary in Miletus. This is the shrine of Apollo Delphinium, the Dolphin God, the patron deity of Miletus. This cult originated in the belief that Apollo, in the guise of a dolphin, always guided the Ionian expeditions when they sailed off to establish their overseas colonies. The oldest elements in the shrine are four altars dating from the sixth century B.C.; these are all that survive from the archaic Delphinium, destroyed when the Persians demolished Miletus in 494 B.C. The stoas that surround these altars date from the early Hellenistic period, with alterations in the imperial Roman era.

We now come to the inner end of the Lion Port, where all of the considerable trade of Miletus was centered. The port quarter here was bordered by a portico called the Harbor Stoa, erected in the imperial Roman era. This was a Doric stoa with a peripheral colonnade of 75 columns, extending for nearly 150 meters along the south side of the port and for 20 meters along its southwest side, with 36 shops at its rear.

Just beyond the southwest extension of the Harbor Stoa there are the remains of a basilica that served as a synagogue in Roman times. This may have been the place where Paul bade farewell to his Ephesian friends in April 57, when he stopped at Miletus on his way to Jerusalem, a moving scene described in *Acts* 20:17-38:

> From Miletus he sent for the elders of the church of Ephesus. When he arrived he addressed these words to them:
> You know what my way of life has been ever since the first day I set foot among you in Asia, how I have served the lord in all humility, with all the sorrows and trials that came to me....I now feel sure that none of you among whom I have gone about proclaiming the kingdom will ever see my face again. And so here and now I swear that my conscience is clear as far as all of you are concerned....
> When he had finished speaking he knelt down with them all and

Lion at Entrance to Lion Port, Miletus

prayed. By now they were all in tears; they put their arms around Paul's neck and kissed him; what saddened them most was his saying they would never see his face again. Then they escorted him to the ship.

Near the southwest corner of the Harbor Stoa there are two Roman commemorative monuments. The largest of these, which has recently been restored, has each of its two ends in the shape of a trireme and is decorated with the figures of tritons in relief. An inscription records the great victory that Octavian (later Augustus) and Agrippa won at Actium in 31 B.C. over Antony and Cleopatra. The small one bears an inscription recording its dedication by a Roman named Grattius during the reign of Vespasian (69-79).

Walking around the eastern end of the Lion Port we pass a Roman bath dating from the first century B.C. Beyond this, at what was once the mouth of the harbor, we find the statues of the two lions that gave the port its name, both of them dating from the Hellenistic period. They were placed here as talismans to protect the port of Miletus, which was closed at this point by a chain. During the medieval era the lions were deeply covered in mud, and though they were unearthed at the beginning of the German excavations they are now half-buried again. They are disappearing once more in the alluvial earth that the Maeander continues to deposit around the site, further marooning the great city that it left to die here among the delta marshes.

There is a small museum near the entrance to the site, with antiquities from Miletus and the surrounding region, including the Ionian city of Myus. The exhibits include objects ranging in time from the Mycenaean age to the early Ottoman period, covering a span of three millennia.

Before leaving the site we will make a brief exploration of the southern end of the peninsula, which was closed off by a stretch of the city walls. The center of this stretch of walls was the site of the Sacred Gate, the main entryway to the city. The Sacred Gate was originally built in the second quarter of the fifth century B.C. and was renovated during the reign of Trajan. The gateway took its name from the fact that it was at the beginning of the Sacred Way, a processional road that led to the temple of Apollo Branchidae at Didyma, the great oracular shrine of the Milesians.

We now head south from Miletus to Akköy and then on to Didyma, a drive of 22 kilometers. The modern road probably follows much the same course as the Sacred Way, which enroute from Miletus to Didyma curved out to the sea at Panormus, a port used by seaborne pilgrims going to and from the shrine of Apollo Branchidae. The road brings us to the village of Yenihisar, which has grown up around the ruins of the temple of Apollo at Didyma. The temple is still magnificent even in its ruins, and travelers have for centuries praised its splendor and the beauty of its setting, as did Richard Chandler when he came upon it in the autumn of 1764:

> The temple of Apollo was...two miles and a half from the shore....It is approached by a gentle ascent, and seen afar off; the land toward

> the sea lying low and level. The memory of the pleasure which this spot afforded will not be soon or easily erased. The columns yet entire are so exquisitely fine, this marble mass so vast and noble, that it is impossible perhaps to conceive greater beauty and majesty of ruin. At evening, a large flock of goats, returning to the fold, their bells tinkling, spread over the heap, climbing to browse on the shrubs and trees growing between the huge stones. The whole mass was illuminated by the declining sun with a variety of rich tints, and cast a very strong shade. The sea, at a distance was smooth and shining, bordered by a mountainous coast with rocky island. The picture was as delicious as striking.

The name Branchidae derives from the family who served as hereditary priests and priestesses at the shrine in the archaic period, supposed descendants of a legendary figure named Branchus who had been given oracular powers when Apollo fell in love with him. During the Hellenistic period the oracle of Apollo at Didyma was the most renowned in the Greek world, surpassing even the famed oracle of Pythian Apollo at Delphi. As at Delphi, the priestess put herself into a trance-like state called *enthusiasmos* (literally "god-withinness"), during which, it was believed, Apollo entered her being and uttered prophecies with her voice.

According to Strabo, the oracle of Apollo Branchidae predated the Ionian settlement at Miletus, indicating that the Milesians took over an already existing Carian shrine and oracle at Didyma. They subsequently linked the oracular shrine to their own city with the Sacred Way, which was at its southern end flanked by huge statues in the Egyptian style. Several of these statues are preserved in the Istanbul Archaeological Museum and in the British Museum, with one solitary archaic lion remaining on the site in Didyma.

Excavations have revealed that the earliest Greek construction at Didyma was an altar dating from the eighth century B.C., which a century or so later was enclosed in a naiskos and peripteral colonnade. Then in the mid-sixth century B.C. a very much larger

Temple of Apollo at Didyma

temple of Apollo was constructed here, apparently on the same grandiose scale as the archaic Artemisium at Ephesus. At Didyma too the principal donor was Croesus, whose mother was a Carian and probably a devotee of the cult. According to Herodotus, Croesus sent rich gifts to the shrine at Didyma comparable to those he had given to Delphi and Ephesus. The oracle at Didyma was one of several that Croesus consulted before embarking on his ill-fated campaign against Cyrus in 546 B.C., but what advice he was given by the priestess here on that occasion is not recorded.

According to Strabo, the archaic temple of Apollo was destroyed by Xerxes in 479 B.C. when he sacked Miletus. The Branchidae surrendered the temple treasury to Xerxes, after which they accompanied him on his return journey to Persia in order to escape retribution from their fellow Greeks, finally settling in Sogdiana. Alexander's army found the descendants of the Branchidae still living in Sogdiana when they arrived there in 327 B.C., and the exiled Greeks greeted the Macedonians as liberators. But Alexander, after conferring with his men, had the Branchidae all executed, thus wreaking upon them the vengeance of Apollo for the treachery of their ancestors.

The temple at Didyma was rebuilt early in the Hellenistic period by Seleucus I of Syria (r. 321-280). The Hellenistic temple, which was five centuries abuilding and never completed, was designed on an even grander scale than its predecessor. It was the third largest temple ever erected in the Greek world, surpassed in size only by the Artemisium at Ephesus and the Heraeum at Samos. Though in ruins, enough of the edifice remains to make out its structure and plan, a process known to architectural historians as anostylosis.

The stylobate measures 109.41 by 51.13 meters. The crepidoma is 3.5 meters in height and has seven steps all the way round except at the middle of the east front, where the pronaos is approached by a flight of 14 steps. The temple is designed in the Ionic order and is of the type known as dipteral decastyle, that is, having a cella surrounded by a double colonnade with ten columns at the ends, while the side columns each have 21 columns. The deep pronaos is tetrastyle *in antis,* with three rows of four columns each between the projecting side walls of the cella.

Between the pronaos and the cella there is an antechamber raised about 1.5 meters above the level of the front porch, with which it did not connect directly. This was the chresmographeion, or oracle room, where the priestess delivered her prophecies. On either side of this room there are passageways opening off from the pronaos, each with an inner stairway ascending to the roof of the chresmo-grapheion and an outer vauted ramp leading down to the adyton in the central courtyard of the cella. The courtyard measures about 54 by 22 meters and its surrounding walls are 25 meters high. At the front of the court a broad flight of steps leads up to the chresmographeion, whose central entryway is flanked by two Corinthian half-columns, with two full columns behind them on the longitudinal axis of the oracle room.

At the rear of the court we see the foundations of a small Ionic prostyle sanctuary dating from the first half of the third century B.C. The sanctuary probably housed the sacred bronze cult statue

Sculptured Column Base of Temple of Apollo, Didyma

of Apollo, made by Kanachus of Sicyon for the archaic temple. This was part of the loot carried away by Xerxes in 479 B.C.; but the statue was brought back from Ecbatana in 300 B.C. by Seleucus I and eventually enshrined again here in the Hellenistic temple.

Directly in front of the temple we see a circular altar where pilgrims made sacrifices, and also a well where they drew water to perform their ritual ablutions. The cracked Gorgon head that we see lying here was part of the frieze above the outer row of columns on the east front of the temple, a work of the second century A.D. The archaic lion formerly stood beside the Sacred Way, a long stretch of which has been unearthed outside the temenos to the northwest of the temple.

Outside the temenos wall to the south there are the scant remains of a seven-stepped stadium. This would have been used in the races connected with the Greater Didymeia, a quadrennial festival that included competitions in both the arts and athletics. All the Greek cities in Asia Minor and the eastern Aegean islands would have been invited.

We now retrace our steps to Akköy, where we turn right and after seven kilometers come to highway 525. We turn left there and drive north across the Maeander valley as far as Sarıkemer. There we turn off to the right on a road that leads to the lakeside village of Avşar. This is half-an-hour's walk from the site of ancient Myus, another city of the Panionic League.

According to Strabo, Myus was founded by a party of Ionians led by Cydrelus, a bastard son of King Codrus of Athens. He also notes that the site was formerly inhabited by the indigenous Carians, who were driven out by the Ionians and had to find refuge elsewhere. Myus originally had one of the most important ports in Ionia, on what was then the Latmian Gulf. The harbor was so large that some three hundred Greek triremes anchored here in 499 B.C., at the beginning of the Ionian Revolt. The city was already in decline by then, for at the battle of Lade in 494 B.C. Myus contributed only three ships, as many as half-abandoned Phocaea, these being the smallest contingents in the Ionian fleet. The decline is also evident in the tribute lists of the Delian Confederacy,

Head of a Gorgon from Temple of Apollo, Didyma

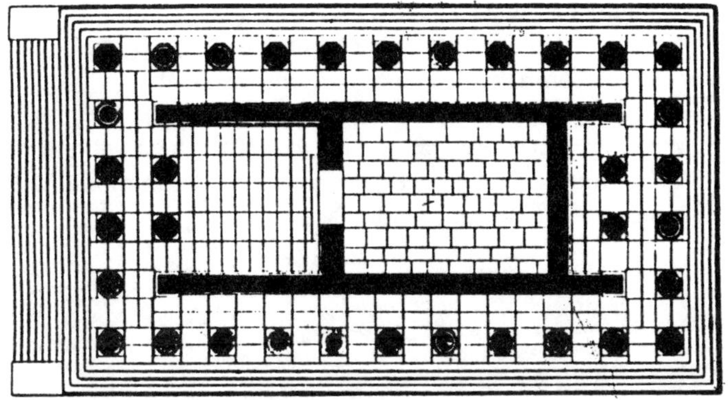

Plan of Temple of Apollo, Didyma

where the normal contribution of Myus was one talent, equal to the lowest among the Ionian cities. The decline was due to the silting up of the port of Myus, which became filled with alluvial earth carried down by the Maeander, transforming the region into a malarial marsh. Eventually the people of Myus were forced to abandon their city and settle in Miletus, as Strabo reports:

> The founders of Myus abandoned their city; it happened like this. That country opened onto a gulf of the sea, though not a very big one, but the river Maeander blocked the channel by silting it up with mud, and transformed the place into a marsh. When the water retreated and the sea was gone, an innumerable swarm of mosquitoes bred in the marsh, until they forced the people to abandon the city. The people from Myus withdrew to Miletus with everything they could carry, including the images of the gods; in my time there was nothing left at Myus but a white stone temple of Dionysus...

All that remains of the temple of Dionysus today are part of its foundations, a supporting wall, and a single column drum of the Ionic order. There are also the exiguous remains of a large temple of the Doric order, which was probably dedicated to Apollo

Terebinthus, the “God of the Terebinth Tree,” mentioned by ancient sources. The most prominent monument on the site is a Byzantine castle on a knoll above the remains of the two temples, indicating that Myus was resettled for a time in the medieval era.

We now retrace our way to highway 525. There we turn right and drive north to Söke, where we complete the third and last of our itineraries through ancient Ionia.

NOTES ON CLASSICAL ARCHITECTURE

Classical Greek architecture has a highly technical vocabulary, whose terminology is explained here with references to diagrams of archetypical Greek temples and drawings of the two major orders of ancient Greek architecture, the Doric and the Ionic. There is also a diagram of a typical Greek theater and drawings showing elements of other orders of ancient Greek architecture, most notably the Corinthian. These and other technical terms in classical architecture are also defined in the Glossary that can be found on pages xiii-xvii at the beginning of the book.

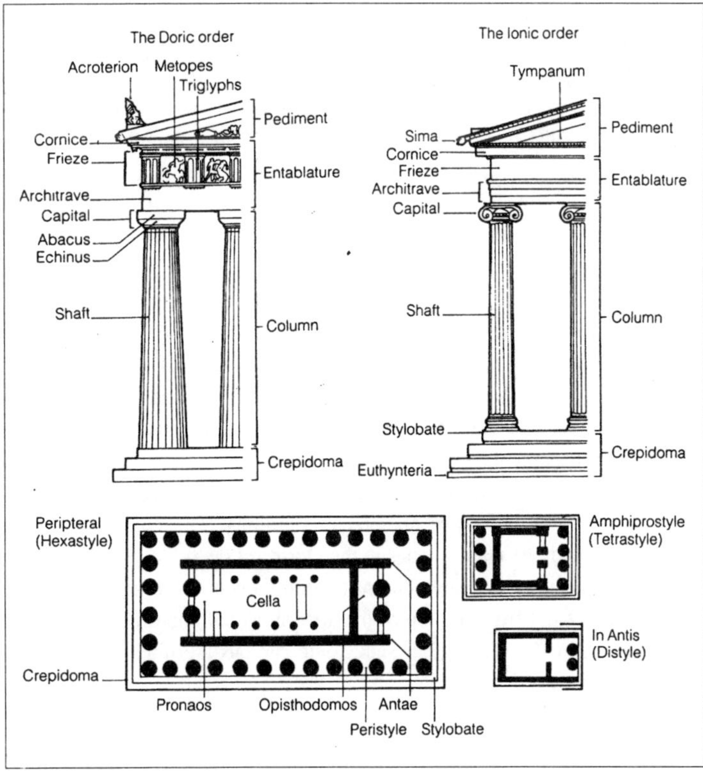

The term cella is used to denote either the central structure of a temple aside from its surrounding colonnade, or, more specifically, the principal chamber. An inner sanctum within the cella is called an adyton, or, if it is small, a naiskos; this sheltered the cult statue of the deity to whom the temple was dedicated. Temples usually face east, except for those dedicated to Artemis-Cybele, which always face west. Many temples have an altar in front of them, standing on the same platform along their longitudinal axis.

The front porch of a temple is called the pronaos, and the rear porch the opisthodomos. Both of these porches are always open, and their side walls terminate in pilasters called antae. The columns of these porches are sometimes between the antae, in which case they are said to be in antis. (A temple whose only columns are between the antae is sometimes called a *templum-in-antis.*) The term prostyle can be applied to a temple if its only external columns are in front of its porch; if it has only a pair of columns between the antae it is called distyle; if it has four columns at its end or ends it is tetrastyle; if it has six it is tetrastyle, etc. If a temple has a surrounding colonnade, the pteron, or peristyle, it is called a peripteros. A temple surrounded by a double colonnade is dipteral. A pseudo-dipteral temple is one with an outer colonnade placed as if it were dipteral, but with the inner colonnade missing. The prefix "amphi" means that the temple has the same arrangement of columns at its front and back.

Beginning at its foundations, the principal structures at the base of a temple, which together are called the crepidoma, are the euthynteria, or leveling course, and the steps (usually three), the topmost one being the stylobate, or temple platform.

Doric columns stand directly on the stylobate, whereas Ionic columns rise from a base with very elaborate mouldings. The columns in both orders are fluted, 20 shallow ones in the Doric, 24 deeper ones in the Ionic. Doric capitals surmount the column through an echinus, a convex moulding that curves out from the top of the uppermost column drum; above this is the abacus, a flat rectangular slab. Ionic capitals are much more elaborate, with characteristic volutes and elaborately carved moulding, known as "egg and dart."

The horizontal members above the columns and their capitals together form the entablature. Surmounting the capitals is the architrave or epistyle; in the Doric order this consists of a plain block; in the Ionic order there are three slightly overlapping slabs. Above the architrave is the frieze, or horizontal zone, which in the Doric order is divided into tri-striated triglyphs and plane-surfaced metopes; this is surmounted by the cornice, which forms the base for the triangular pediment. The frieze was decorated with sculpture; in the Ionic order this was a continuous series of reliefs, but in the Doric order the reliefs were confined to the metopes.

Above the entablature at the ends of the temple are the pediments. The tympanum, or triangular wall within the pediment, is usually decorated with sculpture in the Doric order, but this is rarely done in the Ionic order. Statues called acroteria stood on the summits and corners of the pediments in Doric temples. In Ionic temples the rain gutter was often decorated with lion heads.

The Corinthian order differs from the Ionic principally in its capital, which is decorated with volutes and acanthus leaves. Three other types of capitals are the Aeolic, the Pergamene and the composite, which are illustrated below with drawings, along with the Corinthian.

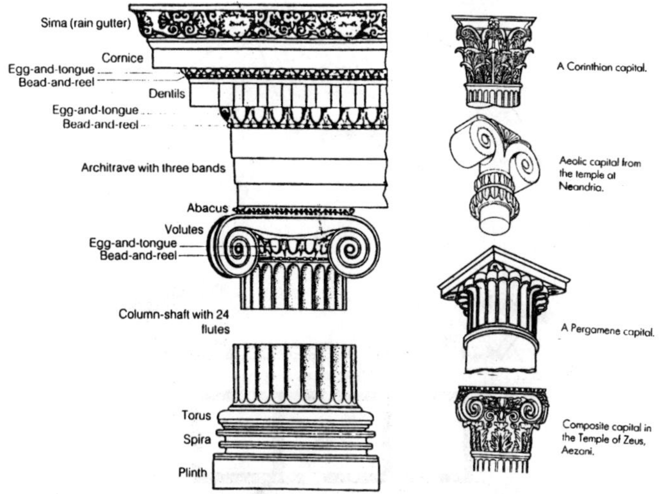

THE IONIC ORDER OF THE TEMPLE OF ATHENA AT PRIENE (LEFT); TYPES OF CAPITALS (RIGHT)

IONIC CAPITAL FROM THE TEMPLE OF ARTEMIS AT SARDIS

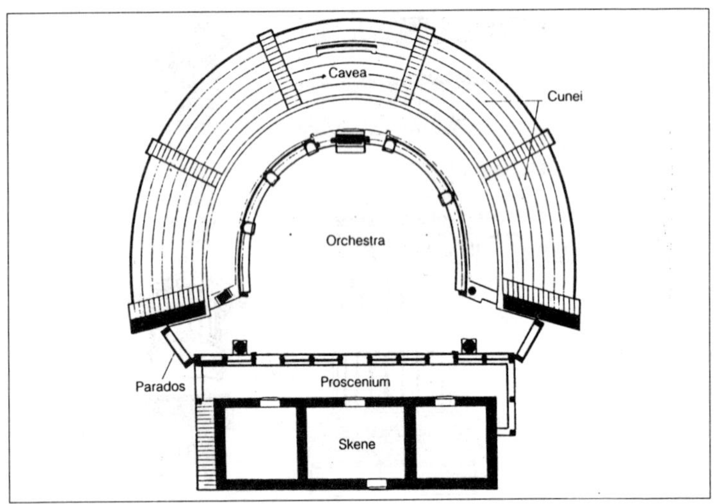

PLAN OF THE THEATER AT PRIENE

CHRONOLOGY

The various periods listed below are approximate dates, and are given for Anatolia in general. These dates can vary from one part of Turkey to another, as, for example, the Byzantine period, which ended earlier in Asia Minor than it did in Constantinople, where it lasted until 1453. Likewise the Ottoman period, which in Istanbul begins in 1453, starts in the early fourteenth period in western Anatolia, overlapping with the *beylik* period.

Palaeolithic period: prior to 8000 B.C.
Neolithic period: ca. 8000 - 4500 B.C.
Chalcolithic period: ca. 4500 - 3000 B.C.
Early Bronze Age: ca. 3000 - 2000 B.C.
Middle Bronze Age: ca. 2000 - 1500 B.C.
Late Bronze Age: ca. 1500 - 1200 B.C.
Mycenaean period: ca. 1500 - 1200 B.C.
Anatolian Dark Age: ca. 1200 - 850 B.C.
Protogeometric period: ca. 1050 - 900 B.C.
Geometric period: 900 - 700 B.C.
Archaic period: ca. 750 - 480 B.C.
Classical period: 480 - 323 B.C.
Hellenistic period: 323 - 129 B.C.
Roman period: 129 B.C. - A.D. 330
Imperial Roman period: 27 B.C. - A.D. 330
Byzantine period: A.D. 330 - early fourteenth century
Selçuk period: 1071 - 1242
***Beylik* period:** 1242 - early fifteenth century
Ottoman period: early fourteenth century - 1923

SELECT BIBLIOGRAPHY

Akurgal, Ekrem. *Ancient Civilizations and Ruins of Turkey.* Istanbul, 1985.

Arrian. *The Campaigns of Alexander.* Translated by Aubrey de Sélincourt. New York, 1971.

Athenaeus. *The Deipnosophists* (Doctors at Dinner). Translated by C. B. Gulick. New York, 1927.

Bean, George F. *Aegean Turkey.* London, 1966.

Cadoux, C. J. *Ancient Smyrna.* Oxford, 1938.

Chandler, Richard. *Travels in Asia Minor, 1764-65.* London, 1971.

Cicero. *The Orations* (4 volumes). Translated by E. W. Sutton and H. Rackham. London, 1920.

Cook, John M. *The Greeks in Ionia and the East.* London, 1962.

—— *The Troad.* Oxford, 1973.

Dinsmoor, William Bell. *The Architecture of Ancient Greece.* London, 1902.

Foss, Clive. *Byzantine and Turkish Sardis.* Cambridge, Mass., 1973.

—— *Ephesus After Antiquity.* Cambridge, Mass., 1979.

Freely, John. *The Western Shores of Turkey.* London, 1988.

—— *Classical Turkey.* London, 1990.

—— *The Companion Guide to Turkey.* London, 1993.

Goodwin, Godfrey. *A History of Ottoman Architecture.* London, 1971

Guthrie, William K. C. *The Greek Philosophers from Thales to Aristotle.* New York, 1966.

Hamilton, William J. *Researches in Asia Minor, Pontus and Armenia.* London, 1842.

Hammond, N. G. L. *A History of Greece to 322 B.C.* Oxford, 1967.

Hanfmann, G. M. A. *Letters from Sardis.* Cambridge Mass., 1972.

Herodotus. *History.* Translated by Aubrey de Sélincourt. Harmondsworth, 1954.

Hesiod, *The Homeric Hymns and Homerica.* Translated by Hugh G. Evelyn-White. London, 1914.

Homer *The Iliad.* Translated by Richmond Lattimore. Chicago, 1951.

—— *The Odyssey.* Translated by Richmond Lattimore. New York, 1965.

Huxley, G. L. *The Early Ionians.* London, 1906.

Imber, Colin. *The Ottoman Empire, 1300-1481.* Istanbul, 1990.

Kuran, Aptullah. *The Mosque in Early Ottoman Architecture.* Chicago, 1968.

Greek Lyrics. Translated by Richmond Lattimore. Chicago, 1949

Livy. *History of Rome* (14 volumes). Translated by B. O. Foster. London, 1919-59.

Magie, D. *Roman Rule in Asia Minor* (2 volumes). Princeton, 1950.

Ostrogorsky, Georg. *History of the Byzantine State.* Translated by Joan Hussey. Oxford, 1968.

Pausanias. *Guide to Greece* (2 volumes). Translated by Peter Levi. Harmondsworth, 1971.

Pedley, John G. *Sardis in the Age of Croesus.* Oklahoma, 1968.

Peters, F. E. *The Harvest of Hellenism.* New York, 1970.

Polybius. *The Histories* (6 volumes). Translated by W. R. Paton. New York, 1922-27.

Stark, Freya. *Ionia, A Quest.* London, 1954.

Strabo. *Geography* (8 volumes). Translated by Howard Leonard Jones. Cambridge, Mass., 1969.

Tacitus. *The Histories* (4 volumes). Translated by C. H. Moore. New York, 1925-37.

Virgil. *The Aeneid.* Translated by W. F. Jackson Knight. New York, 1956.

Vitruvius. *The Ten Books on Architecture.* Translated by M. H. Morgan. New York, 1966.

Xenophon. *The Anabasis.* Translated by Carleton C. Brownson. London, 1922.

INDEX

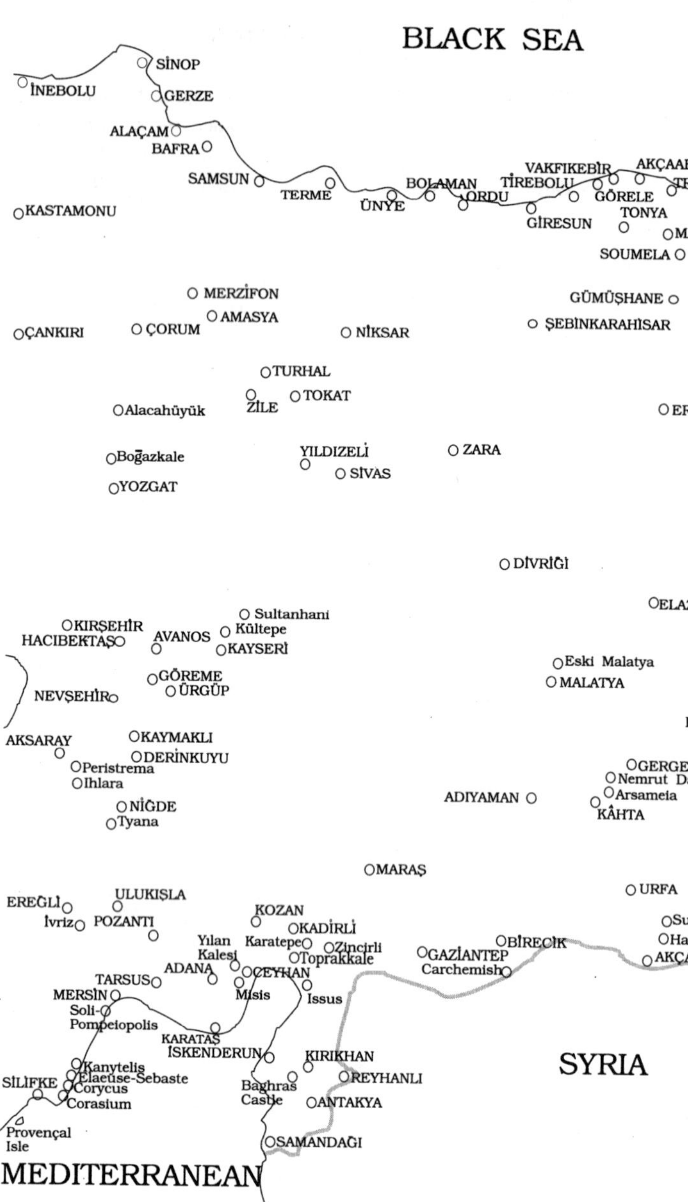
BLACK SEA
SİNOP
İNEBOLU
GERZE
ALAÇAM
BAFRA
SAMSUN
TERME
ÜNYE
BOLAMAN
ORDU
VAKFIKEBİR
TİREBOLU
GÖRELE
TONYA
GİRESUN
SOUMELA
KASTAMONU
MERZİFON
AMASYA
ÇANKIRI
ÇORUM
NİKSAR
GÜMÜŞHANE
ŞEBİNKARAHİSAR
TURHAL
ZİLE
TOKAT
Alacahüyük
Boğazkale
YILDIZELİ
SİVAS
ZARA
YOZGAT
DİVRİĞİ
Sultanhani
Kültepe
KIRŞEHİR
HACIBEKTAŞ
AVANOS
KAYSERİ
Eski Malatya
MALATYA
GÖREME
ÜRGÜP
NEVŞEHİR
AKSARAY
KAYMAKLI
DERİNKUYU
Peristrema
Ihlara
GERGER
Arsameia
ADIYAMAN
KÂHTA
NİĞDE
Tyana
MARAŞ
URFA
EREĞLİ
ULUKIŞLA
İvriz
POZANTI
KOZAN
KADİRLİ
Yılan Kalesi
Karatepe
Zincirli
Toprakkale
GAZİANTEP
Carchemish
BİRECİK
ADANA
CEYHAN
TARSUS
MERSİN
Misis
Issus
Soli-Pompeiopolis
KARATAŞ
İSKENDERUN
KIRIKHAN
Kanytelis
Elaeuse-Sebaste
Corycus
Corasium
SİLİFKE
Baghras Castle
REYHANLI
ANTAKYA
SYRIA
Provençal Isle
SAMANDAĞI
MEDITERRANEAN

GEORGIA
SARP
HOPA
BORÇKA
SAVŞAT
ARDAHAN
ARTVİN
ÇILDIR
ARDANUÇ
ÇAMLIHEMŞİN
YUSUFELİ
ARMENIA
GÖL
OLTU
KARS
Ani
İSPİR
TORTUM
HORASAN
IĞDIR
Mt. Ararat
AŞKALE
ERZURUM
AĞRI
DOĞUBAYAZIT
İSHAK PAŞA SARAYI
IRAN
PATNOS
MALAZGİRT
ERCİŞ
MURADİYE
BİNGÖL
Adilcevaz
Ahlat
Nemrut Daği
MUŞ
LAKE VAN
VAN
Akhtamar
Hoşap Kalesi
TATVAN
GEVAS
ÇAVUŞTEPE
BİTLİS
BAŞKALE
SİLVAN
BATMAN
SİİRT
HAKKÂRİ
Hasankeyf
MİDYAT
Deyrüzzaferan
NUSAYBİN
IRAQ
100
200
300 km.